"Consumers are more active than ever in leveraging digital media for their shopping, purchasing, and even consumption of products and services. Understanding these consumers is critical for the successful entry and profitable growth of international marketers in China. Professors Schultz and Block provided a clear view of the consumer market landscape which can make international marketers' journeys faster, smoother, and more productive. Very important work here!"

— Jie Cheng, Vice President of Analytics and Consumer Insights
   Acxiom, Incorporated

"Economic growth is created and driven by four points—business investment, government expenditures on infrastructure, trade, and consumption. *Understanding China's Digital Generation* demonstrates how consumers will take China consumption from 36% of GDP to the low to mid-40% range in the next 10 years. International marketers want to be a part of this growth."

— David E. Kolan, CPA & Shareholder
   Schneider Downs & Company, Inc.

"Having been a long-time student and practitioner of US and international marketing, e.g. I completed one of the first US deals with China in 1979 following the Nixon Initiative, I have deep respect and admiration for the authors keenly insightful and quite pragmatic assessment of and resultant identified consumer growth opportunities and associated challenges for doing business in China today and in the future. Clearly, the Chinese economy over the past 30 years has been migrating from Turnaround to Transition and aspiring for Transformation. The rapidly-emerging digital generation of 18-34 consumers will be leading the way for the potential Transformation. Those international marketers who strive to optimize their respective opportunities to capitalize upon the emerging consumer migration would be well advised to view this book as a potential strategic and tactical road map for doing so, albeit requiring some strong degree of commitment and patience"

— Robert "Kam" Kamerschen
   Successful Business Leader, Private Investor
   Senior Adviser and Board Member

"As a former CEO and board member of international companies, who opened and operated in markets around the globe, I can only wish I had these types of consumer insights and resources 20 years ago. This is a must-read for international marketers who want to succeed in today's growing Chinese consumption economy."

> — John Mariotti, Retired CEO, Author, Speaker, and Consultant
> Columbus, Ohio

"The authors provide the valuable keys that unlock the insights to the Chinese consumer. This is an essential building block in a market laden with complexity and scale. Masterful."

> — J. Alfonso A. de Dios, Founder & Managing Partner
> Telos Media Works, Ltd., Beijing

"Born and raised in Chicago, Illinois (USA), but having lived and raised a family in China for nearly 20 years, I've seen and been a part of driving China's shifting and growing consumer dynamics. *Understanding China's Digital Generation* provides a clear picture of the opportunities that lie ahead for Consumption growth."

> — Gregg Loveall, Founder & Managing Director
> Consumer Dynamics, Ltd. (Hong Kong & Shanghai)

Understanding China's Digital Generation

Books Brought to You by Prosper Publishing

Understanding China's Digital Generation:
A marketer's guide to understanding young Chinese consumers
www.www.goProsper.com/chinabook

The Changing American Consumer
www.ChangingConsumer.com

Understanding China's Digital Generation

A marketer's guide to understanding young Chinese consumers

Heidi Schultz   Martin P. Block   Don E. Schultz

Understanding China's Digital Generation: A marketer's guide to understanding young Chinese consumers
by Heidi Schultz, Martin P. Block and Don E. Schultz in cooperation with the Prosper Foundation

ISBN: 978-0-9848756-1-0

Library of Congress Control Number: 2012921749

Printed in the United States of America

10 9 8 7 6 5 4 3 2 1

Published by Prosper Publishing
Website: www.goprosper.com

Prosper Publishing books are available at special quantity discounts to use for sales promotions, employee premiums, or educational purposes. To order or for more information, please call 614-846-0146 or write to Prosper Publishing, 400 West Wilson Bridge Road, Suite 200, Worthington, OH, 43085.

Book Design by Sun Editing & Book Design (www.suneditwrite.com)

World and local economic growth is driven by four platforms: infrastructure, trade, investment, and consumption. When the authors conceived this book in 2012, consumption represented about 35% of China's gross domestic product (GDP)—well below the 50–70% levels of the United States, Western Europe, Japan, and South Korea. However, McKinsey forecasts that by 2020, consumption in the world's second-largest economy will exceed 43% of GDP.

One of the key demographics growing China's GDP is its young. They are keenly embracing purchases of cars, clothing, household goods, groceries, electronics, cell phones and digital devices, and health and beauty care products, as well as new opportunities to eat out, travel, and much more. At the same time, jobs, lifestyles, cities and infrastructure, trade, and investment economies in China are evolving rapidly. The resulting social and economic shifts will greatly impact the whole world.

This thought-provoking book is dedicated to the marketing, merchandising, financial, and operations professionals who will successfully play a role in China's healthy evolution to a consumption economy and society.

—R. S. S.

Contents

Thank you for purchasing *Understanding China's Digital Generation*. Most of the insights found in this book are obtained from the ProsperChina InsightCenter™. Ongoing access to trends analyzed in the text and additional insights are available to users on a complimentary basis. This exciting service provides marketers with a direct link to the heart and mind of the young Chinese consumer.

The ProsperChina InsightCenter is an advanced cloud-based platform for the visualization and delivery of key insights and answers on the financial outlook, lifestyle, and media consumption of 1.3 billion Chinese consumers. It identifies through easy-to-understand graphs how Chinese consumers feel about China's economy, changes they are making in reaction to economic fluctuations, where they are shopping, how they are using media (including digital), and much more.

Whether your company is already located in China or you are looking to expand into the Chinese market, the ProsperChina InsightCenter goes beyond traditional point-in-time data reports to trended insights in one easy-to-use, decision-ready format. And best of all, it's available via tablet app or online for users at any level within your organization can gain the knowledge needed to effectively market to the Chinese consumer.

Register today! Visit http://www.prosperchinaic.com/chinainfo/ for more information.

Foreword

Here's a secret about many of the marketers at leading multinational companies in China: They know they should be investing heavily in digital media programs that are engaging, entertaining, relevant and interactive, but they have no idea how to go about it. Unsurprisingly, only a handful of companies such as Nike, always an early adopter, have achieved real success online—either in trying to build brand awareness or push sales through e-commerce.

Their confusion is understandable. Digital media can become a powerful marketing tool in China to accelerate brand engagement, activation, leads and sales, but even marketers in the West are still trying to figure out the best ways to calculate the effectiveness of online campaigns, especially when social media is involved. When you take the challenge to China, an entirely new ecosystem is involved. Forget about Google, YouTube, Facebook, Twitter, Amazon, eBay, Yahoo, Groupon and other American Internet giants. They are minor players in China or absent altogether. Instead, you'll want to consider Baidu, Youku/Tuduo, Sina Weibo, Taobao, AliExpress, Tencent QQ and the numerous other digital innovators across mainland China.

More importantly, Chinese use the Internet differently and for different reasons than their Western counterparts, as you'll learn in *Understanding China's Digital Generation*. The China Internet Network Information Center (CNNIC) points out that there are nearly 500 million netizens in China, with 40 to 50 million more being added each year. That is larger than the total population of the United States. Marketers are mistaken if they believe they can build a business in China without this knowledge.

For instance, Chinese are more likely to watch video entertainment online than on television—a trend based as much on what they don't like about TV as what they do like about computers. Strict regulations on mass-media programming lead to boring, watered-down content with little appeal, and most family homes, typically with three generations under one roof, have one TV set in the family room and a remote controlled by grandma. Few teenagers or young adults living at home—still a common scenario before marriage—have personal TV sets in their bedrooms but many own a computer and a mobile phone.

The Internet also gives them access to friends. Most urban, white-collar Chinese were subject to the one-child policy so today's digital generation largely grew up without siblings. A desire to make friends online partly explains the rise of local social media platforms such as Sina Weibo, Tencent's WeChat and Renren, but online interaction hardly stops there. As *Understanding China's Digital Generation* rightly states, even online shopping is seen as an opportunity for entertainment and socializing.

This book also provides a helpful examination of the uncertainty and risk felt by many Chinese today, including the degree of distrust of things unknown and foreign. As the authors point out, Chinese consumers do not immediately gravitate to imported products or brands simply because they come from the West. Marketers need to understand how being foreign can help or hurt brands, because social media gives consumers a powerful mouthpiece that can destroy brands run by careless or naive managers.

Understanding China's Digital Generation details these and other trends, making it a valuable handbook for anyone who needs to understand the behavior of netizens in the world's largest Internet market.

Normandy Madden, Senior Vice President,
Content Development Asia/Pacific at Thoughtful Media Group, Hong Kong
(Former Asia editor, *Advertising Age Magazine* and editor, *AdAgeChina.com*)

Preface

This book is about a remarkable generation: young Chinese consumers between 18 and 34 years old and the potent role they play in the Chinese marketplace. It is about what they do as consumers—how they shop, what they buy, how they live their lives, how they spend their time, what media forms they use—and some fact-based suppositions on why those behaviors occur.

We say "fact-based" because all the concepts and information in this book have come directly from Chinese consumers themselves. They have reported their views, activities and purchasing behaviors to the ProsperChina™ Quarterly Study (PCQS). This online survey maintained by ProsperChina.com, a service from Prosper Business Development, has collected consumer data for the past half-dozen years. Thus, the information you will find in this text is not based on hypotheses, opinions or marketplace snapshots, but on what Chinese consumers have reported to PCQS every quarter since 2006.

The PCQS is based on similar US consumer surveys from BIGinsight.com, another service of Prosper. The US surveys include the Monthly Consumer Survey™, and the Media Behaviors & Influence™ Study (MBI™), both of which have a ten-year history.

This book is intended primarily for Western managers of consumer-oriented products and services who are seeking to expand their marketing activities from the US to China. Grasping the complexities and dynamics of the Chinese marketplace is no small undertaking, and should not be approached cursorily. Many excellent books have been written in recent years about the broad economic, social and technological advances that characterize China, and this book is not intended to replace any of those resources. However, we have found relatively little has been written about Chinese consumers themselves, and few books provide concrete, research-based data on their marketplace behaviors.

Quite simply, this book aims to be the most specific, most detailed book on any segment of customers that has been published about China. Two questions should be addressed upfront: 1) why use an age-based approach and 2) why choose 18–34-year-olds as the focus of our book? There are several compelling reasons.

First, market segmentation is a hallmark of modern-day marketing, and no method is more basic, straightforward or ubiquitous than segmentation by age. It is readily applied to media strategies, as most TV, broadcast, print and Internet organizations provide details by age segments. It is an approach familiar to most consumer products marketers, and can be applied to most product categories. While some Western marketers may use more sophisticated segmentation techniques such as lifestyle, psychographics, values or needs-based methods, data on such approaches is extremely rare in China. Therefore, a focus on age provides a common reference point that we feel is useful to the greatest number of marketers.

Second, the 18–34 age segment is a priority target for most marketers, especially when they are entering a new territory and looking to build their brand for the long term.. Consumers in the early stages of adulthood are generally a relatively high spending segment, a fact that is particularly true in a market such as China where there is a rapidly expanding middle class. They are at the point of finishing their education, launching a career, beginning their first household, perhaps starting a family and planning for their future. And, they are establishing habits, consumption behaviors and brand preferences that they are likely to sustain for many years to come. Yes, managers of products geared specifically to middle-age and older adults (hair restorers, anti-wrinkle cream, retirement planning) may not benefit from this text as much as those that have an inherent need to reach young people. However, since this is the first book that has focused on a specific demographic group within China, we believe the 18–34 group has the greatest utility to the greatest number of marketers.

Finally, and most compelling, is the fact that this generation is unlike any that has come before in China—or perhaps anywhere in the world. They were born at a pivotal point in the country's history: at the onset of a host of economic, technological and societal changes that fundamentally transformed China and which continue to this day. Their lives have been shaped not only by the extraordinary economic success and dizzying transformation that China has witnessed, but also by the advent of new communication systems that connect them directly to each other and to the rest of the world. They are the first "post-revolution" generation, and the first cohort of the "one-child" policy. As consumers, these young adults have greater spending power, a greater variety of products available to them and more tools with which to gather product information than any previous generation.

The economic pillars that have supported double-digit growth each year over the first decade of the century have been manufacturing, infrastructure and financial investment. However, going forward, it is critical that China expand its economy to include greater domestic consumption. According to the *Wall Street Journal*'s Tom Orlik, "To foster sustainable growth, China needs to shift to a new model, where investment takes a break and household consumption steps up as the new engine."[1]

---

1. Tom Orlik, "Internal-Consumption Engine Poised to Rev?" *Wall Street Journal*, April 8, 2012, http://online.wsj.com/article/SB1000 1424052702304023504577319682208442906.html

Importantly for marketers, the young adults who are the focus of this book will be in the vanguard of China's growing consumption economy. In 2012, China began the second year of the Twelfth Five-Year Plan. A stated objective of this plan is to increase the role of consumption in China's gross domestic product (GDP). Outgoing premier Wen Jiabao, addressing the annual National People's Congress in March 2012, pointed out, "Boosting consumer demand is the year's first priority, with the government looking to wean the economy off its reliance on external demand and capital investments. We will improve policies that encourage consumption."

Thus, marketing managers operating in China are well served to take the time to understand this unique and economically powerful group, the factors that have shaped them, their beliefs, their media usage and their purchasing behaviors.

Because Western managers are accustomed to dealing with US consumers, whenever possible we will try to put the information on Chinese consumers into perspective by comparing and contrasting it with the parallel data on 18–34-year-old consumers in the US.

Thus, the consumers explored in this book share two important characteristics: they are all 18–34; and they participate in online activities, including the surveys on which the data is based. What makes the insights in this text so useful and practical is the ability for marketing managers to compare and contrast what young adult Chinese consumers say and do with their counterparts in the US. We believe that provides an informed framework for managers to adapt and adjust their marketing strategies to the realities of the Chinese market.

The structure of the book is straightforward. We start with a general picture of young adult Chinese, and then provide more granular detail on their behaviors and beliefs about specific activities and product categories. Chapter 1 sets the stage for understanding the context in which young Chinese adults live their lives, and provides a very brief glimpse into the cultural, geographic and economic factors that shape their consumer behavior. In Chapter 2, we discuss the methodologies used to gather data in both China and the US, and provide a basic comparative demographic profile of the two groups, including such key indicators as education, income and occupation, and how these differ among major cities according to their "tier" classifications. Subsequent chapters examine specific aspects of their lives: leisure activities, media usage and influence, online activities. We also examine purchasing and use behavior across a range of individual product categories—such as digital media, telecommunications, health and beauty, entertainment and amusement, fashion and apparel, durable goods and financial services. We conclude with a summary and some thoughts on the challenges and opportunities Western managers face in creating effective, relevant and sustainable marketing programs for young Chinese adults.

Knowing the marketing similarities and differences between the US and Chinese young adult consumers, we *laowei* (Chinese for "outsider") can take a big step in developing effective strategies and tactics for the reaching young adults in the world's fastest growing and perhaps most challenging consumer market. That is the goal of this book.

The authors wish to thank the staff of the Prosper Foundation for granting us access to the consumer insight databases, and their assistance throughout the process. In particular, we wish to thank Gary Drenik and Phil Rist for their long-term friendship, support and constant encouragement to expand our thinking. To Roger Saunders we owe a great debt for his valuable insight, based on his own deep experience in China. And, finally, we wish to express our very special thanks to Chrissy Wissinger, without whose hard work, dedication and great organization this book could not have come to fruition.

Heidi Schultz
Martin P. Block
Don E. Schultz
December 2012

Chapter 1

The First Post-Revolution Generation

In 1978, Mao Zedong had been dead for two years, yet the country was still struggling in the aftermath of the Cultural Revolution he had fostered with the aim of imposing a strict Maoist orthodoxy across the People's Republic of China. The economy was in tatters, millions had been killed or displaced, hundreds of cultural and religious sites had been ransacked and the country was isolated from the international community. For two years, various party leaders had been jockeying for position as his successor, but finally in December 1978, Deng Xiaoping assumed control as paramount leader of the Communist Party of China.

While Deng was never officially the head of state, over the next fourteen years he would go on to dramatically alter the direction of China. He is credited with developing the concept of "socialism with Chinese characteristics," reforming the educational system, opening China's door to international trade and pushing the leadership and fledgling business community toward

1

the goal of creating a "socialist market economy." Under Deng the path to reform was not without its detours, perhaps most notably the incidents in Tiananmen Square in June 1989. However, Deng's rise in 1978 set in motion a chain of events and sequence of economic, legal, educational and political changes that are still being carried on today, and thus it marks a pivotal year in the history of modern China.

The children born in 1978 and the years that followed represent the first post-revolution generation. It is that generation—now between the ages of 18 and 34 years old—that are the focus of this book. They are the first generation born under the one-child policy (initiated in 1979) and have grown up with the privileges (and the pressures) of being the focal point for their parents' aspirations for the future. Where their parents and grandparents had known little but decades of war, upheaval and deprivation, these children grew up hearing that "to get rich is glorious." They have seen the country open up to the West and embrace, as least in part, values, ideas and concepts that were previously unheard of in the Middle Kingdom. They have seen their country rise as a global economic power, and have participated in major international events such as the Beijing Olympics and Shanghai's Expo 2010. Also, they are becoming knowledgeable, astute customers of a range of consumer products that their parents and grandparents could not have imagined back in 1978.

Those born in 1978 grew up in a world very different from the one their parents and grandparents had experienced. Yet their growth was profoundly shaped by the traditions, the history, the culture and the economic realities of China during the years before their birth.

To understand what has influenced the attitudes, feelings and behavior of today's young Chinese adults, it is useful to briefly examine the cultural, social, geographic and economic context in which they live, and the implications these may pose for marketers.

Cultural and Social Context

A critical element in understanding the Chinese consumer market is understanding how it has evolved and adapted to both internal and external pressures, opportunities and challengers over the years.

The history of China is a rich tapestry spanning more than 5000 years. Over the millennia, China has mostly been a highly civilized society, with sophisticated literature, music and visual arts, and a highly refined system of social mores. It has been a society that has emphasized learning, resourcefulness and ingenuity—resulting in innovations such papermaking from pulp, the compass, gunpowder and printing (the so-called "Four Great Inventions") as well as thousands of other contributions to the modern world, including porcelain, the rotary fan, the non-friction match, toilet paper, tofu and the merit system of advancement based on performance on civil service examinations.

Yet China has also had its dark days: periods of invasions, corruption, revolutions, famines and natural disasters—periods when advancement came to a seeming standstill. The highs and lows of history have given the Chinese a deep sense of their ability to endure, to overcome hardship, to persevere and to bravely face challenges with hard work, dedication and sacrifice. These are lessons that have been passed down for thousands of years, and in spite of the turmoil and change that Chinese citizens have experienced, are still relevant today.

Westerners often make the mistake of assuming that China is totally homogenous from ethnic and linguistic standpoints. While the majority (approximately 92%) of China's 1.3 billion citizens are Han Chinese, the government officially recognizes 55 ethnic minorities. Among the major minority ethnic groups are Zhuang (18 million), Uyghur (11.2 million), Manchu (10.6 million), Hui (10 million), Miao (9 million), Tujia (8 million), Yi (7.7 million), Mongol (5.8 million), Tibetan (5.4 million), Buyei (2.9 million), Yao (3.1 million) and

Korean (1.9 million). [1] Since each group has its own strong traditions, customs and language, marketers entering a region with a large ethnic minority should be sensitive to cultural distinctions and practices.

Standard Mandarin, *Putonghua*, is the official language, and the one commonly taught in the schools. However, China has a great and complex diversity of tongues. Overall, there are eight distinctly different, mutually unintelligible language families used across the country, each with dozens of local variations and dialects. Each ethnic minority has its own language and dialects, but even Han groups have local languages that are virtually unintelligible from one region to the next. This can pose complications for marketers. While most students will learn standard Mandarin and be fluent by the time of graduation from high school, local customs and traditions are often still expressed in the regional dialect. This diversity of language is not a phenomenon that only pertains to rural or less developed areas. While marketers can generally assume that Mandarin will be the language of choice for most people in Shanghai and Beijing, consideration must be given to an area such as Guangzhou where Cantonese is still the lingua franca. Other major language groups include Mongolian, Tibetan, Uyghur (a Turkic language spoken in the Xinjiang Uyghur Autonomous Region in Western China) and Zhuang (Guangxi Zhuang Autonomous Region in Southern China).

A final observation about language in China: One of the initial educational reforms introduced under Deng's leadership was the re-introduction of English into the school curriculum. Today English is a prerequisite for most university programs. While exact statistics are difficult to come by, various sources estimate that 300–350 million Chinese are learning English on some level, with approximately 10 million deemed fluent. By contrast, roughly 2 million Americans are estimated to speak some form of Chinese (mostly Cantonese) with a

---

1. "Ethnic Minorities in China," *Wikipedia*, last modified on Aug 19, 2012, http://en.wikipedia.org/wiki/Ethnic_minorities_in_China

high proportion being immigrants and their children who speak the language at home.[2] While Mandarin is increasingly being offered in as an elective in US schools, the Chinese place far, far more importance on learning English than US schools place on learning any foreign language, Mandarin included.

Confucian Heritage

Much of Chinese culture is deeply rooted in Confucianism, a philosophical system of beliefs and ethics dating to the fifth century BC. Its central values were humanism (the belief that humans are teachable and improvable), filial piety (respect for one's parents) and respect for ritual (the proper way of doing things, in the deepest sense).[3] And as Confucianism evolved over the centuries, it became a sophisticated, interconnected set of virtues—honesty, loyalty, etiquette, integrity, kindness, frugality, modesty and bravery—which guide how individuals should behave.

The victory of the Communists in 1949 ushered in a new era for China, and along with it introduced many new elements into the cultural and social fabric. During the period of the Cultural Revolution great emphasis was placed on values such as agrarian socialism, nationalism, patriotism, political orthodoxy, revolutionary class struggle and disdain for capitalists and the bourgeoisie. While the excesses of the period may be history, it is a mistake to underestimate the power that some of these concepts still hold today.

If the Confucian heritage represents one facet of the Chinese culture, and socialism represents another, in recent years some Chinese have also begun to embrace ideas flowing from the West such as

---

2. Him Mark Lai, *Becoming Chinese American: A History of Communities and Institutions* (Lanham: AltaMira Press, 2004) as quoted in *Wikipedia* article "Chinese American," http://en.wikipedia.org/wiki/Chinese_American

3. *Routledge Encyclopedia of Philosophy*, vol 7, (New York: Routledge, 1998)

consumerism, economic advancement and individual achievement. Professor Pierre Xiao Lu of Fudan University aptly summed up the conflicting cultural influences that confront modern-day Chinese[4]:

> Today, the Mainland Chinese consumer's 21st century value system is comprised of three salient parts: the traditional Chinese value system persists, the socialist Chinese value system (dominant), and the Western value system which is often regarded like a trend. The updated Chinese socialist value system of Deng's reform and opening policy brings modernity, wealth, achievement and success, while the Western values bring personal liberty, post-modernism, also modernity, achievement and success. Together, the Chinese consumer's 21st century value system is a veritable melting pot; strong values of modernity, wealth and success are dominant.

Marketers wishing to appeal to young adult Chinese consumers would be best served to keep this cultural "melting pot" in mind. It is easy to assume because young adults are wearing Western clothes and listening to Western music that they are evolving into being like their Western counterparts in every other aspect. Nothing could be further from the truth.

There are several other cultural factors that distinguish Chinese consumers from their US counterparts. Two that we will address here are (a) how the individual sees himself or herself in relation to society, and (b) attitudes toward uncertainty and risk.

Communal Society

Like almost all Asian cultures, China is predominantly a communal society. In such cultures, an individual's sense of identity is derived

---

4. Pierre Xiao Lu, "Luxury Consumer Behavior in Mainland China: What Exists Behind the Facade of New Wealth?" *European Business Journal* (Sept 2010)

from the groups to which he or she belongs (particularly family, village, community, school or workplace unit). In communal societies, the broad, extended family is paramount, with several generations (and often multiple branches of one generation) living or working together. Reciprocity, loyalty and mutual obligations form the heart of communal societies, where there is a strong obligation to get along, to foster harmony, to seek compromise, to sacrifice personal desires for the greater good or group, and in general to behave in a way that is acceptable to others or which will be admired by others. This has a great deal of influence on the products individuals buy, the clothes they wear, the places they go, the media they use, and so forth. As we will see in later chapters, young adult Chinese consumers rely heavily on word-of-mouth recommendations from family or friends, and their use of digital media is an important method by which opinions are solicited and distributed.

By contrast, Americans and most Northern Europeans tend to be far more individualistic. While ties to the immediate family are strong, that loyalty extends primarily to parents and siblings, not the broader, extended family of aunts, uncles and cousins. In individualistic societies, there is a strong emphasis on being your own person, on personal liberty and freedom, on privacy and on creating a distinctive, unique individual persona and sense of style. Marketers accustomed to targeting young adults in the US are adept at appealing to their sense of individuality, vanity, competitiveness and even rebelliousness. Such approaches are usually not relevant to Chinese audiences and must be adapted or recast.

Communal societies place a great deal of importance on defining who is "in" a group—whether it is a family, village or other social unit—and who is "out," that is, outside the group and not subject to the same mutual obligations and loyalties. Thus communal societies often tend toward exclusion of outsiders while conserving resources for those within the group. There may be fear or mistrust of those from outside the society ("foreigners"), and there may be a consequent, built-in dislike of foreign goods, especially if they are not already a well-known name.

Another related factor that is often a conundrum to Westerners is the high degree of inter-connectedness in China that can be very difficult to pierce from the outside. It is necessary to understand that a person's status within a group is built up over years of mutual favors, friendship and services to others in the same group, with the expectation that these will be repaid someday. Thus, an intricate network of favors, preferential treatment or privileges often determines how business is conducted, how agreements get signed and deals are made. As with so many things, the Chinese have a word for it—*guanxi*—and it is a fact of communal life in China.

Feelings about Uncertainty and Risk

In general, the Chinese are deemed to have a relatively high tolerance for ambiguity and uncertainty[5]. While Westerners tend to see the world in concrete terms—black or white, yes or no—the Chinese are comfortable maneuvering in the space in between. In fact, it is considered impolite to give a direct "no" to a question or request, so they will often reply with an all-purpose "maybe." In business they are often able to turn their skill with ambiguity to their advantage, by keeping negotiations open and fluid until a final solution is found that satisfies all partners. And, the willingness to take business risks has been a major contributing factor to the rise of the new entrepreneurial class.

However, there is a strong risk aversion when it comes to buying and using certain categories of consumer products. Those fears are a complicated mix of cultural history and recent quality issues, and marketers must take them into consideration.

---

5. Geert Hofstede, Gert Jan Hofstede and Michael Minkov, *Cultures and Organizations: Software of the Mind* (New York: McGraw Hill, 2010)

On one hand, as mentioned above, there is a degree of distrust of things unknown and foreign. Contrary to common Western assumption, Chinese consumers do not immediately gravitate to imported products or brands simply because they come from the West. In fact, foreign origin can sometimes be a significant barrier, especially with consumers outside of Tier 1 cities (see below). Brands that have been highly successful in China have usually gone to considerable lengths to adapt to local tastes and cultural milieu. For example, according to a study conducted by the Boston Consulting Group, Procter & Gamble's Tide Detergent has done such a thorough job of acculturating to the Chinese market that is actually considered by consumers to be a local brand.[6] Even though McDonald's is recognized as an American brand, it, too, has adapted its menu and promotion to be relevant to Chinese tastes and sensibilities. For example, the company created a special Chinese New Year's meal that included a grilled chicken burger, curly fries, a horoscope with the twelve animals of Chinese astrology, and a traditional red packet for monetary gift giving, symbolizing good luck.

On the other hand, consumers in China have seen product recall after product recall, and often do not have faith in domestic manufacturers to produce products that are safe, reliable or durable. With limited financial resources (which we will discuss in more detail in later sections), they are often torn between buying products that are a good value and those that they can trust. In a nation where one child is still the norm (even as the policy is being loosened in some areas), the wellbeing, safety and good health of the "little emperor or empress" is of paramount importance to young parents. Products that have demonstrable functional reliability, purity or other benefits will have an advantage—but those attributes must be communicated in a clear, believable fashion.

6. Matt Anestis, Hubert Hsu, Vivian Hui and Carol Liao, "Foreign or Local brands in China?" BCG Perspectives, Boston Consulting Group, (2008)

Geographic Context

Mainland China comprises 3,705,407 square miles, only slightly larger than the US 3,676,486 [7]. Yet is has a population of 1.3 billion people—approximately 4.5 times that of the US (310 million). And because much of the country is mountainous or desert, the population density in those areas that are inhabited is significantly greater than even these comparisons indicate.

As shown on the map below (Figure 1-1), China is divided into 33 administrative units:

- 22 provinces—the most common form of regional government, led by a local committee secretary and governor.

- 4 municipalities—Beijing, Shanghai, Tianjin and Chongqing, which are directly under the central government. Their status is theoretically equal to that of the provinces.

- 5 autonomous regions—areas with large ethnic minority (non Han) populations, which have been granted a degree of autonomy for local governance, namely, the Uyghurs in Xinjiang, the Mongols in Inner Mongolia, the Tibetans in Tibet, the Huis in Ningxia and the Zhuangs in Guangxi.

- 2 special administrative regions—Hong Kong and Macau, areas that were returned to China in the late 1990s from Britain and Portugal respectively. They come directly under the central government and enjoy a high degree of autonomy.

---

7. "China," *Wikipedia*, last modified on September 16, 2012, http://en.wikipedia.org/wiki/China

FIGURE 1-1: Provinces of the People's Republic of China

Source: Reproduced from http://en.wikipedia.org/wiki/Provinces_of_the_
People%27s_Republic_of_China

Understanding the Tier Classification

If there has been one overriding change in China since 1978, it has been the stunning increase in urbanization. Up until that time, China had been primarily an agrarian society, with cities designed to be administrative centers of commerce and trade. Today, however, it is home to several of the most populous, modern and dynamic cities in the world.

Its two largest cities, Shanghai and Beijing, each have a population estimated at 22–23 million—or more than the entire state of

New York (19 million) and about the same as the entire country of Australia (22 million). There are over 160 cities in mainland China with a permanent population of more than 1 million residents, and hundreds more in the 500,000–999,999 range.

Making sense of this rapid urbanization has been a challenge for marketers entering China, especially those accustomed to having readily available and up-to-date demographic and market research information. As a result, an unofficial framework has been developed to classify mainland Chinese cities into tiers. This framework, broadly outlined below, takes into account a range of factors including population, economic influence, political influence (provincial/county capitals), provincial GDP, disposable income, cultural and historical significance, and similar characteristics.

Tier 1: Major megalopolises, notably Beijing, Shanghai, Guangzhou and Shenzhen. These are cities with modern, developed infrastructure and relatively high per capita income and per capita retail sales.

Tier 2: Approximately 30 cities, mostly provincial capitals such as Hangzhou, Chengdu, Ningbo and Xian with populations of at least 5 million.

Tier 3: Approximately 150 county capitals, typically with population of at least 1 million, including Hefei, Guilin, Baoding and Changzhou.

Tier 4: Approximately 400 of the smaller and less affluent county-level capitals, with populations generally less than 1 million.

Tier 5: Thousands of smaller cities and towns, sometimes divided into as many as five additional tiers.

To date, much of the focus of Western marketers has been in developing a presence in the Tier 1 cities. These cities have seen tremendous inward migration growth since 1978, the start of economic reform, as thousands of workers poured in from smaller cities, towns and villages in search of education and employment. The Tier 1 cities still dominate the economic and political landscape, but they have begun to see the price of progress in overcrowding, high land costs, congestion, rising cost of living, growing income disparity and pollution. Continued migration into Tier 1 cities would only worsen the situation, so a concerted effort is being made to shift growth to Tier 2 and Tier 3 cities in the future. In fact, Euromonitor International anticipates that "it is the rapid rise of the 'second tier' cities that is changing the urban landscape," and predicts that the current Tier 1 cities will come to experience a decline in relative demographic and economic importance.[8]

Economic Context

The Five-Year Plans

With the advent of reform in 1978, China began to take shape as a modern economy. Until that time, the Chinese marketplace was essentially closed to the outside world. Its economy was centrally managed through a series of Five-Year Plans (5YP), which directed almost every area of industry, agriculture, manufacturing, mining and finance. Even after the era of economic reform commenced, the central government continued to use the 5YP as the primary mechanism for managing the economy, although the goals and objectives have evolved dramatically over the years.

---

8. Stephane Lesaffre and Amy Wang, "Multinational Retailers' Quest for Gold in China's Tier 2 and Tier 3 Cities," Knowledge@Wharton, January 26, 2011, http://knowledge.wharton.upenn.edu/article.cfm?articleid=2688

The First Five-Year Plan (1953–57) focused on industrial growth and the socialization of society. The key elements of that plan were to concentrate all efforts on (a) developing the country's industrial base through construction of roughly 700 large and medium-sized industrially based projects, (b) to develop agricultural producers co-operatives to assist in the socialist transformation of the agriculture and handicraft industries, and (c) to put capitalist industry and commerce on track toward a move to state capitalism. In other words, the goal was to gain control of both the direction and operation of all forms of industry and commerce.

We mention this first plan because it provides a noteworthy benchmark by which to view how the plans have evolved. The changes became apparent by the early 1980s, when the government slowly began to open the country to a limited amount of external trade, and allowed foreign companies to participate in joint ventures with state-owned companies. Furthermore, it established special economic zones, particularly in southern China in the areas around Shenzhen and Guangzhou, to experiment with more market-based and entrepreneurial approaches to business. It is in these areas that manufacturing of low-cost consumers goods destined for export markets became established, thereby triggering one of the most dramatic economic turnarounds the world has ever seen.

The 5YPs are still an important instrument over which the central government has maintained control. However, the plans have grown significantly in economic sophistication and breadth, and have evolved in recognition of China's growing role in the world. For one thing, they are now positioned more as broad "guidelines," to more accurately reflect China's move away from Soviet-style planning to a "socialist market economy."

The most recent 5YP—the twelfth, covering the period 2011–15—represents several developments and shifts in focus that are of significant importance to anyone doing business in China.

For example, a KPMG analysis[9] of the twelfth plan identified the following goals:

- Boost domestic consumption to increase the country's overall GDP, relying less on low-end export manufacturing and more on consumer purchasing of Chinese products within the country.

- Use a new set of economic tools to orchestrate higher consumer spending. Today, Chinese consumers are among the most frugal in the world, that is, they tend to save, not spend. To create a consumer economy, spending and consumption is critical. The government believes this can be done through a set of specific tactics:

  - Improve the social welfare network, thus reducing the need for consumer saving.

  - Boost wages to make more purchasing power available.

  - Create new jobs by shifting to the production of consumer products and services.

  - Promote urbanization and support affordable housing.

  - Adjust taxes to encourage consumer spending.

  - Increase consumer goods imports, which, by making more goods available, will unlock the savings of Chinese consumers.

- Increase the income level of all citizens using many of the tools listed above, specifically to:

  - Increase the disposable income of urban residents by 7%.

  - Increase the new income of rural residents by over 7% each year.

---

9. KPMG, *China's 12th Five-Year Plan: Overview*, (2011) http://www.kpmg.com/CN/en/IssuesAndInsights/ArticlesPublications/Publicationseries/5-years-plan/Documents/China-12th-Five-Year-Plan-Overview-201104.pdf

As a result of those changes, the Chinese governmental planners expect overall household income to more than double from the current US$3.8 trillion to US$8.9 trillion in 2015. Further, China's retail sales are expected to more than double to US$6.4 trillion in 2015 from today's US$2.4 trillion because of increased consumer spending.[10]

China's economic focus has shifted—from the primacy of developing and expanding industrialization and manufacturing, particularly of low-cost products for export, to the development of the consumer market and increased consumer spending and consumption. In its report on the twelfth plan, KPMG believes the primary reason for this shift in emphasis is that Chinese domestic consumption, as a percentage of GDP, fell from 45% in 1999 to 36% in 2009. This is supported by McKinsey & Company reporting that Chinese domestic consumption fell even further in 2010 to 33% of GDP—considerably lower than the proportion that consumer spending represented in the US (71% of GDP) and the UK (65% of GDP).

To reverse this trend, the Chinese government is focusing on improving and enhancing social safety networks such as pensions, health insurance, public education and affordable housing, thus, making more private funds available for the purchase of consumer goods and services.

McKinsey suggests the government's efforts to retool the Chinese economy via the 5YP and boost domestic consumption will result in benefits to many consumer-facing industries such as airlines, consumer products, food, pharmaceuticals, shipping and tourism. McKinsey believes these industries will benefit from a favorable environment for profit growth and a reasonably free, less restricted market. Further, McKinsey also argues these industries will also benefit from the government's attention to social harmony and the

---

10. At the time of writing, the official conversion rate was US$1 = RMB 6.31. This rate is used throughout this text for converting renminbi into US dollars.

"green" environmental area.[11] Should all these occur, the goals of the Twelfth Five-Year Plan may well be accomplished.

To capture the greatest growth opportunities during the current 5YP, McKinsey believes marketing organizations must increase their market penetration and offer tailored products for their core customer segments. That's a long step from the low-cost, commoditized product approach that fueled much of the Chinese manufacturing growth and economic development over the past twenty years. Whether or not the entire Chinese economy can be retooled is a major question, but it is an inherent aim of this 5YP.

In short, most consultants and experts see the next five years as being ones of great opportunity, particularly for consumers and consumer products in the Chinese market. All the governmental and social indicators point in that direction.

Yet, the success of all those governmental plans will ultimately be driven by consumer behaviors. What consumers think and believe are really the key element in understanding what will actually happen within the country. While the government can decree, the people must respond.

Five Key Takeaways

1. China's digital generation—young adults age 18–34—are the first born under the one-child policy, and the first to grow up under the post-revolution era ushered in by Deng Xiaoping in 1978.

2. It is erroneous to assume that this generation is becoming inexorably Westernized. They are deeply rooted in China's Confucian heritage, as well its more recent socialist past, and combine elements of all three cultural systems in a unique and thoroughly Chinese fashion.

---

11. Guangyu Li and Jonathan Woetzel, "What China's Five-Year Plan Means for Business," *McKinsey Quarterly* (July 2011)

3. While much of the economic development over the past three decades has been focused in the major cities, notably Beijing, Shanghai, Guangzhou and Shenzhen, growth increasingly is shifting to Tier 2 and Tier 3 cities, with attendant opportunities and challenges for marketers hoping to grow brands in these areas.

4. The central government has recognized that China cannot continue to thrive simply by being a low-cost producer of cheaply manufactured goods. Its most recent Five-Year Plan places heavy emphasis on policies to encourage domestic consumption, namely, improving the social welfare network, and thereby freeing up more income for discretionary spending by consumers.

5. Marketers operating in China will face increasing competition to capture the heart, minds and wallets of the digital generation. It will be critical to understand the finer points of their needs, wants, motivations and aspirations in order to develop appropriately tailored products, services and marketing approaches.

Moving On

The goal of this chapter was to set the stage for understanding some of the key factors that shape the lives of Chinese consumers. Having given a broad overview of the cultural and economic setting in which they live, we can now turn our attention to understanding young adult Chinese consumers on their own terms.

Chapter 2

Comparing Young Adult Consumers in China and the US

We begin our examination of young adult Chinese consumers by first explaining the research methods used to gather the data in this book, and by examining the basic demographic profiles of those in the 18–34 age group. This sets the stage for the following chapters that discuss their behavior and preferences in specific product categories.

Throughout this book we will put the data on young Chinese consumers in perspective by comparing their profiles, behaviors and attitudes with those of their contemporaries in the US. While we do not provide point-by-point comparison on all factors, we believe the data on 18–34-year-old Americans is a useful reference point for Western managers more accustomed to marketing in cities such as New York, Dallas and Seattle than Shanghai, Shenzhen and Chengdu.

How the Profiles Were Developed

The data in this book are drawn from online syndicated studies from ProsperChina.com and BIGinsight.com, both services of Prosper Business Development, a business acceleration firm based in Columbus Ohio (http://www.goprosper.com). Since 1990, Prosper has helped its clients maximize productivity and grow revenues. In 1996, Prosper entered the China market. Since then it has been helping companies expand in China through consultative services that include market intelligence.

The information is generated using large, online panels—conducted via e-mail—of adults age 18–54 in China and over 18 in the US. While our purpose in this book is to focus on the generation of 18–34-year-olds, the broader databases contain extensive information across additional adult age groups in both countries, with samples balanced to meet known demographic criteria of age and gender along eight segments in China and fourteen segments in the US studies. These sample bases are dynamically balanced against available census data records for a proper reflection of males and females age 18–24, 25–34, 35–44 and 45–54 in China, plus two added brackets in the US, 55–64 and over-65.

In 2006, the first ProsperChina™ Quarterly Survey (PCQS) was launched in China, via e-mail, in order to gather parallel information on Chinese consumers.

The key advantages of using these two databases is that they provide information that is consistently gathered over time, using similar questionnaires and methodologies, to achieve a high level of comparability between the studies. Often Western managers find to their dismay that the data they are accustomed to receiving in the US is not available in China, or that it has been collected with such a different method, or using different questionnaires, that it is difficult or misleading to draw comparisons between two groups of consumers.

Another frequent challenge for Western marketers is that they often must depend on "point-in-time" research that merely depicts consumer attitudes, feelings or reported behaviors at that given juncture. However, by drawing on the cumulative databases we are able to investigate changing attitudes and behaviors longitudinally—that is, over time. During the periods covered in this analysis, the questionnaires and methodology have remained consistent, therefore, we can make longitudinal comparisons with confidence.

This is of critical importance in providing useful views of the consumers in the two nations. By providing trends spanning four or five years, we can remove the monthly or yearly variations that occur in many types of research data gathering. Therefore, the results reported are more likely to reflect actual consumer belief and behaviors than the typical one-point-in-time "snapshot" research studies, which often reflect anomalies rather than facts. To make rational business decisions, managers must have information that shows trends and that only comes from tracking behavioral data over time.

We will briefly review the nature of the databases used in this and the following chapters.

ProsperChina™ Quarterly Studies (PCQS)

The data on Chinese consumers in this book has been drawn from the ongoing ProsperChina™ Quarterly Study (PCQS). These PCQS gathers responses from large-scale panels of online participants across all geographic areas of China. Since its inception in 2006, the PCQS have received over 232,000 cumulative consumer responses, making it one of the largest and most comprehensive of all available Chinese consumer databases.

A key factor in the success of the PCQS is the anonymity it provides respondents. In a culture that frowns upon expressions of personal preference and attitudes, especially when dealing with strangers, it is difficult for researchers to gather information using traditional techniques such as personal interviews, telephone surveys or focus groups.

However, by getting respondents to answer online in a confidential, anonymous setting, these studies have been able to generate participation from large numbers of willing and candid consumers. The most recent panel reflected in this book consisted of over 16,000 consumers who responded to the questionnaire during the fourth quarter of 2011.

The PCQS studies are very broad and far ranging. Not only are a large number of consumers surveyed and their responses tabulated and aggregated, the PCQS respondents provide information on a wide variety of subject areas, such as consumer confidence, employment outlook, investor confidence, practical purchasing needs versus wants and budgeting, consumer finances, planned discretionary purchases, online shopping, online research and media influence. Quite simply, these studies are the most comprehensive data source available on Chinese consumers today.

The primary users of the PCQS data have been retailers, consumer goods manufacturers, media managers and others interested in marketing in China. They have used the information to help them understand the exceedingly complex and rapidly evolving Chinese consumer marketplace.

US Studies of Media Behavior and Influence

The data on US consumers in this book are drawn primarily from the ongoing Media Behavior & Influence™ Study (MBI) from BIGinsight.com, a biannual online survey of media usage and influence on buying behavior. Each group of respondents is balanced against US census data to assure it is representative of the nation at large. As with the PCQS, the MBI relies on large respondent bases to assure the accuracy and projectability of the data. Each study wave normally generates approximately 22,000 to 25,000 responses and has gathered more than 300,000 cumulative responses since its inception in 2002. This continuity of data gathering, as well of the consistency in research questions, provides a unique longitudinal view of the US consumer and marketplace.

Similarities Between the Chinese and US Databases

The PCQS and MBI are designed to be quite similar in structure and have a considerable degree of overlap and consistency in the questions and areas of inquiry. Thus, we are able to make insightful comparisons and contrasts between the two populations quite easily.

Both studies ask consumers to report on the attitudes, preferences and use of nine broad product categories:

- apparel
- automobiles
- eating out
- electronics
- financial services
- groceries
- home improvement
- medicines and health and beauty aids
- telecommunication and wireless services.

Purchases in these categories make up a significant portion of all consumer purchasing activities in both countries. Behaviors and attitudes about these product categories will be detailed in the subsequent chapters.

Comparative Profiles on Young Adults in China and the US

By definition, in this analysis, we know that our two groups of Chinese and American consumers share two traits: they are between the ages of 18 and 34, and they participated in the online survey used to gather the data. Beyond those shared characteristics, there are some very telling differences between the groups, as summarized in Figure 2-1.

FIGURE 2-1: BASIC DEMOGRAPHIC CHARACTERISTICS
CHINESE AND AMERICAN CONSUMERS

	China 18–34	US 18–34	Index
Male	51.7	51.2	100.9
Female	48.3	48.8	99.0
Married	36.8	30.1	122.1
Living with partner	11.9	14.1	84.3
Divorced or separated	0.8	4.1	20.7
Widowed	0.5	1.0	47.2
Single, never married	50.0	49.5	101.0
Children	45.2	41.5	108.9
Baby	26.3	25.7	102.2
Size	3.84	2.96	129.8
Income (in US$)	$9,438	$55,184	15.4

Source: ProsperChina.com

The proportion of males is somewhat higher in the Chinese than in the US respondent group, and conversely, the proportion of females lower. Additionally, at this age the Chinese are far more likely to report being married (36.8% in China, 30.1% in the US). And, given the disproportionate number of young marrieds, the Chinese are also more likely to have a baby or a child in the household, which would, in part at least, account for the greater average household size (3.84 persons in China, 2.96 in the US).

While the young Chinese adults are more likely to be married, the traditional nature of Chinese household becomes apparent when we see that they are far less likely to be living with an unmarried partner, or to be divorced or separated.

Nevertheless, those in the 18–34 category are still relatively young, and a significant proportion in each country (50.0% in China and

49.5% in the US) have never been married. This has an important influence on how discretionary income is spent. As we will see later, there is great interest in spending on apparel, electronics, vacations and leisure activities—items that often have to be put on the back burner once a baby comes into the picture.

A final point to be made about Figure 2-1 is the considerable gap that still exists in income between the Chinese and American in the 18–34 age group. The Chinese report an average income of US$9,438, only about 15% of the income of their US counterparts. And while the cost of living in China is well below that in the US, there are also fewer government- or workplace-provided benefits and safety nets. Thus, frugality, saving for the future and "smart" spending (read "value consciousness") are still extremely important to young Chinese, as we will discuss further in coming chapters.

FIGURE 2-2: HOUSEHOLD STATUS
CHINESE AND AMERICAN CONSUMERS

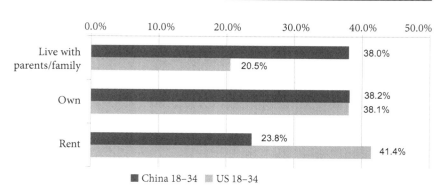

Source: ProsperChina.com

Further data about Chinese living arrangements are shown in Figure 2-2. We find that 38.0% of Chinese 18–34-year-olds report that they live with parents, compared with only 20.5% in the US. Multi-generational households are still very common in China, often extending well past the time a son or daughter is married and has a child of his or her own. While on one hand, young Chinese are more likely to live with their parents, on the other, they are also more likely to own their own home or apartment. Renting is far less common among young Chinese adults than in the US (23.8 versus 41.4%). Bear in mind that China has gone through a tremendous real estate boom in recent years, with a great deal of marketing emphasis on owning a home or apartment in a new development. What these figures tell us may be the tendency of young Chinese adults to stay at home to save money in order to make that first real estate acquisition.

While a large number of demographic characteristics are gathered in both the Chinese and US studies, over time, we have learned that two are the most revealing in terms of illustrating the primary differences between the Chinese and US consumer populations: education and occupation. Those comparisons are shown in Figures 2-3 and 2-4 below.

FIGURE 2-3: EDUCATIONAL ACHIEVEMENT
CHINESE AND AMERICAN CONSUMERS

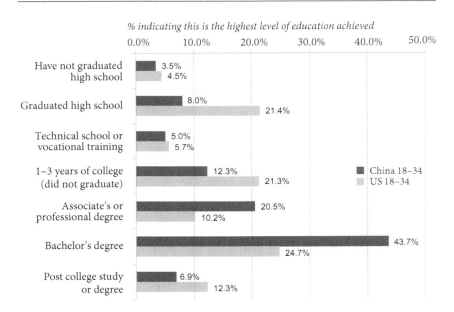

% indicating this is the highest level of education achieved

Source: ProsperChina.com

There are particularly sharp differences between the two countries when looking at the highest level of education achieved. The US group is heavily weighted toward respondents who have graduated high school and attended (but did not graduate) college. Respondents to the Chinese study are more than twice as likely to hold an associate's or professional degree, and are almost twice as likely to have completed a bachelor's degree. While Americans have a slight edge in post-college degrees, this is still a relatively small proportion of the population in either country. And, with the tremendous increase in graduate programs in China in the past decade, especially executive MBAs and other professional graduate programs, we would expect the gap on this statistic to narrow in the coming years.

FIGURE 2-4: OCCUPATIONAL CATEGORIES CHINESE AND AMERICAN CONSUMERS

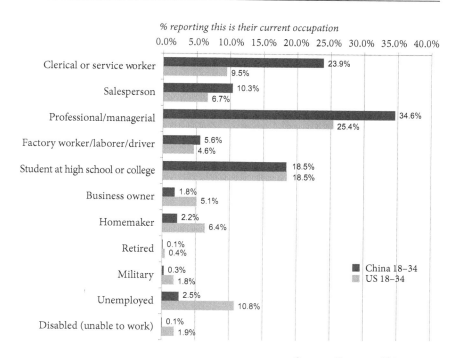

Source: ProsperChina.com

In terms of occupation, the Chinese respondent base is weighted more toward professional/managerial, salespersons and especially clerical or service workers than the US. The US 18–34-year-old respondents have a higher proportion working as business owners or in the military. They are also more likely to be homemakers, students, unemployed or disabled—that is, not part of the workforce. And overall a significantly lower percentage of American 18–34-year-olds are currently employed outside the home, 53.0%, than in China, 76.6%. This difference should be kept in mind when reviewing the comparisons in the remaining chapters.

As discussed in Chapter 1, Chinese cities are categorized by tiers, according to factors such as population, provincial GDP and economic growth and other criteria. It is beyond the scope of this book to present a detailed analysis of Chinese consumers in all tiers. Furthermore, few Western companies have the resources, scale or capabilities to market across the vast consumer environment that is modern day China. However, while most multinational marketers have focused their efforts so far on the Tier 1 cities, many recognize the growing economic importance of cities in Tiers 2 and 3. Therefore, this text will share relevant insights into consumers in Tiers 1–3, and how important differences between the tiers may require alternative marketing approaches. For many marketers already operating in China, Tiers 2 and 3 represent the "next step" expansion opportunities, but success will require adaptation of their marketing approaches to the realities of these regional consumers.

One of the first factors to become apparent in studying the data by tiers is the disproportionate number of young women who are in Tier 1, and the disproportionate number of young men in Tier 3. For the young women, they are likely drawn to the Tier 1 cities by the opportunities for work in offices or on light manufacturing assembly lines, while some men find more opportunities in heavy industrial manufacturing and mining in Tier 3 cities. Nevertheless, this imbalance creates some anomalies that have important implications for marketers.

FIGURE 2-5: KEY DEMOGRAPHIC CHARACTERISTICS TIERS 1–3
* CHINESE CONSUMERS BY TIER

	Tier 1	Tier 2	Tier 3
Male	42.0	51.4	54.3
Female	58.0	48.6	45.7
Married	44.6	36.1	31.3
Average age	26.8	25.8	25.0
Average household size	3.5	3.7	3.9
Average household income (US$)	$13,977	$9,891	$7,227
Professional/managerial	45.9	35.9	29.9
Clerical or service worker	27.9	24.9	21.8
Factory worker/laborer/driver	2.9	4.5	5.7
Student	9.2	17.9	24.0
Bachelor's degree	55.7	47.1	40.0

Source: ProsperChina.com

For example, individuals in Tier 3 cities are less likely to be married. This may be because of few opportunities for finding a partner or because of lower incomes associated with these areas. In spite of this, the average household size in Tier 3 cities is larger than in Tier 1 and 2 areas. Most likely this is a reflection of a greater number of multi-generational family units living in the same residence.

Most telling is the dramatic differences in income across Tiers 1–3. Whereas the average income in Tier 1 is US$13,977, it falls significantly for Tier 2 (US$9,891) and even more for Tier 3 (US$7,227). This would be expected given the greater proportion of professional and managerial occupations in Tier 1, and the high proportion of industrial and laborer jobs in Tier 3. As we will discuss in more detail in later chapters, it is imperative for marketers to recognize the financial constraints of consumers in these markets, as well as the importance they attach to frugality, value and tradition.

Educational levels also differ by tier, with a higher percentage of the respondents in Tier 1 stating they that have completed a bachelor's degree (55.7%). For Tier 2 the figure drops to 47.1%, and for Tier 3 it drops to 40.0%. It should be kept in mind, however, that in the US the percentage of 18–34-year-olds with a bachelor's degree is only 24.6. Even adding in those with post-graduate study (12.2%), the combined total (36.8%) is still less than the percentage with a bachelor's degree in Tier 3 cities. Furthermore, a significant percentage of respondents in Tiers 2 and 3 report that they are students, and thus have not completed their education.

Five Key Takeaways

1. The data in this text is derived from ongoing, large-sample online research among Chinese and Americans age 18–34, a critical group of consumers in the early phases of their careers and household formation. The two databases used in this text—the ProsperChina Quarterly Study (PCQS) and the biannual US Media Behavior & Influence Study (MBI)—provide insights and trends on consumer attitudes, preferences and intentions spanning nine product categories.

2. For Western marketers seeking to appeal to China's digital generation, it is useful to use Americans of the same of age cohort as a point of reference, and to compare and contrast the demographics, economic and lifestyle characteristics of the two groups.

3. For example, the Chinese respondents more frequently report being married, having a child and living with their parents. Additionally, the Chinese respondents have higher educational levels than the Americans do, yet have an average income that is less than one fifth of their US counterparts.

4. A greater proportion of the Chinese report being actively engaged in the workforce while the US respondents are more likely to be unemployed, homemakers, disabled or unable to work or in the military.

5. Demographic differences within China are important as well. For example, currently, respondents in Tier 1 cities tend to be better educated, more often professional or managerial and more affluent—a gap that will likely narrow as growth continues to shift to Tiers 2 and 3. Nevertheless, marketers hoping to penetrate Tiers 2 and 3 need to recognize that cultural, linguistic and economic differences still play an important role in these regions, and should adapt their plans accordingly.

Moving On

Following this background to the studies in China and the US, in the next chapter, we move to one of the most important areas of comparison: media consumption. Which media consumers access and use, we argue, defines what they do and can indicate what they are likely to do in the future.

Chapter 3

Digital Generation Lifestyle and Leisure Activities

In the last chapter, we drew a profile of China's digital generation and their counterparts in the US using basic demographic information. That provided an initial insight into some of the factors that shape their attitudes, behaviors and habits. In this chapter, we will go a step further by examining what they do in their day-to-day activities, the life-changing events they are experiencing and what pastimes they enjoy.

Young adulthood is universally a period of change and transition. In China, however, personal maturation for the digital generation is played out against a background of rapid, incessant change on the societal level. As we will see throughout this book, this context of transformation is an important factor in shaping the different lifestyles, behaviors, beliefs and aspirations of both Chinese and Americans of the same generation.

Much has been written about young Americans in the 18–34 age bracket—often referred to as "Millennials," "Gen Y" or "Generation Next." They came of age in a time shaped by increasing American concerns about international terrorism, two ongoing wars and the "Great Recession." A full exploration of the experience of American Millennials is beyond the scope of this book, but the interested reader is directed to an excellent report produced by the Pew Research Center, *Young, Underemployed and Optimistic*.[1] Following are some of the key characteristics of 18–34-year-old Americans from the report:

- They are the most educated generation in the history of the country, yet they are currently facing high unemployment or underemployment.

- The negative job outlook has led to many to return to school for more education or training, in spite of already carrying record levels of education debt.

- They place a high value on marriage and parenthood, but are de-ferring marriage or having a baby until their situation improves.

- They embrace digital technology and are highly connected.

- They believe they have it harder than did their parents.

- They are less acquisitive than previous generations and less brand loyal in their buying habits.

- They are nevertheless optimistic about their future, and expect that by going "small and simple" they will be able to earn enough for their needs and to save for the future.

While we do not have a comparable qualitative study of Chinese of the same generation, some broad lifestyle differences can be noted. Young Chinese are generally very optimistic about their chances to succeed, and see they have greater opportunities than were available

---

1. Pew Research Center, *Young, Underemployed and Optimistic, Coming of Age, Slowly, in a Tough Economy*, Feb 9, 2012, http://www.pewso-cialtrends.org/2012/02/09/young-underemployed-and-optimistic/

to their parents. Along with that, however, comes tremendous pressure to excel and to live up to their parents' expectations. They are caught between rapidly rising prices for housing, healthcare and food, and their desire for luxury branded goods to demonstrate their success. They embrace the idea that "to get rich is glorious," and are willing to work extremely hard, defer gratification and sacrifice for the future, but they also see some of the negative consequences: ever increasing demands from superiors and family, toll on health and lack of personal time. While many believe this is "China's century," their optimism is often tempered by fears that economic or political developments in the West could set back the pace of progress in their country.

Life-Changing Events

Both the ProsperChina Quarterly Studies (PCQS) and the Media Behavior & Influence Studies (MBI) ask respondents about the life-changing events they are currently undergoing, although the study in China covers a longer list of potential changes. The comparisons are shown in Figure 3-1.

FIGURE 3-1: LIFE-CHANGING EVENTS PLANNED OR ANTICIPATED IN COMING SIX MONTHS

	China 18–34	US 18–34
Starting a new job	40.3%	N/A
Starting or developing your own business	36.6%	N/A
Getting married	20.3%	9.1%
Expecting a baby	13.9%	7.9%
Moving to a new city	12.5%	N/A
You or your child starting college or graduate school	6.4%	11.7%
Separated or divorced	1.2%	2.6%

Source: ProsperChina.com

Across the board, young adult Chinese report a higher incidence of undergoing almost every type of life-changing event, with many evidently experiencing more than one. Over a third of the Chinese respondents state that they are either starting a new job and/or launching a new business. (The study in the US does not include these career-related questions, so we do not have comparable data.) Furthermore, a fifth of the Chinese respondents (20.3%) report that they are getting married, twice the rate reported by the Americans in the same age group. And, 13.9% of the Chinese say they are expecting a baby, compared with only 7.9% in the US. It was noted in Chapter 2 that young adult Chinese more frequently report being married and having a child, so these data reinforce the idea that the Chinese generally marry earlier and begin their families sooner than their American counterparts.

The one area of change the Chinese participants report less frequently than Americans is starting college or graduate school. However, it should be kept in mind that, as noted in Chapter 2, the Chinese respondents far more frequently report having already attained an associate's, professional, or bachelor's degree than do the respondents from the US. And, as noted in the Pew study, many young Americans are returning to school because they either cannot find a job, or hope to obtain a better one through additional education or training.

Another key statistic that has important implications for marketers is the number of young Chinese consumers who say they plan on moving to a new city—12.5%. As discussed in Chapter 1, over the past three decades China has undergone a huge migration of workers from the countryside and smaller towns and cities to the giant Tier 1 cities. Increasingly, this ongoing population shift now also includes inward migration to Tier 2 and 3 cities. Many (if not most) of these urban immigrants are young people looking for work in factories and offices, or seeking an education. While there is no exact statistic, it is safe to conclude that a significant proportion of the post-revolution generation currently lives away from the town or city where they grew up. As we will see in later sections, this has a tremendous influence on their attitudes and behaviors—from how they spend their leisure time, and with whom they spend it, to the goods and services they consume as part of their free time activities.

Taking all of these life-changing events together, we can see that members of China's digital generation are on the move, literally and figuratively, and represent tremendous buying opportunities for marketers who can be relevant to them during their time of transition.

This much rapid change, however, carries with it a number of stresses. So, how do these busy young adults relax, unwind and spend their leisure time? In the following sections, we examine the leisure activities reported by young adult Chinese and American consumers. As we will see, while there are commonalities, there are also major differences in how the young Chinese and Americans spend their free time.

Leisure Pursuits

Figure 3-2 illustrates the percentage of respondents in China and the US who report engaging in each listed activity during the most recent study period.

The most widely reported activity by Chinese respondents is surfing the Internet (77.4%) followed by listening to music (64.2%). While these are also quite popular with the Americans (65.3 and 65.7% respectively), in the US the most popular pastime is watching TV (71.7%)and going to movies (66.1%), both of which rank lower with the Chinese (52.1 and 46.8% respectively).

Generally speaking, Americans are more likely to favor activities that require an outlay of money—namely eating out, going to an amusement park, movies, concerts or live theater, or going

FIGURE 3-2: FAVORITE LEISURE ACTIVITIES
CHINESE AND AMERICAN CONSUMERS

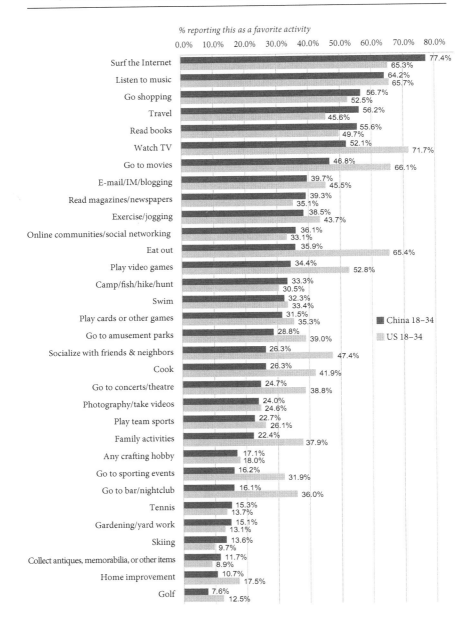

% reporting this as a favorite activity

Activity	China 18–34	US 18–34
Surf the Internet	77.4%	65.3%
Listen to music	64.2%	65.7%
Go shopping	56.7%	52.5%
Travel	56.2%	45.6%
Read books	55.6%	49.7%
Watch TV	52.1%	71.7%
Go to movies	46.8%	66.1%
E-mail/IM/blogging	39.7%	45.5%
Read magazines/newspapers	39.3%	35.1%
Exercise/jogging	38.5%	43.7%
Online communities/social networking	36.1%	33.1%
Eat out	35.9%	65.4%
Play video games	34.4%	52.8%
Camp/fish/hike/hunt	33.3%	30.5%
Swim	32.3%	33.4%
Play cards or other games	31.5%	35.3%
Go to amusement parks	28.8%	39.0%
Socialize with friends & neighbors	26.3%	47.4%
Cook	26.3%	41.9%
Go to concerts/theatre	24.7%	38.8%
Photography/take videos	24.0%	24.6%
Play team sports	22.7%	26.1%
Family activities	22.4%	37.9%
Any crafting hobby	17.1%	18.0%
Go to sporting events	16.2%	31.9%
Go to bar/nightclub	16.1%	36.0%
Tennis	15.3%	13.7%
Gardening/yard work	15.1%	13.1%
Skiing	13.6%	9.7%
Collect antiques, memorabilia, or other items	11.7%	8.9%
Home improvement	10.7%	17.5%
Golf	7.6%	12.5%

Source: ProsperChina.com

to sporting events, a bar or nightclub. This is, in part, a result of their higher income, as we saw in Chapter 2. However, it is also a reflection of how the Chinese prefer to spend the funds they have. Thus, going shopping is more popular in China (56.7 versus 52.5% in the US), as is travel (56.2 compared with 45.6% in the US). This gap is not simply due to the impact of the recession on US shopping and travel since both of these activities rated lower with the Americans than the Chinese even prior to the economic downturn.

Another point to be made about the leisure activities of these young adults is that Americans more commonly mention activities that are done with one or more companions (eating out, going to amusement parks, and so on), while the Chinese more often cite activities that are done alone such as various online activities, listening to music and reading. The Chinese respondents report socializing with family and friends less often than the American group (26.3 versus 47.4%). They also engage in family activities less often—22.4% for the Chinese respondents compared with 39.7% for the Americans. These findings appear counterintuitive for a communal society, in which group and family connections are paramount. However, it must be kept in mind that the 18–34 age group are the first generation of the one-child policy, and thus generally come from small families. Since they are more likely to be married or live with their parents, or both, they may not see spending time on family activities as a pastime. Finally, as discussed in the previous section, a large proportion live away from the town or city where they grew up and thus are not near their parents or childhood friends, and so would have less opportunity to spend time with them.

Differences by Gender

Within the Chinese respondent group, there are important differences in how men and women choose to spend their leisure time, as shown in Figure 3-3.

FIGURE 3-3: FAVORITE LEISURE ACTIVITIES
CHINESE CONSUMERS BY GENDER

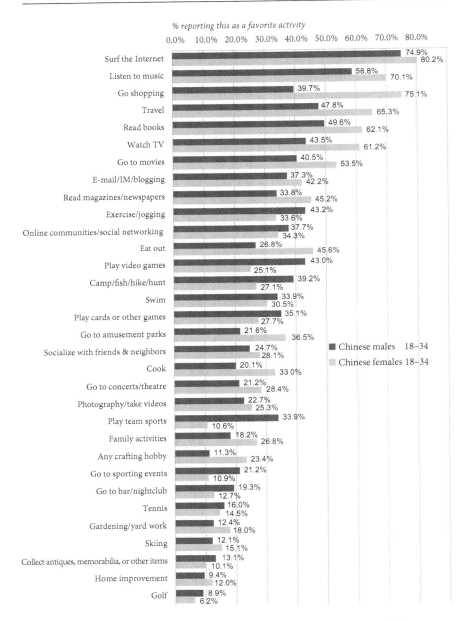

Source: ProsperChina.com

Surfing the Internet is the most frequently mentioned pastime by both genders. Young women, however, far more frequently cite activities such as shopping, travel, listening to music, reading a book, magazine or newspaper, watching TV, eating out and cooking. In fact, the young women overall tend to answer that they participate in more types of leisure activities than the men.

On the other hand, the young men are less interested in shopping as a leisure pastime, and lean more towards such typically masculine pursuits such as playing video games, going camping/fishing, playing cards and team sports and going to sporting events.

Interest in Physical Activity and Sports

One of the most popular leisure activities around the world is physical activity to keep fit, and this is certainly true for Chinese men and women. In particular, exercise activities such as tai chi, jogging, hiking and swimming have long been popular in China—all of which do not necessarily require expensive equipment and can be done in public places. More recently tennis and golf have begun to gain a following in China, in part as a way to demonstrate social status and sophistication.

Additionally, since professional and amateur sports have increasingly become major sponsorship opportunities within China, it is worthwhile understanding which sports are most heavily favored by young adults. Basketball in particularly has become hugely popular in China, thanks in no small part to the success of Yao Ming, and more recently Jeremy Lin, in the NBA. Both US and domestic teams are followed with great excitement, and pick-up courts are now a common sight in Chinese cities.

Major team sports as known in the West are relatively new in China, although interest appears to be growing. In a September 2011 PCQS, respondents were asked, "Which sports do you like to watch?" Basketball was mentioned by 49.6% of the respondents. This was followed by badminton (42.9%), swimming (40.2%), table tennis (37.4%) and gymnastics (33.3%), all of which are primarily individual sports. However, three major Western team sports are making inroads into the Chinese psyche: baseball, American football and hockey. While the awareness level is still relatively limited, appealing to only about 7–9% of 18–34-year-olds, interest in all three has been growing steadily over the past few years. It may be that the growth in followers of these sports can be attributed to the greater television exposure that is now available in China. Or it may represent an interest in Western team sports, and the fact that American sports celebrities are becoming better known around the world. Whatever the reason, it would seem there are opportunities for each sport to cultivate new fans in China, with resulting sponsorship opportunities for marketers.

Having given an overview of the favorite leisure activities of young Chinese and Americans young consumers in Figures 3-2 and 3-3, we will now explore some key leisure areas in greater depth: watching TV, travel, going to the movies and eating out.

Watching TV

Probably nothing tells marketers more about a culture or a population than the television shows the people in that market watch. Even if some of this viewing is dependent on what is being aired, the choices and selections consumers make often clearly indicate their interests and preferences.

It should be noted that Chinese television has been highly regulated over the years. China Central Television (commonly known as CCTV), the state-owned network comprising 22 channel of diverse programming, continues to be the dominant outlet. Today, however, major changes are occurring as regional television has enhanced their offerings while satellite and dish-TV networks have expanded their coverage across the country.

Of particular interest to marketers is the role that TV plays in delivering marketing communication. According to Group M China, the media arm of WPP, one of the world's largest advertising groups, TV is still the most important medium in terms of ad spending, with an estimated US$31 billion spent in 2011, or approximately 58% of all ad spending within the mainland.[2] With such a large proportion of advertising budgets spent on TV, competition is strong among advertisers jockeying for prime positions, and rates have steadily increased in recent years as more multinationals enter the market and demand among domestic marketers has increased. Given the tremendous expense of running a TV campaign in China, any marketer doing so must be very cautious in media planning and carefully direct their investment towards channels and programs that are relevant to their particular target audience and product category.

In Figure 3-2 it was noted that young adult Chinese mention watching TV as a favorite pastime less often (52.1%)than their US counterparts (71.7%). However, when asked what type of shows they watch "regularly," the Chinese show a keen interest in many programming formats, as shown in Figure 3-4.

Movies are the most popular form of programming among both the Chinese (62.2%)and the Americans (55.3%). However, whereas the Chinese list news as their second-most regularly watched format (54.2%), only 24.6% of the Americans report regularly watching news programs. The Chinese also report more regular viewership of drama shows, game shows, talk shows, documentaries and soap operas. The Americans, on the other hand, are far more regular viewers of cartoons, sports, reality TV, cooking and home improvement.

---

2. "Group M Forecasts 17% Ad Spend Growth in China Next Year," *Advertising Age*, Sept 14, 2011

FIGURE 3-4: TV PROGRAMMING WATCHED REGULARLY
CHINESE AND AMERICAN CONSUMERS

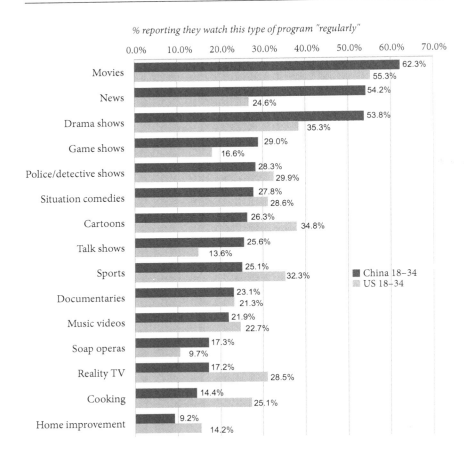

Source: ProsperChina.com

Within the Chinese respondent group there are some noteworthy differences by gender that should be kept in mind when planning TV advertising campaigns. Young women report they watch drama shows much more often than men (65.2 versus 43.2%). Women also more frequently report being a regular viewer of soap operas and cooking shows. In contrast, men regularly watch news more often than women, as well as game shows, sports and documentaries.

FIGURE 3-5: TV PROGRAMMING WATCHED REGULARLY CHINESE CONSUMERS BY GENDER

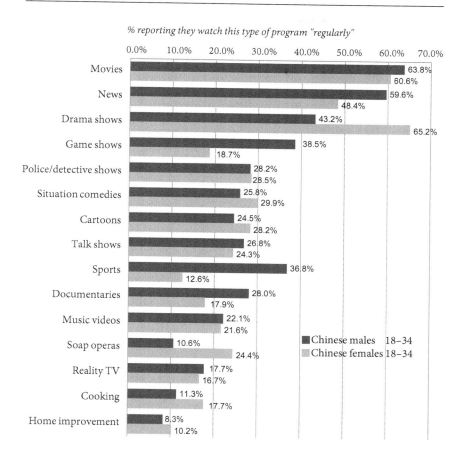

% reporting they watch this type of program "regularly"

Source: ProsperChina.com

We will return to the question of TV viewership in Chapters 4 and 5 when we take a closer look at how the digital generation consumes all forms of media, traditional as well as digital, and how these media forms influence their purchasing behaviors.

Travel

Travel and tourism have expanded greatly in the past thirty years within China, and are now recognized as an important growth industry. Increased wealth, improved infrastructure and easing of restrictions on domestic and international travel have helped to fuel a boom in all areas of travel services—airlines, trains, hotels, tour operators and so on. Additionally, the growing commercial sector has led to greater incidence of business travel, spurring demand for executive-level travel services.

Overall, the Chinese travel industry consists of three main components that are important to marketers: inbound travel by foreign visitors; domestic travel by Chinese consumers and business people; and outbound travel by Chinese tourists and executives to international destinations. By any measure, all three segments are experiencing rapid expansion. In fact, the World Tourism Organization projects that by 2020 China will become the world's most popular destination and the fourth-largest source of outbound tourists. Recognizing the importance of the travel industry, China declared tourism a strategic pillar of its national economic policy in 2009, and continues to make investments in infrastructure and services to encourage domestic and international travel.

A prime time for travel within China is one of the seven public holidays celebrated each year. Of these, the Chinese New Year, Labor Day and National Day celebrations have been extended by the government for as long as a week (the so-called Golden Weeks) in order to encourage workers to return to their home city to celebrate with their family, or take the opportunity to travel for a domestic or international vacation.

In the previous figures, we saw that travel ranks quite high as a leisure activity, especially with young Chinese women. For them, it is often combined with one of their other favorite pastimes, shopping.

Retail tourism—the "shop till you drop" trip or the "sweeping goods tour" (as it is called in Chinese)—is increasingly popular among Chinese of all ages, including those in the 18–34 age bracket. For this reason, fashionable destinations such as Hong Kong, Macau, Paris, New York and Milan are seeing significant increases in travelers from China. According to the *International Herald Tribune*, Chinese travelers accounted for 62% of the total amount spent on luxury goods in Europe in 2011[3]. Top of the shopping list are items such as watches, leather goods, eyewear, cosmetics, scents and jewelry. Like generations before them of the newly affluent (think Americans in the 1880s and 1890s or the Japanese of the 1970s and 1980s), Chinese consumers are creating their own "Grand Tours" in order to become more knowledgeable about the world around them, to hone their language skills, to develop insights into other cultures and societies and to victoriously drag home bags and bags of merchandise acquired abroad.

If shopping is one reason for travel, rest and relaxation is another. Destinations such as Phuket and Hawaii now compete with domestic locations such as Hainan Island and Yellow Mountain (in Anhui province) for those seeking natural beauty, panoramic vistas, clean air and opportunities for favorite leisure activities including hiking, camping, swimming and photography.

Vacation travel is an important activity among most 18–34-year-old Chinese, with 91% saying they regularly or occasionally take vacation trips (Figure 3-6). It is notable that over a third say they take a vacation trip two or more times a year, a figure which rises to 51% for those living in Tier 1 cities.

---

3. Harvey Morris, "Chinese Tourists to the Rescue", *International Herald Tribune*, February 3, 2012, http://rendezvous.blogs.nytimes.com/2012/02/03/chinese-tourists-to-the-rescue/?scp=1&sq=luxury&st=cse

FIGURE 3-6: HOW OFTEN DO YOU TAKE VACATION TRIPS? CHINESE CONSUMERS BY GENDER AND TIER

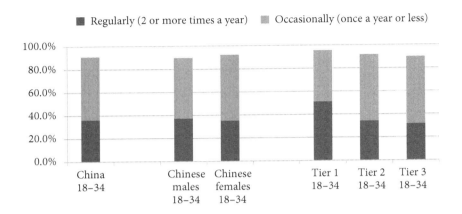

Source: ProsperChina.com

Overall, 79.9% of the Chinese consumers in the study report they are planning on taking a vacation trip within the coming six months. However, across the country there is distinct difference as to the mode of travel. Those living in Tier 1 cities most often report they will travel by airplane (66.0%) compared with 43.5% for all respondents in the age group. Outside of Tier 1 cities, train travel is still the mode of choice, with 35% in Tier 2 cities saying they will travel by train, as well as 46.4% of those in Tier 3 cities. Relatively few individuals expect to travel by car, bus or other modes of transport. While car ownership is increasing in China (see Chapter 8), there are obstacles to the type of "cross country" driving vacation popular in America and Europe. The distances are vast, the costs of gas is high, rural roads are often in poor condition and much of the landscape away from the coast is inhospitable. The government has initiated a program to build a national expressway network connecting all provincial capitals with Beijing and one another, but traveler services (hotels, motels, restaurants, gas stations) along the way are still limited in many areas.

FIGURE 3-7: Will you be traveling by...?
◆ Chinese consumers by tier

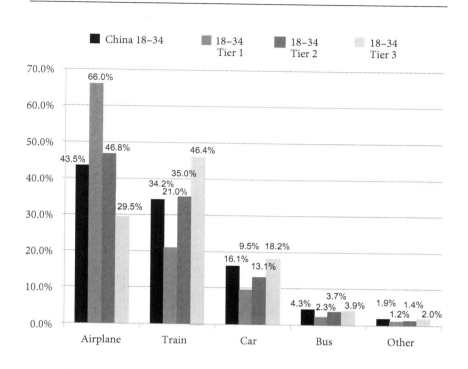

Source: ProsperChina.com

Travel for Business

The importance of business travel to this generation of Chinese consumers is seen in Figure 3-8, with over two-thirds reporting that they travel either regularly or occasionally on business. The percentage reporting regular business travel is higher for men (23.4%) than for women (12.9%), and is higher in Tier 1 cities (27.1%). However, keeping in mind that this is still a relatively young group, it can be expected that their level of business travel will increase as they advance in their careers.

FIGURE 3-8: DO YOU TRAVEL FOR BUSINESS?
CHINESE CONSUMERS BY GENDER AND TIER

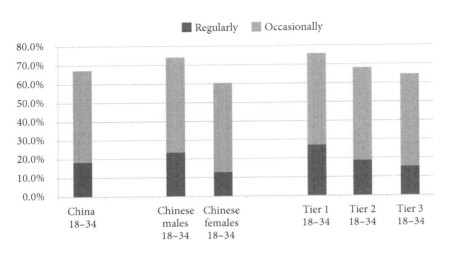

Source: ProsperChina.com

Going to the Movies

Chinese and American consumers have somewhat different attitudes about seeing movies. While both list movies as the type of TV programming they watch most regularly, it is a different story when it comes to going to a theater to see a movie. As noted in Figure 3-2, 66.1% of Americans cited going to the movies as one of their favorite pastimes, compared with 46.8% of the Chinese. However, this still translates into a sizable movie-going audience in China, especially in the larger cities. Figure 3-9 summarizes the responses of those who report they go to the movies at least once a month, as well as the average amount spent per trip.

FIGURE 3-9: GO TO THE MOVIES AT LEAST ONCE A MONTH AND AVERAGE SPEND PER VISIT ✦ CHINESE CONSUMERS BY GENDER AND TIER

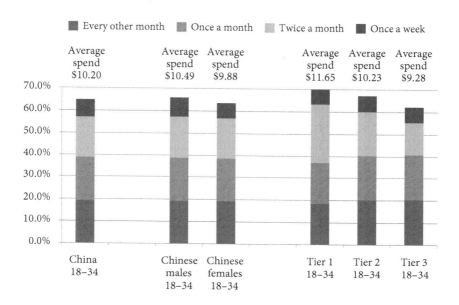

Source: ProsperChina.com

The Chinese movie industry is plagued by many of the same challenges facing its counterparts in the West—declining attendance, competition from readily available DVDs, streaming from the Internet, and so on. The situation is exacerbated in China by the wide availability of pirated DVDs sold quite openly on the streets. The industry has responded, in part, by building sleek multiplexes in shopping malls, improving the in-theater experience with plush seats, wider snack choices, digital surround sound, and creating specialized large-format theaters (such as Imax)—all enhancements that cannot be replicated on a pirated disk.

Recently, the government has become concerned about the high price of movie tickets and is considering both putting a cap on ticket prices and requiring theaters to offer more half-price screenings.[4] Given the average amounts spent shown above, and considering the relatively low income levels discussed in Chapter 2, a night out to see a movie is a costly event indeed.

Eating Out

A final leisure activity to be discussed is eating out, more specifically, going to fast-food restaurants. This is a segment of the dining industry that is growing rapidly not just in Tier 1 cities, but also in Tiers 2 and 3. According to Research and Markets, the industry has sustained an annual growth rate of 10–20% for the past ten years, and expects growth to remain robust for the foreseeable future.[5]

Overall, young Chinese report eating at fast-food restaurants about as frequently as their US counterparts: 4.6 times per month for the Chinese compared with 4.5 for the Americans. Figure 3-10 details the average number of visits and average amount spent per visit by gender and tier. Considering the disparities in income levels across the country, there is relatively little variation between the geographic segments. It would be expected that the more affluent Tier 1 cities would show higher frequency and expenditures, which they do, yet the differences are relatively minor, indicating that fast food is of growing importance in Tier 2 and 3 cities.

---

4. Laurie Burkitt, "China May Cap Prices of Movie Tickets," *Wall Street Journal*, Jan 9, 2012, http://online.wsj.com/article/SB100014 24052970203436904577150670046923492.html

5. Research and Markets, "Research Report on China Fast Food Industry – 2011-2012" published January 2011, http://www. researchandmarkets.com/reports/1511788/research_report_on _china_fast_food_industry

FIGURE 3-10: In an average month, how many times do you eat at a fast-food restaurant? ◈ Chinese consumers by gender and tier

	China 18–34	Chinese males 18–34	Chinese females 18–34	Tier 1 18–34	Tier 2 18–34	Tier 3 18–34
Average visits per month	4.6	4.7	4.5	5.1	4.6	4.6
Average spend per visit (US$)	$8.06	$8.06	$8.06	$8.75	$7.94	$7.83

Source: ProsperChina.com

Figure 3-11 shows the fast-food restaurants young Chinese say they go to most often. The restaurants have been grouped in two sections: Western chains, sorted in decreasing order of popularity; and domestic Chinese restaurants, again in decreasing order.

Yum! Brands' KFC is by far the most popular and most frequently visited fast-food restaurant chain, followed by McDonald's and Pizza Hut (also owned by Yum! Brands). The dominance of KFC is attributable in part to their long history in China, having entered the country in 1987, and their breadth of distribution across the country (over 3,000 stores in 650 cities). The company has been very aggressive in building scale not only in Tier 1, but also in Tiers 2, 3 and beyond. Additionally, they have extensively modified their menus to appeal to Chinese tastes, utilized local sourcing where possible and even created special regional variations of menu items.[6]

McDonald's entered China later than KFC, and its approximately 1,400 stores are more concentrated in the larger urban areas. However, it has announced plans to expand to 2,000 stores by 2013,

6. Maggie Starvish, "KFC's Explosive Growth in China," *HBS Working Knowledge*, Harvard Business School, Jun 17, 2011, http://hbswk.hbs.edu/item/6704.html

and is working on new, more comfortable and inviting formats and expanded menu offerings. Its new ad campaign directly addresses Chinese concerns about food safety, with a strong emphasis on freshness and quality.

FIGURE 3-11: FAST-FOOD RESTAURANT EATEN AT MOST OFTEN
CHINESE CONSUMERS

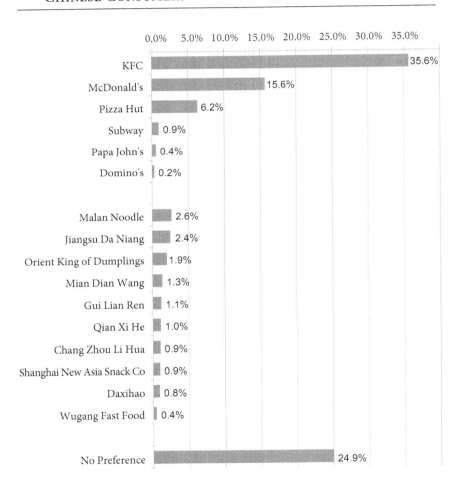

Source: ProsperChina.com

The competitive race between these Western giants is far from over. In reviewing the other fast-food providers on the list, it is important to keep in mind that the fast-food industry is still highly fragmented, and therefore demand is spread across a wide range of regional chains and small entrepreneurial operations. As noted by Michael Kelter of Goldman Sachs, "China today is essentially the US of the 1950s, which means there are decades to come of compounding growth as the restaurant market matures."[7]

The last bar on the chart confirms this important point: 24.9% indicate they have no preference in fast-food restaurants. While Western brands have captured a strong share of wallet, there is still a sizable segment who have not yet been won over to any one provider. As the local chains expand, improve their operational efficiencies, develop more standardized internal processes and gain greater presence around the country, they will likely become more formidable competitors.

It is insightful to see why people prefer the restaurants they frequent the most often, as seen in Figure 3-12. It is often assumed that KFC or McDonald's are popular because they offer diners an opportunity for a truly Western experience, albeit one adapted to Asian tastes. However, the Chinese have far more practical reasons for preferring these brands—namely cleanliness, service and location. In a highly price- and value-conscious society, price is only the fourth-rated attribute. This is a pattern we will see in other categories as we move forward. While Chinese consumers are notoriously concerned about price, they have other issues that often take precedence. Understanding those concerns is critical for being competitive and building brands in China.

---

7. Laurie Burkitt, "McDonald's to Tout Quality in China" Wall Street Journal, February 29, 2012, http://online.wsj.com/article/SB100014 24052970203833004577250832595756206.html

FIGURE 3-12: REASONS FOR EATING AT MOST FREQUENTLY
VISITED FAST-FOOD RESTAURANT ◆ CHINESE CONSUMERS

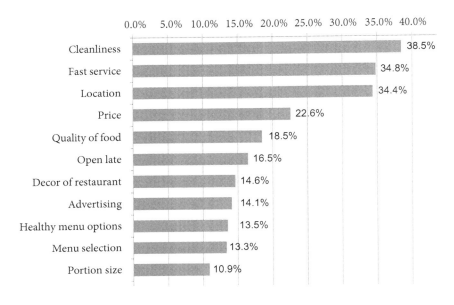

Source: ProsperChina.com

Five Key Takeaways

1. China's digital generation is living through rapid change in their personal lives as well as in the society around them.

2. Leisure time is often spent alone, to a greater extent than for counterparts in the US—on the Internet, reading or listening to music.

3. Young Chinese women of the digital generation are avid shoppers, and in general mention more leisure activities than do men of the same age, especially travel, reading and watching TV.

4. Travel is an important leisure activity, often combined with other interests such as shopping, hiking, swimming or visiting family.

5. Increasing income, time pressures and concerns about food safety have helped to foster increasing attendance at fast-food restaurants in China among the digital generation.

Moving On

Clearly, we can learn much about the differences between Chinese and US consumers in the 18–34 age category by looking at what they say they do for leisure. As we saw, for Chinese and American consumers surfing the Internet and watching TV are two very popular activities. However, they are, of course, exposed to many additional types of media every day: traditional media (TV, radio, print), personal interactive media (Internet, blogs, chat), as well as media encountered in retail establishments. The extent to which the American and Chinese digital generations consume each of these— and the impact each has on their purchasing behaviors—will be the focus of Chapters 4 and 5.

Chapter 4

Media Usage

In both the ProsperChina Quarterly Study (PCQS) and the US Media Behavior & Influence Study (MBI) much of the focus has been on trying to understand, and ideally predict, what consumers might do in the future. The longitudinal nature of these two research databases makes this attempt at prediction more practical than when the views are based on a one-time research snapshot since it allows the establishment of trend lines, which are commonly more predictive of future results. Thus, the primary value of the PCQS and MBI is in helping managers determine directionally what they might do today to impact short-term results tomorrow. It also helps managers understand the likely impact those short-term activities might have on longer-term results.

The PCQS and MBI data are useful to marketers since they provide information on factors that are commonly not measured by syndicated or external research organizations. In particular, most marketers have traditionally focused on message distribution, that is, the number of customers or prospects that are supposedly reached by a given medium (TV stations, magazines or newspapers). Commonly, they ignored message consumption—that is, the number of people who actually use each medium and who are likely to access the marketer's message. These marketers also ignored what customers and prospects would like to see or hear and, more importantly today, the messages and information they would like to acquire from the marketer through some type of interactive communication.

Today, we call this a "push" marketing system—where sellers are continuously sending out marketing programs and communication messages in an attempt to influence or persuade consumers to respond in a certain way. As a result, most marketing and communication measurement systems are focused on measuring the distribution of those programs and activities. Less attention is paid to the "receiver"—that is, the consumer who is supposed to respond—other than the fairly traditional demographic classifications. In truth, in today's multimedia, multi-alternative marketplace where the consumer is in control—even in an emerging market such as China—these approaches are hopelessly archaic. Importantly, they are gradually being superseded by new concepts and ideas that are much more relevant and are discussed in this chapter.

When consumers have access to a wide range of media forms, from which they can pick and choose, and when technology makes the selection and consumption of those media forms increasingly simple and easy, what the marketer sends out in the form of marketing programs and communication messages becomes less important than what consumers access, consume and respond to. Thus, the PCQS and MBI purposefully were designed not to measure marketing communication *distribution*, but, instead, to measure consumer marketing message *consumption*. In other words, we are focused on what customers and prospects do, not what marketers do.

In truth, no matter how pervasive or creative or engaging the marketing and communication activities are, if the consumer doesn't access the media form the marketer is using, no response can ever occur. In short, if consumers don't see or hear the marketing activity, the investment is wasted. It's that simple, and it is also that critical.

Two Key Marketing and Communication Measures

Two key elements in the PCQS and MBI studies allow managers to understand and be able to compare consumer behaviors in the two markets over time:

- *media usage*—the consumption of media forms, that is, the amount of time the consumer reports spending with each medium, as well as the combination of media he or she may choose to use at the same time.

- *media influence*—the consumer's view of how each media form influences his or her purchasing in specific product categories.

Media Usage

Importantly, the media forms consumers choose commonly define and determine what shopping behaviors they will exhibit in the future. This is because those media choices generally determine which marketer's messages they will be exposed to, which, in turn, commonly lead to the behaviors they eventually exhibit in the marketplace. It is a very simple concept: consumer consumption of the marketing and media messages are what really matter, not the marketer's media plan. Unfortunately, this simple concept is one that is too often overlooked or forgotten by supposedly sophisticated marketing organizations. Customer exposure to marketing messages often equals potential influence. No exposure results in no influence. This simple equation has eluded many marketers for too many years but is critical in today's multi-media marketplace.

In this chapter, we review consumer media consumption among young adult Chinese and US consumers, and discuss the trends that are shaping their use of all forms of traditional and non-traditional media. That data provides a baseline for how media consumption by Chinese consumers can be used to plan more effective marketing and communication programs in the future.

Media Influence

We all have favorite media forms. If we want to see what movies are playing at the local theater, we will commonly pick up a newspaper or go online. If we're interested in finding a silversmith to repair a treasured heirloom, we likely will turn to some type of specialized directory or web search system. If a computer purchase is being considered, we might ask a friend or pick up a technology-related magazine. And our musical tastes are often influenced by songs we hear on radio. In short, most consumers have some idea which media forms give them the most valuable information on a particular product or service. And, for the most part, they can report the value of those media forms by product category through a questionnaire response device.

The PCQS and MBI studies provide just such a consumer-oriented view of media usage and influence. These studies span more than 20 media forms—including traditional mass media, digital and new media, as well as in-store and other forms of ambient media. The studies ask consumers which media forms have the most influence on their current or future purchases in specific product categories. Since the influence of media exposure on purchase behavior by media form is very product category specific, further examples and illustrations of those comparisons will be held for Chapter 5. More details will be provided by product category as each is discussed in later sections.

Consumption of Traditional Media

In the following sections, consumption of a number of traditional media forms will be compared for Chinese and US consumers age 18–34. Some of the results will likely be surprising. For others, the response may well be: "That's just common sense." But, all the consumption comparisons are insightful in terms of helping managers develop and implement effective marketing and media programs in China.

In the PCQS and MBI, consumers are asked how many minutes per day they spend with various media forms by day-part. In the sections that follow, we will examine the amount of time spent on each major media form by young adults in China and the US. Notable trends for the period 2008–11 will be discussed as well.

One of the interesting findings of these comparisons is the changing media consumption patterns we see in both countries. Some of these can be explained simply by consumers having more media available to them, and thus greater choices for how they might spend their time. In China especially, some of the changes come from the increasing availability of television (both an increase in the number of television sets owned as well as increases in regional stations and satellite TV) and the substantial number of new newspapers and magazines that have been founded over the past few years in the country as well. The most dramatic changes, however, have been in the area of online communication and the rapid consumer adoption of mobile and wireless devices.

We will first look at daily consumption of each of the traditional, advertiser-supported media forms that are of greatest interest to marketers, followed by an examination of how consumers use "new media" forms. That is followed by a discussion of the implications for marketers in developing their communication plans.

TV Consumption

Figure 4-1 compares the minutes per day that Chinese and US consumers age 18–34 report they spend watching television. Clearly, US consumers consistently spend much more time watching television than do the Chinese—on average, 40–50% more—and that continues to be the case in the most recent period. What is notable, however, is that average per day viewing time is declining steadily in both countries among the 18–34 cohort. (In this and the following figures, the dotted line represents the moving average trend line showing the general direction of usage, up or down, over the period) In the US, the average growth rate (AGR) in time spent watching TV has fallen by -3.08% a year for the periods shown. It has declined even more (-5.43%) among Chinese 18–34-year-olds. We believe these declines clearly indicate the growing popularity of new media forms in both countries at the expense of TV viewership.

FIGURE 4-1: TV CONSUMPTION IN MINUTES PER DAY
CHINESE AND AMERICAN CONSUMERS

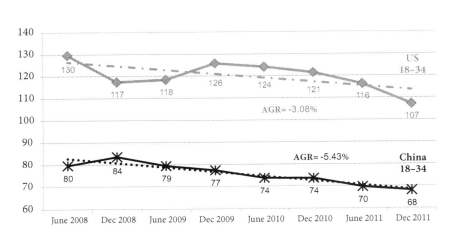

Source: ProsperChina.com

Newspaper Consumption

Since the 1980s, China has seen a dramatic increase in the number of national, regional and local newspapers, as well as a large number serving specialized interests (business, workers, military or specific industries). While newspapers are still owned by state or party-aligned organizations, this growth has given consumers a greater variety of information sources, thus, daily newspaper reading has grown fairly rapidly. During this same period, but particularly since the late 1990s, the American newspaper industry has faced persistent contraction in circulation and the amount of time consumers spend reading has declined as well.

Figure 4-2 illustrates the trends in newspaper consumption among the 18–34 cohorts for the two counties since 2008, as measured in self-reported minutes per day.

FIGURE 4-2: NEWSPAPER CONSUMPTION IN MINUTES PER DAY
CHINESE AND AMERICAN CONSUMERS

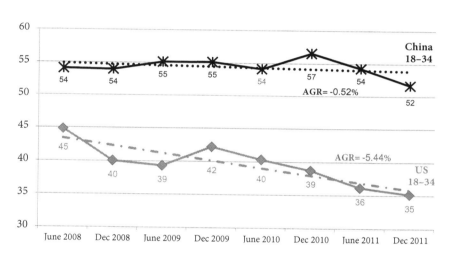

Source: ProsperChina.com

During the period June 2008–10, Chinese newspaper reading among 18–34-year-olds varied within a narrow range of 54–55 minutes per day. After a modest increase in 2010 to 57 minutes, time spent reading appears to be declining, to an average of 52 minutes per day at the end of 2011. However, this is substantially higher than the 35 minutes per day reported by Americans of the same age. Overall, newspaper consumption in the US has declined among 18–34-year-olds—averaging a -5.44% a year decrease in time spent since 2008. Since many marketers, especially retailers, are commonly heavy investors in newspaper space to promote their products and services, this should be a critical factor in terms of understanding how to reach and motivate customers and prospects in the Chinese marketplace.

Magazine Consumption

Consumer magazines have been a growth medium in China for the past several years. In many cases, these are Western titles such as *Vogue*, *Harper's Bazaar*, *Forbes* and many others, which have been licensed to Chinese publishers. However, a number are homegrown Chinese publishing ventures, such as *Caijing*, *Duzhe* and *Ray Li*. Many of these new publications have become quite successful since the market has become relatively stable. That is shown by the amount of time Chinese consumers spend with magazines in general. Such is not the case in the US, as we see in Figure 4-3.

FIGURE 4-3: Magazine consumption in minutes per day
❖ Chinese and American consumers

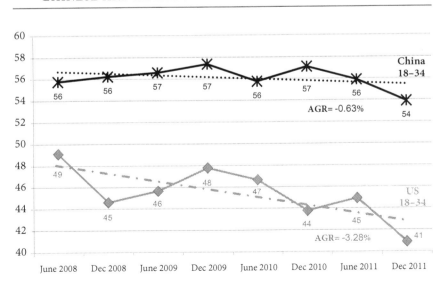

Source: ProsperChina.com

Chinese consumers typically spend a little over 50 minutes per day with magazines compared with the US consumer's time investment of only about 41 minutes in 2011. More importantly, consumer use of magazines has been fairly stable in China during the measurement period while the US has been on a downward trend. For the period illustrated, Chinese consumer time spent with magazines has declined slightly, with an AGR of -0.63%. While US consumer time spent with magazines has declined more markedly, by -3.28% during the same period.

Direct Mail Consumption

Direct mail has been a latecomer to the Chinese marketing communication scene. Early on, the lack of lists and customer databases limited the use of this media form but these issues have been at least partially overcome in the past few years. There has been a significant growth in catalog distribution and usage, which accounts for much of the time spent with this media form.

FIGURE 4-4: DIRECT MAIL CONSUMPTION IN MINUTES PER DAY CHINESE AND AMERICAN CONSUMERS

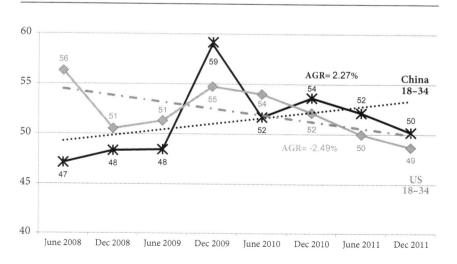

Source: ProsperChina.com

Consumer usage time with direct mail in China generally increased during the measurement period with the exception of the first quarter of 2010. As Figure 4-4 shows, direct mail had a huge spike in the last half of 2009 and then receded somewhat in the following quarters. Overall, the AGR since 2008 has been 2.27%.

Consumer usage of direct mail in the US is not as robust. From a peak of 56 minutes per day spent with direct mail in June 2008, it had declined to less than 50 minutes per day in December 2011. More disturbing, however, is the fact that the sheer amount of time US consumers spend with direct mail has been trending downward for the entire four-year measurement period, with an AGR of -2.49% since 2008.

With this look at media forms that are primarily advertiser supported, we now turn to the increasingly important electronic media forms.

Electronic Media Usage in China and the US

Based on consumer usage, electronic media of all forms is flourishing in China and the US, although perhaps in different ways. Of course, one of the challenges of electronic communication is simply the definition. While there are a number of vehicles available, we have selected four areas that seem to be quite important in both countries: e-mail and instant messaging; blogs; video games; and, relatively new to China, terrestrial and web-based radio. As will be seen, while most of these are popular with young adults in both countries, there are differences in how and when they are used.

Internet Consumption

The most prominent electronic medium, of course, is the Internet. Comparing time spent by consumers in the two markets on the Internet over the measurement period is quite revealing.

FIGURE 4-5: INTERNET CONSUMPTION IN MINUTES PER DAY CHINESE AND AMERICAN CONSUMERS

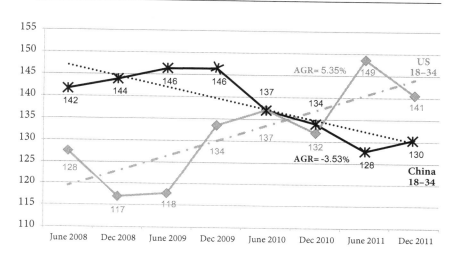

Source: ProsperChina.com

The use of the Internet by consumers presents a considerably different usage pattern between the US and China. As shown in Figure 4-5, the amount of time spent by consumers in the two markets crossed in June 2010, as Chinese usage time declined and US consumption increased. Chinese Internet time peaked in the fall of 2009 and has continued to decline for several subsequent periods (although there was a small increase at the end of 2011). Overall this represents an AGR of -3.53% since 2008. On the other hand, US Internet usage has increased, with an AGR of 5.35% over the same period.

Part of the reason for the decline in Chinese consumers' Internet usage can be attributed to the relatively slow download speeds for DSL service via telephone lines within China. However, in the past few years there has been a rapid conversion from computer-based access (desktop, laptop, notebooks) to mobile devices such as smartphones, tablets and other handheld devices that use Wi-Fi and advanced cellular technologies. The recent growth in the use of mobile telephone and other wireless devices has been phenomenal in China. For example, mobile telephone subscribers in the country now number more than 879 million. Among these, 303 million are mobile Internet users, almost more than the entire population of the United States.[1]

In the PCQS and MBI studies, the Internet is taken to be computer based. While both the computer and mobile devices use the same technology, consumers see and use them differently. We believe that likely accounts for the reported decline in Internet usage in the Chinese market. While we may see some convergence in usage between the two countries in the future, for the present, consumers in China and the US view and use the various media technologies quite differently.

E-mail and Instant Messaging

Figure 4-6 illustrates the usage of both e-mail and instant messaging (IM) among Chinese and American consumers age 18–34. It is interesting to note how the different technologies have evolved in the two nations, and how that has impacted usage over time.

For example, US consumers historically have relied primarily on desktop and laptop computers, both in their business and their personal lives. Thus, they have come to be heavy users of e-mail for personal and commercial communication. Until recently, instant messaging in the US was associated mainly with providers such as Microsoft and Yahoo, and generally was used as a supplement to e-mail—if indeed it was used at all. However, with the introduction of smartphones and other handheld wireless devices, and with the growing popularity of Twitter, Facebook and similar immediate communication services, there has been a dramatic increase in all forms of IM in the US since 2010. Thus, looking at the two

---

1. "April 2011 Asia-Pacific Data Snapshot," BBH Labs, (April 2011), http://bbh-labs.com/introducing-bbh-asia-pacific-data-snapshots

methods in the US since 2008, we see that e-mail usage peaked in 2009 at an average of 133 minutes per day for personal communication, decreasing to 113 minutes per day by the end of 2011. During the same period, levels of IM activity were initially flat in the US, averaging only about a half hour per day, until they began to grow in 2010 and 2011 to slightly over one hour per day. Combining the two methods, we can say that in the US those in the 18–34 respondent group are spending more time than ever before communicating through a combination of e-mail and IM—a combined average of 182 minutes per day.

FIGURE 4-6: E-MAIL & IM CONSUMPTION IN MINUTES PER DAY CHINESE AND AMERICAN CONSUMERS

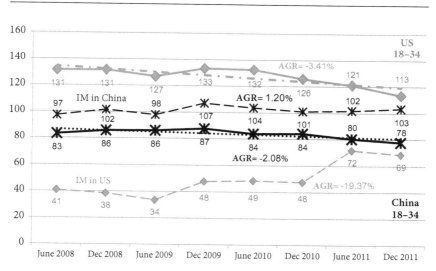

Source: ProsperChina.com

In China, however, advanced, mobile phone-based IM technologies have been available for several years, most notably the popular QQ service offered by Tencent Holdings. As mentioned earlier, Chinese consumers are heavily reliant on mobile devices for accessing the Internet, so it is not surprising that their use of IM has consistently exceeded their use of e-mail. At the end of 2011, they reported spending an average of 103 minutes per day on IM, and 78 minutes per day on e-mail. Combining the two results in an average of 181 minutes per day—just about the same amount of time as their US counterparts.

Marketers accustomed to reaching prospective or current customers via e-mail in the US will need to expand their communication skill sets, and embrace a range of new technologies. QQ, Sina Weibo, Renren and other services in China are advanced and sophisticated interactive marketing environments, with their own vernacular, customs and practices that must be mastered in order to effectively reach young Chinese consumers.

Usage of Blogs

A related electronic media form that has captured the interest of the Chinese is the use of blogs, as shown in Figure 4-7.

FIGURE 4-7: BLOG CONSUMPTION IN MINUTES PER DAY CHINESE AND AMERICAN CONSUMERS

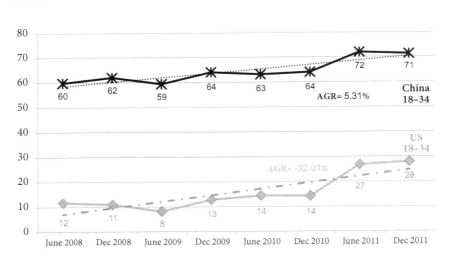

Source: ProsperChina.com

Chinese consumers spend more than twice as much time each day blogging than US consumers. In a society that traditionally has limited the expressing of opinions in public, the opportunity offered by blogs to comment on a wide range of subjects is compelling. And, the fact that such comments can be made under a nickname, an avatar or other assumed identity makes it even more appealing. While the censors will step in on certain sensitive subjects—mostly political issues or topics deemed obscene, derogatory or in bad taste—there are still many areas of modern life on which Chinese can, and do, comment actively. Hence, they spend an average of 71 minutes per day blogging, compared with less than half an hour spent by their US contemporaries.

Video Game Usage

An interesting area for analysis is the use of video games by young adult Chinese and US consumers. While traditional marketers may not consider a video game as a media form, it is something on which the young people of China and the US spend considerable time and where advertisers in both countries are trying to penetrate. Additionally, some marketers are finding that inserting their promotional messages within the context of a video game can generate good results for specific product categories, and many have even created or sponsored their own games.

In Figure 4-8, the comparison of time spent with video games shows that Chinese consumers have been much heavier users of video games than their US contemporaries until recently.

As shown, the Chinese consumers spend over 60 minutes a day with video games, and this has been relatively constant since 2008. On the other hand, in 2008 US consumers spent only about half that time on video games, but usage has increased significantly since then. Part of the huge spurt in video gaming in the US can be attributed to the introduction of the iPad in spring 2010, and its popularity as a birthday or holiday gift that year. Additionally, several successful gaming apps for the iPad were introduced around this period (*Angry Birds, Grand Theft Auto*, and so on). While US video game usage has grown at an average rate of 27%, in China it has actually declined slightly, with an AGR over the measurement period of -0.54%. In China, the stability of video game usage is due to video game parlors where games are rented rather than purchased for home use. That difference in where Chinese and American consumers access and play video games doubtless accounts for some of the differences in the amount of time each spends gaming.

FIGURE 4-8: Video game consumption in minutes per day Chinese and American consumers

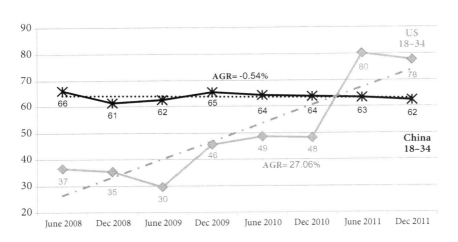

Source: ProsperChina.com

Terrestrial and Web Radio Consumption

Our final example in this initial description of media consumption is that of terrestrial and web radio. These are either satellite delivered or available via streaming feeds on the Internet. Consumption of both these media forms is shown in Figure 4-9.

Terrestrial or satellite-delivered radio was available in both markets during the measurement period 2008–11. Terrestrial radio started fast in the US and then dropped off sharply in terms of consumers' reported time spent with the media form, with consumption dropping by almost one third between the July and December 2008 studies. While there have been some slight ups and downs in reported consumer usage in the US, terrestrial radio still represents roughly one hour per day for American consumers. The AGR for the period is distorted by the high initial consumption and then rapid decline, and does not reflect the relative stability the media form has enjoyed since then.

FIGURE 4-9: TERRESTRIAL AND WEB RADIO CONSUMPTION IN MINUTES PER DAY ◆ CHINESE AND AMERICAN CONSUMERS

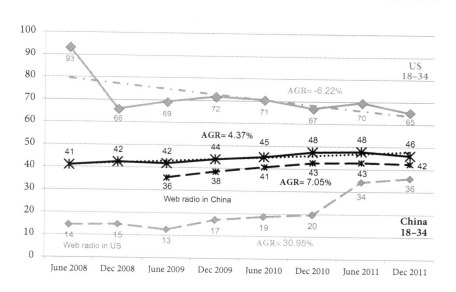

Source: ProsperChina.com

Chinese use of terrestrial radio has been much more stable from the outset. While about one-third less time is spent by Chinese consumers on the media form on a daily basis, namely, over 60 minutes for the US and over 40 minutes per day for the Chinese, the upward trend in Chinese usage is becoming more important, with an AGR of +5.64 for the measurement period.

A particularly interesting media phenomenon has been the introduction of web radio in China. As shown in the chart above, web radio was an established media form in the US, with consumers reporting spending about 15 minutes per day with the medium as of June 2008. That usage has now increased to approximately 36 minutes (December 2011), an AGR of around +31% in the 2008–11 period. So, while still a minor media form in terms of consumer usage, it is a relevant media vehicle for a portion of the US respondents.

However, in China, web radio only started to appear in the studies in June 2009. At that point, Chinese consumers reported they were using web radio about 36 minutes per day. That usage has now grown to approximately 42 minutes per day in the latest PCQS. That growth provides an AGR of +7%—a healthy increase, even if from a small base.

The most important thing about the Chinese consumers' use of web radio is the capability of the PCQS and MBI studies to identify new media forms and begin to track their success and, in some cases, failure over time. For example, the high initial numbers for US consumers' use of terrestrial radio followed by a quick decline. And, the identification of web radio as a potential major media form in China, although we may find a similar early interest and then declining use pattern over time. It is the longitudinal tracking provided by PCQS and MBI that gives the manager a much more informed view of the marketplace than other point-in-time or limited view research studies, which are so often used.

Key Differences in Media Consumption within China

Within the overall respondent base of Chinese young adults, there are some notable differences in media usage by gender and geography that warrant a brief discussion.

Figure 4-10 illustrates the key differences by gender. Generally speaking, young women tend to be heavier users of the almost all major media forms, especially the Internet, IM, e-mail, TV and blogging. Consistent with what we have seen earlier, young males are likely to spend more time with video games.

FIGURE 4-10: TIME SPENT WITH EACH MEDIUM IN CHINA ◆ CHINESE CONSUMERS BY GENDER

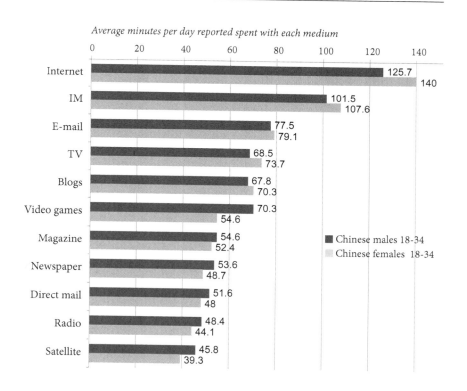

Source: ProsperChina.com

Interestingly, media usage in almost all forms is higher in Tier 1 cities than either Tiers 2 or 3, as depicted in Figure 4-11. This is to be expected, as growing affluence and education often means that households have greater access to, and greater wherewithal to own or subscribe to more media forms.

FIGURE 4-11: Time spent with each medium in China
Chinese consumers by tier

Source: ProsperChina.com

As of the end of 2011, young Chinese adults in Tier 2 and 3 cities spend slightly less time with most media forms than those in Tier 1. However, the relative ranking is essentially the same: in each area the Internet receives the most time, followed by IM, e-mail, blogs and TV. Only in video gaming do those in Tier 2 and 3 cities spend more time than those in Tier 1. As noted earlier, Tier 2 and 3 cities tend to have a greater preponderance of single young males, who are more likely to spend time with video games.

Simultaneous Media Usage

A key issue in planning a communication program is identifying the most appropriate context in which to deliver a brand message. That includes not just the media form to be used, but also understanding the way in which the consumer may be accessing and consuming the information from that medium.

Traditionally, advertising campaigns have been planned on the basis of the number of people supposedly exposed to an individual medium at a point in time—for example, the assumed viewership of a particular TV program, or the readership of a particular issue of a magazine. The data for these calculations usually came from various audience estimates provided by either third party research organizations (such as the Nielsen ratings) or from the media organizations themselves. Unfortunately, the underlying weakness of all such audience measurement is that each methodology only examines one particular medium at a time. For example, the Nielsen TV ratings consider only the number of households that have the TV turned on, and of those, how many households are "watching" program X or program Y. It tells us nothing about whether that is the only medium being consumed. Thus, while someone may have the television on, they may also be flipping through a magazine, surfing the net, talking on the phone or a multitude of other attention-distracting activities.

This weakness in audience measurement systems has become much more critical as the various forms of electronic media are factored in to the equation. Increasingly we are a society of multi-taskers, and that applies to our media consumption as well. And nowhere is that more apparent than among the digital generation. Where their parents and grandparents may have sat down to read a newspaper, and when finished, turned on the TV, young people are more likely to do both at once (and perhaps even a few more things as well).

What does this mean for media planning in China? Consider Figure 4-12 regarding TV viewership. Chinese respondents were asked to indicate what, if any, other media forms they occasionally or regularly use while they are watching TV. Of those who watch TV, over a third indicate they also go online, while 23.9% say they read a magazine and 23.7% read a newspaper. Somewhat surprisingly, even 16.5% say they listen to the radio. This challenges the way advertising on TV and other media has traditionally been bought and sold. For example, it means that the audience an advertiser thought was being delivered by a TV commercial may be frequently distracted by other media-consuming activities, making it less likely that the advertiser's message will be seen or understood. Advertising time is sold on the basis of the size of the expected audience, yet the advertiser is often not getting the full attention of the audience for which they have paid. That is a factor that is becoming increasingly important to advertisers as the media spectrum expands.

FIGURE 4-12: "WHEN YOU WATCH TV DO YOU ALSO...?"
CHINESE CONSUMERS

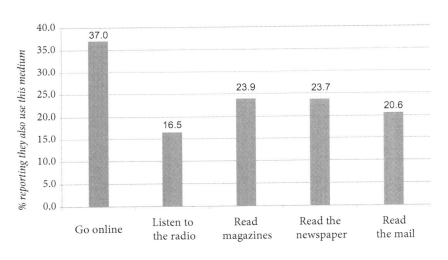

Source: ProsperChina.com

A similar situation occurs when we look at what people do when they are online, as shown in Figure 4-13. This shows that of those who go online, 37% report they are also watching TV, while approximately one quarter are also either listening to the radio, reading a magazine or newspaper, or scanning their mail. Again, the development of multi-tasking with various media forms creates a challenge for advertisers in both countries.

FIGURE 4-13: "WHEN YOU GO ONLINE DO YOU ALSO...?"
CHINESE CONSUMERS

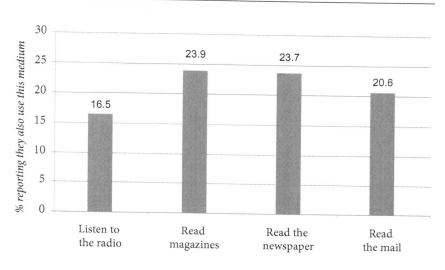

Source: ProsperChina.com

Simultaneous media usage is a fact of life with the digital generations in the US and China. It means that marketers must take a holistic, integrated approach that encompasses all media forms, and not plan one form in isolation. Additionally, taking advantage of synergies between media that are used simultaneously becomes a critical planning skill.

Five Key Takeaways

1. Traditionally, media planning has been done on the basis of message distribution, that is, the supposed audience size of various media forms (TV, newspapers, magazines, and so on), and media planning research has tended to focus on one medium at a time. Today, however, consumers have access to a growing range of media platforms, from which they pick and choose, and which they will often use in combination.

2. Chinese respondents typically report spending less time per day watching TV than do their US counterparts, and they report more average time per day reading newspapers and magazines.

3. Overall, consumption of traditional media (TV, newspapers, magazines and direct mail) is generally declining in both China and the US among 18–34-year-olds.

4. Chinese members of the digital generation are heavy users of instant messaging and blogs, while their US equivalents tend to favor e-mail as a mode of communication.

5. Multitasking and simultaneous media usage must be taken into consideration when developing media plans. Fragmented attention spurred by the use of multiple devices (TV, Internet, smartphone) at the same time can seriously erode the impact of a communication plan unless it is approached holistically and with an eye to creating synergies across the various platforms.

Moving On

Media usage is only one part of the marketing communication planning challenge. With this overview of media consumption by Chinese consumers, we move on to the next major factor in the media planning process, that is, the influence each media form has on potential purchasing activity.

Chapter 5

From Media Usage to Media Influence

While the amount of time consumers spend with various media forms is the traditional way media value has been determined, a much more important factor is the amount of influence consumers say the media form has on their current and future purchases. Simply having the marketer's message available is of limited value if there is no effect or impact. Thus, knowing which media form has the most influence on a consumer's purchasing decision can help marketers greatly improve the returns on their communication investments.

In this chapter, we build on the notion of media consumption discussed in Chapter 4, and extend it to a relevant and practical media-planning framework based on the ProsperChina Quarterly Study (PCQS) and the Media Behavior & Influence Study (MBI). We will also include some practical examples of how these data can be applied in making media decisions for reaching young adult Chinese consumers in different product categories.

To this point, we have illustrated what media forms Chinese and US consumers say they use, the amount of time spent with each and have given some insights into the data available on simultaneous media usage. When we factor in an "influence measure" we begin to see how all these factors come together at the customer level. We also begin to understand how they provide some strong direction for the marketer in terms of where marketing communication investments should be made. We'll illustrate how all these pieces fit together in the last part of this chapter when we discuss a CHAID analysis approach that assists in planning media activities.

Influence by Media Form

The final factor in our media-planning model is the influence consumers say each media form has on their product category purchase decisions. For each of the nine product categories (apparel, automobiles, eating out, electronics, financial services, groceries, , medicines, health and beauty aids, telecommunication and wireless services) on which consumers report their media behaviors in the PCQS and MBI they also identify the media form they say is most relevant to them in making purchase decisions. These self-reported influence measures, we believe, are strong indicators of where the marketer should invest available marketing communication funds. This consumption approach provides greater insights for the marketer than the traditional measures that simply attempt to relate the consumer exposure to the media form based on factors such as demographics or geographic location. The supposition that demographics are good indicators of purchase potential for any but a few consumers and product categories continue to be challenged as we learn more and more about consumers.

In both the PCQS and MBI, respondents are asked to rate the various media forms in terms of the influence that each medium has on their purchase decisions in the nine specific product categories mentioned above. From this, we can determine which media form, or combination of forms, would provide the best opportunity for the marketer to reach and influence the potential customer.

In the following section, we will look at the overall influence that Chinese and American consumers age 18–34 attribute to each of the media forms analyzed in the PCQS and MBI studies. In later chapters, we will provide details on how consumers say this influence varies from one product or service to another. In this chapter, we look at the aggregated data across all nine categories to provide a baseline for the material that comes later.

To simplify the discussion, in the figures below we have consolidated the information into four groupings: traditional mass media, personal interactive media, retail media and miscellaneous media. In each exhibit there are four columns:

(a) the percentage of Chinese respondents age 18–34 reporting that media form has an influence on their purchases.

(b) the percentage average growth rate (AGR) of the reported media influence in China, positively or negatively, over the period 2008–11.

(c) the percentage of US respondents age 18–34 reporting that media form has an influence on their purchases.

(d) the percentage average growth rate (AGR) of the reported media influence in the US, either positively or negatively, over the period 2008–11.

Traditional Mass Media

Figure 5-1 details the average reported influence for traditional mass media across all nine product categories. In China, television has the greatest overall reported influence, followed closely by word of mouth. Nearly one quarter of the Chinese respondents (24.9%) say that TV influences their purchase decisions, and 23.9% say they are influenced by word of mouth. In the US sample, however, consumers say word of mouth is substantially more influential than television (33.6% versus 22%). What is interesting about this finding is that culturally China is much more communal than the US. One would have expected word of mouth to have been the more dominant media form in China than in the US, and, thus, more highly rated. But, that is not what consumers say. It may be that the Chinese rely more on other shared electronic media forms such as instant messaging (IM) or personal blogs to communicate with friends and relatives, but current measures do not reflect that distinction. Also, culturally, word of mouth is almost continuous in China as consumers always recognize that product acceptance comes as much from their friends, relatives and associates as it does from the outside world. Nevertheless, both TV and word of mouth are still the two most influential media forms in both countries across all media forms across all nine product categories, and are major factors in the development of any communication program.

FIGURE 5-1: REPORTED INFLUENCE FOR TRADITIONAL MASS MEDIA ● CHINESE AND AMERICAN CONSUMERS

	China 18–34	Average growth rate 2008–11	US 18–34	Average growth rate 2008–11
TV	24.9	3.8%	22.0	-0.6%
Word of mouth	23.9	0.9%	33.6	0.2%
Cable	16.6	0.8%	14.1	-0.1%
Internet	14.3	1.4%	12.7	2.3%
Outdoor	12.0	0.4%	7.2	0.9%
Magazine	10.5	-4.0%	16.3	-1.3%
Web radio	10.2	9.0%	2.9	5.8%
Newspaper	8.5	-4.4%	18.1	-0.4%
Radio	7.0	3.3%	12.5	0.2%

Source: ProsperChina.com

Cable, Internet and outdoor all have substantially lower reported average influence in China and the US, although as we will see in later chapters, this varies significantly between product categories. Reported influence of the Internet on purchase decisions has seen a small increase in both countries. Magazines and newspapers have seen declines in their reported influence among both Chinese and American consumers—the only media forms to have lost influence in both countries. Areas of growing influence include regular radio (China) and web radio (China and US)—although from a relatively modest base.

It is this type of understanding of the changes that are occurring over time that can be of great benefit to marketers who are making future media commitments. Only longitudinal data such as that found in the PCQS and MBI studies can identify these types of critical change. Single point-in-time measures simply can't reveal this type of impact and effect of media for planning purposes.

Personal Interactive Media

The influence attributed to various forms of personal interactive media is shown in Figure 5-2. While there are a number of definitions of personal interactive media, for the PCQS and MBI reports, these were defined as video on a cell phone, text messages, mobile telephone, e-mail, instant messaging and social media, such as Facebook, Twitter, YouTube and their Chinese counterparts QQ, Sina Weibo and so on.

Again, the percentages shown are the average of the purchase influence in the nine categories found in the PCQS and MBI. As can be seen, the AGR for all forms of personal interactive media in China and the US is increasing. IM has long been the staple of interactivity in the Chinese market and continues to be. As Chinese consumers transition to new media forms, such as mobile and social media, it is not surprising to see that IM, while still deemed the most influential form of personal interactive media, has stabilized in favor of some of these new, more innovative interactive communication tools.

FIGURE 5-2: REPORTED INFLUENCE FOR PERSONAL INTERACTIVE MEDIA • CHINESE AND AMERICAN CONSUMERS

	China 18–34	Average growth rate 2008–11	US 18–34	Average growth rate 2008–11
IM	13.1	0.7%	3.3	5.5%
Social media	11.5	2.2%	8.2	8.5%
E-mail	7.5	2.6%	12.6	3.9%
Text	7.4	6.8%	3.5	12.2%
Video on cell	5.5	9.9%	3.1	4.9%
Mobile	4.3	3.6%	5.8	15.7%

Source: ProsperChina.com

The primary difference between the two countries is that the Chinese respondents report IM and social media as the most influential media forms in the overall classification. In the US, more respondents say e-mail is influential. This difference is likely a reflection of the technological developments in the two markets as noted earlier. In China, the use of 4G and other forms of interactive and digital communication is quite advanced compared with that available to US consumers. While these new digital tools have not had a major impact at this point, as the technology is expanded and enhanced, we will likely see these areas becoming increasingly important to all levels of marketers.

It bears noting that the influence of all forms of personal interactive media is growing rapidly in both countries. As the dizzying pace of technological advancement is not likely to abate any time soon, it is incumbent upon anyone marketing to the digital generation to stay abreast and adapt programs to suit the full range of these dynamic platforms.

Retail Media

The third media grouping is what we have termed retail media, or media forms used to promote sales at the retail level. Those include in-store promotions, coupons, newspaper advertising inserts and direct mail. We should note that these media forms are very closely related to mass merchandisers and large supermarket chains that have developed and matured in the US and Western Europe. In some cases, these media forms are relatively new in China, having been introduced in only the past few years. That helps explain some of the results shown in Figure 5-3.

FIGURE 5-3: REPORTED INFLUENCE FOR RETAIL MEDIA CHINESE AND AMERICAN CONSUMERS

	China 18–34	Average growth rate 2008–11	US 18–34	Average growth rate 2008–11
In-store promotion	20.4	-0.5%	20.3	3.5%
Coupons	16.2	0.7%	26.9	1.8%
Ad insert	13.2	-1.3%	21.2	-1.6%
Direct mail	7.5	2.3%	18.5	0.7%

Source: ProsperChina.com

Almost all forms of retail media appear to exert a fairly strong influence over consumers in both China and the US. One fifth of Chinese and US respondents say they are influenced by in-store promotion, making this one of the most influential forms in all classifications. While coupons are mentioned less frequently by the Chinese (16.2%) than the Americans (26.9%), it must be noted that China does not yet have the extensive, sophisticated infrastructure for distributing and redeeming coupons that has been developed in the US. Similarly, the system for distributing advertising inserts is not as well developed either, especially the use of free-standing inserts which are so commonly found in US Sunday newspapers.

We expect that the influence of all retail media forms will continue to gain strength in the coming years in China. As shoppers, Chinese consumers are highly value conscious, and will go to considerable lengths to obtain the best price for a desired item. Retail media efforts that provide immediacy, the perception of good value and relevant incentives will be an important component of successful marketing programs aimed at Chinese consumers.

Miscellaneous Media

The three classifications of traditional, personal interactive and retail media account for the majority of the media influences in China and the US. In the spirit of completeness, however, we have also included a chart for what we have termed miscellaneous media. These might be termed specialized media, and for the most part, play an important role in helping marketers round out their media plans.

FIGURE 5-4: REPORTED INFLUENCE FOR MISCELLANEOUS MEDIA ▪ CHINESE AND AMERICAN CONSUMERS

	China 18–34	Average growth rate 2008–11	US 18–34	Average growth rate 2008–11
Read article	16.9	2.6%	18.9	0.0%
Product placement	12.4	7.3%	9.0	2.9%
Blog	7.9	1.1%	3.5	8.7%
Yellow pages	4.9	8.0%	7.1	-1.4%
Video games	4.7	7.8%	3.3	11.5%

Source: ProsperChina.com

The miscellaneous media form "read an article" is considered as the surrogate for public relations in the PCQS and MBI questionnaires. Among both China and US respondents, articles are a powerful source of influence, ranking on a par with some forms of retail media in their ability to stimulate purchase intentions. From a marketing communication standpoint, this is influenced by public relations efforts to obtain positive media coverage. We note that "read an article" was mentioned by over 16% of Chinese respondents, and over 18% of those in the US, illustrating the importance of public relations in generating conversations with customers and prospects in both countries.

The second most influential miscellaneous media form is product placement in both China (12.9%) and the US (9.0%). Product placement is the paid inclusion of branded products by the marketing organization within the content of entertainment programs such as movies and television shows. This is an area that is growing rapidly in China (+7.2% average growth), but its current growth rate has slowed in the US, probably because of its already widespread usage.

It should be kept in mind that while some of the miscellaneous media forms shown in the figure are fairly small now, in terms of consumer usage, one must remember that most of these did not exist at all until quite recently in China. Yet, as shown, they are growing rapidly in influence.

While all these comparisons are useful and interesting, the real question is how the media planner or marketing executive can use them in creating better media plans. In the final section of this chapter, we offer a unique planning methodology that combines much of the data found in the PCQS and MBI in a new and meaningful way. Before we address that, however, we will look for some key differences within the Chinese digital generation.

Differences Among Chinese Consumers

Having compared the influence of various media forms on Chinese and American consumers in the 18–34 age group, we will briefly comment on some key variations among the Chinese respondents by geography and gender.

There are few material differences in media influence among Tier 1–3 cities. While various forms of personal interactive media may have a slightly greater influence on respondents in Tier 1 cities, the gap is only a few percentage points, at most. Where there are notable differences, however, is in the reported influence by gender, as shown in Figure 5-5.

Young Chinese females are far more likely to report being influenced by TV, word of mouth, in-store and coupons than are the male respondents. They also more frequently mention magazines, outdoor and product placement, but these differences are minimal.

Young men, on the other hand, say they are influenced more often by the Internet, IM, blogs, video games and mobile.

These gender characteristics have important variations, which will be examined further in the discussion of specific product categories.

Practical Applications to Media Planning

While all these comparisons are useful and interesting, the real question is how a marketer or media planner could use them in creating better media plans. In this section, we offer a unique planning methodology that combines much of the data found in the PCQS and MBI in a new and meaningful way.

We have used a statistical analytical technique called CHAID (CHi-squared Automatic Interaction Detection). Quite simply, this is a computer algorithm that identifies, in descending order, the value the customer places on that media form in terms of its influence in a specific category, such as eating out (fast foods) or apparel.

FIGURE 5-5: Reported media influence on purchase decisions ✦ Chinese consumers by gender

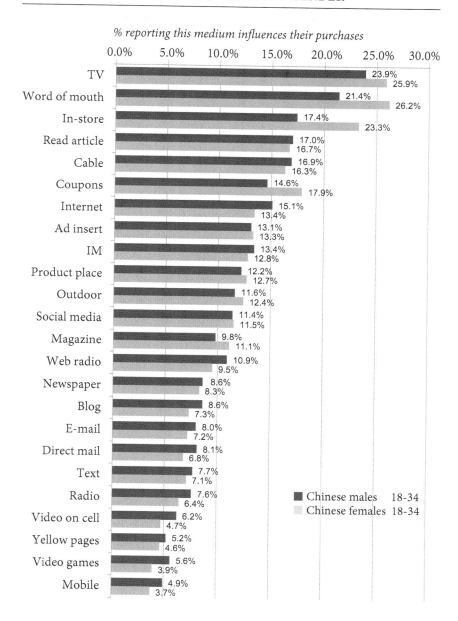

% reporting this medium influences their purchases

Source: ProsperChina.com

In other words, the system sorts out which media form has the greatest reported usage (time spent) and combines that with the media form that has the greatest influence and creates a tree-like output, as shown in the following examples. Note that these are "pruned" CHAID trees, that is, they show only the most relevant branches of the analysis, based on consumers' reported media usage and influence in each category.

In the first example, Figure 5-6 we examine fast food. Our purpose is to identify the best combination of media to reach frequent fast-food customers in China age 18–34. Further, we refine our analysis to specifically identify which media forms are most important in order of use by high-frequency customers, in other words we want to identify the media form which is most often used by the largest number of "heavy users" of fast-food restaurants. This is based on their media usage and the influence these consumers report each medium has on their decisions relating to fast- food restaurants.

Overall, the young adult Chinese in the study report visiting a fast-food restaurant an average of 4.78 times per month, or a little over once a week. Those who report using social media, and who say it influences their purchase in the category, also eat at fast-food restaurants more often: 5.38 visits per month. When social media is combined with mobile and gaming (the next most popular media forms among this group), the average frequency increases to 6.93 times per month. By using these media forms in combination, a marketer could target a narrow but lucrative segment of very high-frequency fast-food users. On the other hand, 87.5% of the respondents in China said they are not influenced by social media in the decision to dine out. These only average 4.69 visits per month. In this case, the best option would be to utilize web radio, as it is the next most influential medium rated by this group and results in a target group with an above average frequency of 5.07 visits per month.

FIGURE 5-6: FREQUENCY OF FAST FOOD VISITS PER MONTH

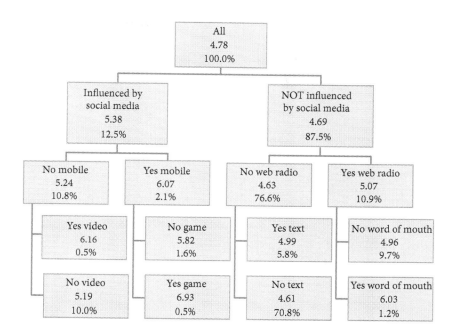

Source: ProsperChina.com

Our second example (Figure 5-7) looks at monthly spending on apparel. The goal in this case is to identify the best media combinations to reach the highest spending customers in this category. That will be based on their reported media usage and influence. Overall, the respondents in the study spend an average of US$58.68 per month on apparel. Those who use and are influenced by video spend well above the average, at US$77.97 per month, while those who use both video and inserts spend even higher US$90.89 per month. When that combination is supplemented with the yellow pages, the average increases to US$103.73 per month.

FIGURE 5-7: AVERAGE MONTHLY SPEND (US$) ON APPAREL

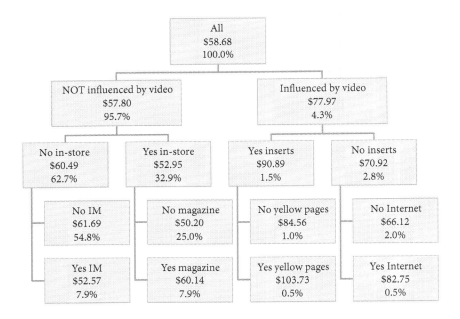

Source: ProsperChina.com

The final example is for a considered purchase, that is, those who state they plan to buy an automobile in the coming six months. For the sake of simplicity, we are not factoring in the expected purchase price, just whether or not they plan to purchase a car. Overall, 21.6% of the young Chinese consumers said they planned to purchase a car within the next six months. We have commented earlier on the popularity of blogging in China, and in this category it is a medium that is highly used and highly influential. Among those who participate in blogging, fully 35.5% say they plan to buy a car within six months. This presents a somewhat different challenge for the marketer or media planner, as blogging is primarily the exchange of opinions between individuals. While corporations can and should attempt to participate in these conversations, it is far less promotional than more traditional forms of marketing communication. When activities within the blogosphere are combined with other forms of digital communication, especially e-mail and text messaging, the likelihood that a prospect is planning on buying a car within six months increases to 61.3%. Thus, we once again see the importance of viewing media forms in combination, not just separately and individually.

FIGURE 5-8: PLAN TO PURCHASE AUTOMOBILE IN NEXT 6 MONTHS

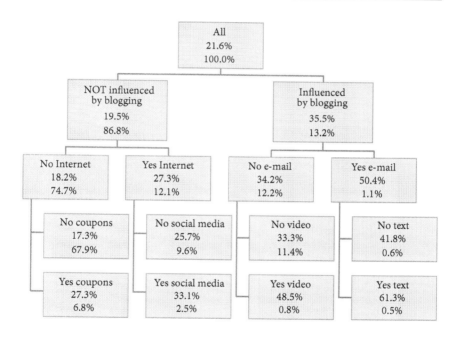

Source: ProsperChina.com

These are just three examples of how a more sophisticated analysis of media usage and media influence data can be used to improve media planning within China. As the three examples point out, there are certainly major differences by product category and what media forms are most widely used and which are most influential. Those topics will be addressed in coming chapters. In addition, clearly, different communications objectives would produce appropriately different pathways in the CHAID analysis. However, these examples do illustrate the power of the data in the PCQS database which allow planners to hone highly targeted, purpose-built media plans

Prosper MediaPlanIQ™

Sophisticated analytical tools such as the CHAID analysis, as illustrated in the previous section offer marketers a robust solution to solving complex media planning issues. From a pragmatic standpoint, however, marketers often do not have the resources—time, data or statistical skills—to develop customized CHAID models.

A practical alternative is to utilize the Prosper MediaPlanIQ™, a cloud-based application that brings the power of the Prosper databases to the planning process. MediaPlanIQ has been in place for several years in the US, and has recently been introduced into China. It is available in both English and Standard Chinese, and users can easily toggle from one language to another, facilitating use by multinational, multilingual staff.

MediaPlanIQ provides marketers with fast, accurate and easy-to-use online tools to determine the best allocation of media forms, given consumers' stated usage of each media form, the influence they say each medium has on their buying decisions and their purchasing behaviors in nine product categories. This is just one of the many new, more sophisticated media planning tools that are required in the very complex media systems which now exist in China.

Five Key Takeaways

1. The influence a given medium has on consumer decision making is a critical, but frequently overlooked, factor in media planning. Such influence differs significantly from one category to the next, but some broad generalizations can be made by media form.

2. China's digital generation rates TV, word of mouth, in-store promotion and "read an article" as the media forms that most influence their purchase decisions. Americans of the same age group tend to favor word of mouth, followed by coupons, TV and ad inserts. The popularity of coupons and ad inserts does not mean that Americans are necessarily more promotion oriented, but likely reflects the more highly developed infrastructure in the US for the distribution, processing and redemption of promotional offers.

3. Personal interactive media—especially IM, social media and mobile—is increasingly shaping purchasing decisions in China and the US.

4. Chinese woman more often report they are influenced by media than do men of the same generation. In particular, Chinese women most often report being influenced by word of mouth, TV, in-store promotion and coupons.

5. Analytical tools such as CHAID or the Prosper MediaPlanIQ can assist marketers in determining the most effective combination of media to use in specific product categories, given consumers' reported media usage and the influence they say each form has on their buying decisions.

Moving On

Following this general discussion of media influence, we move on to a closer examination of how the digital generation in China and the US use the Internet for online activities—especially surfing, searching and online shopping.

Chapter 6

Online Activities:
Surfing, Searching and Shopping

The era of digital communication in China had its unofficial beginning on September 20, 1987 when, after months of work, the first Internet connection was made between Beijing's Institute of Computer Applications and Karlsruhe University in Germany. The first e-mail message to be sent from China to Germany read simply but prophetically: "Across the Great Wall we can reach every corner in the world."[1]

The oldest members of China's digital generation were still young children at the time, and some were not even born. However, their lives would forever be changed in ways that no one could have anticipated in 1987. And, in spite of ongoing government regulation and censorship of sensitive topics, young Chinese have indeed seen beyond

---

1. "The Internet Timeline of China 1986~1996," China Internet Network Information Center, June 26, 2004, http://www1.cnnic.cn/html/Dir/2003/12/12/2000.htm

the Great Wall, and become active netizens of the global digital communication system.

Explosion of Internet Usage in China

Growth in the number of Internet users in China was initially slow. Infrastructure was limited, connection speeds were sluggish and computers were beyond the means of most people. By the turn of the millennium the US had amassed 121.7 million Internet users, while China had only 22.5 million. However, the rate of growth in China quickened throughout the early 2000s—the result of improving technology, increasing wealth, development of consumer-oriented online services and the introduction of digitally enabled mobile phones. According to the World Bank, by early 2007 China could lay claim to over 226 million users, the largest Internet community in the world—roughly a tenfold increase in only seven years.

China continues to experience explosive increases in the number of connected users, with growth now shifting to Tier 2 and 3 cities. There are now about a half a billion users in China—greater than the combined populations of the United States, Canada and Mexico—yet penetration is still only about 38% of the total Chinese population. For comparison, the World Bank estimates Internet penetration in the US, Japan and Korea to be around 80% of the population. Thus, it is likely that as the Chinese economy continues to expand and mature, and as less expensive devices become available, the population of Chinese Internet users will see robust growth for many years ahead.

Evolution of Social Media in China

Many of the earliest Internet applications in China that consumers embraced were those that connected individuals with one another—bulletin board systems (BBS), chat rooms, forums, instant messaging (IM) and so on—in which participants were able to seek advice, express opinions, trade insights and make friends online.

According to McKinsey, the beginnings of social media in China can be traced back to 1994, with the first online forums and communities, and further expansion with the arrival of IM in 1999. The next advancement came in 2003 with the introduction of user review sites, followed by rapid increases in blogging in 2004. In 2005, social networking sites with chatting capabilities such as Renren began to gain followers. More recently, Sina Weibo launched micro-blogging with multimedia in 2009, and Jiepang began offering location-based services in 2010. [2]

Although the government has kept tight control of discussions on certain sensitive or taboo subjects, Chinese online users have had, for the first time, relative freedom to converse on a wide range of other issues with people whom they do not necessarily know. Much of the early BBS and chat sites were based on assumed user identities—nicknames, screen names, avatars and so on—that gave users an additional sense of freedom from the strictures of Chinese social interactions. It became common for Chinese consumers to maintain multiple accounts for different online identities and different purposes. To this day, nickname-based sites are still extremely popular, although after the unrest in spring 2012 the government initiated efforts to require real name-only registration for blogs, micro-blogs and online forums.

For the digital generation in China and the US, the Internet has come to be one of the key defining factors shaping their lives. Nevertheless, there are important practical differences that marketers need to keep in mind. How each nationality uses the Internet, the types of activities they undertake and the types of sites they frequent influences the context in which online marketing communication will be consumed.

---

2. Cindy Chiu, Chris Ip and Ari Silverman, "Understanding Social Media in China," *McKinsey Quarterly* (April 2012), https://www.mck inseyquarterly.com/Understanding_social_media_in_China_2961

Surfing the Web for Fun, Information and Connections

In Chapter 3 we learned that Chinese and American consumers frequently mention surfing the Internet as one of their preferred leisure activities. In fact, for the Chinese, it was the favorite pastime among both men and women, as well as across Tiers 1, 2, and 3. While, in the US, it was the fourth-most popular activity, behind watching TV, going to movies and listening to music. It makes sense, then, to begin our exploration of online behaviors by looking first at the types of activities Chinese and American netizens do online for fun, as detailed in Figure 6-1.

Staying connected with friends and family is a key online activity in both China and the US. However, note the differences in the applications used to connect with others. The Chinese respondents are much heavier users of IM and chat than are respondents in the US (54.5% in China compared with only 32.8% in the US), reflecting the much stronger role both of these applications have historically played in China. Americans, on the other hand, are more likely to use online communities and social networking to stay in touch with family and friends (35.2% in the US compared with 23.6% in China). Adding the two categories together shows that overall, the Chinese use the Internet much more intensively for interpersonal communication. Among the Chinese, 78.1% report using either IM and chat and/or online communities and social networks, versus only 68.0% of the Americans. While marketers are already aware that social media is a critical resource for engaging with the digital generation in either country, it is incumbent on them to appreciate the technological differences as well as more subtle cultural nuances in how Chinese and American consumers use the Internet.

Beyond using the web for interpersonal communication, both groups frequently use the Internet for various forms of entertainment and information gathering, especially downloading music or videos (42.1% in China and 37.6% in the US). Celebrity gossip is much more popular among Chinese respondents, with 39.8% saying they

FIGURE 6-1: ACTIVITIES DONE ONLINE FOR FUN CHINESE AND AMERICAN CONSUMERS

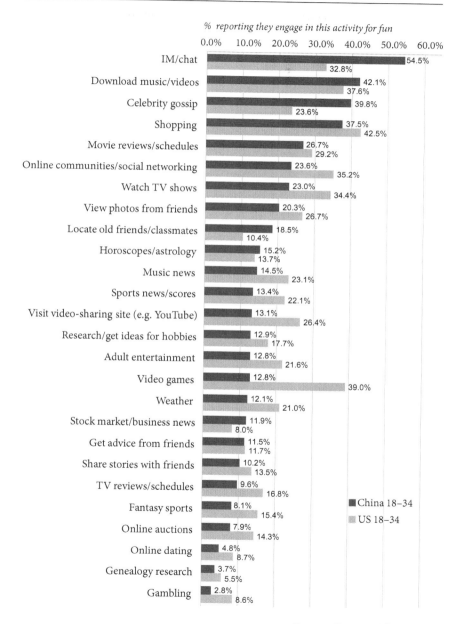

% reporting they engage in this activity for fun

Activity	China 18–34	US 18–34
IM/chat	54.5%	32.8%
Download music/videos	42.1%	37.6%
Celebrity gossip	39.8%	23.6%
Shopping	37.5%	42.5%
Movie reviews/schedules	26.7%	29.2%
Online communities/social networking	23.6%	35.2%
Watch TV shows	23.0%	34.4%
View photos from friends	20.3%	26.7%
Locate old friends/classmates	18.5%	10.4%
Horoscopes/astrology	15.2%	13.7%
Music news	14.5%	23.1%
Sports news/scores	13.4%	22.1%
Visit video-sharing site (e.g. YouTube)	13.1%	26.4%
Research/get ideas for hobbies	12.9%	17.7%
Adult entertainment	12.8%	21.6%
Video games	12.8%	39.0%
Weather	12.1%	21.0%
Stock market/business news	11.9%	8.0%
Get advice from friends	11.5%	11.7%
Share stories with friends	10.2%	13.5%
TV reviews/schedules	9.6%	16.8%
Fantasy sports	8.1%	15.4%
Online auctions	7.9%	14.3%
Online dating	4.8%	8.7%
Genealogy research	3.7%	5.5%
Gambling	2.8%	8.6%

Source: ProsperChina.com

go online for this, while only 23.6% of the US group reports that as a fun activity. Respondents in the US are much more likely to use the Internet to obtain information on weather, sports scores and music and news. Additionally, playing video games online is much more popular in the US (39.0% versus only 12.8% among the Chinese). This may at first seem counterintuitive, since we know from Figure 3-1 that video games are very popular among young Chinese men of the digital generation. However, as we also stated, much of their gaming takes place in retail video gaming parlors rather than online at home. Hence the significant gap in the frequency with which the Chinese and American mention gaming as an online activity.

Another area that is more frequently mentioned by US respondents, compared with their Chinese contemporaries, is adult entertainment (21.6% in the US compared with only 12.8% in China). This category is highly controlled and censored by the Chinese government, while the US is much more lenient. As might be expected, Chinese men are more likely to report going to adult entertainment sites than are Chinese women.

Websites Most Often Visited

Chinese netizens have a diverse range of online platforms from which to choose—everything from news and information to bulletin boards, search, social networking, blogging, micro-blogging, file sharing, gaming and e-commerce sites (see sidebar A Short Guide to Major Chinese Digital Media). While many platforms began as a clone of a successful Western site, such as Facebook, Flickr, Twitter or YouTube (all of which are blocked in China), in several cases the Chinese versions have added technological enhancements and functionality, thereby "leapfrogging" the applications they set out to emulate.

The most popular of these are Tencent Holdings' QQ and its sister social network Qzone, as shown in Figure 6-2 where Chinese consumers were asked which sites they visit regularly (that is, "routinely") or occasionally ("no set pattern, as the mood suits").

FIGURE 6-2: How often different sites are visited
◆ Chinese consumers

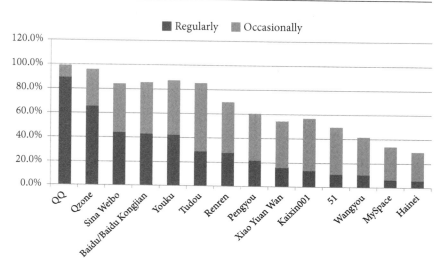

Source: ProsperChina.com

Nearly every 18–34-year-old respondent in the study reports using QQ on a regular or occasional basis, with regular usage at an astounding 89%. There are two services provided under the QQ rubric. The first, the exceptionally popular Tencent QQ instant messaging service, originated under the name OICQ in 1999 and now claims over 711 million active user accounts. In addition to IM, Tencent QQ also supports chat rooms, games, personal avatars and Internet dating services. It pioneered the use of the Q Coin, a virtual prepaid currency used to facilitate micro-transactions such as buying ringtones, playing games or acquiring virtual goods for avatars. Parent company Tencent Holdings also offers QQ.com, a domain name it acquired in 2004, as a popular news, information and entertainment portal. Qzone was launched in 2005 as an assumed-name social network, and has grown rapidly thanks, at least in part, to the massive QQ user base.

Of the 14 sites listed in Figure 6-2 that Chinese consumers use regularly or occasionally, social media platforms dominate. Baidu is a search engine, and Xiao Yuan Wan refers to campus intranets students use to access the web. Youku and Tudou are both video-hosting sites, now merged into a single company Youku Tudou Inc. The remaining 10 sites all enable social interaction under either real or assumed names. QQ provides IM, chat and gaming, Sina Weibo provides micro-blogging, and the rest are social networks, some with specialized orientation such white-collar workers, youth, students, alumni groups or arts and entertainment. Whereas Facebook is by far the dominant social network in the US, followed by Linked-In for business networks, it is apparent that social networking in China is much more diverse, narrowly focused and fragmented. The challenge for marketers is to master the unique character, vernacular and intricacies of each platform and communicate in ways that are appropriate to the context, technology and specific audience that each delivers.

Of course, there are many other sites that are frequently used by Chinese consumers, depending on the purpose, information to be gathered or desired activity. When asked which site they most visited for fun and entertainment, the 5 most frequently mentioned sites were QQ.com (29.7%), Sina.com (27.9%), 163.com (8.7%), Xunlei.com (8.0%) and Tianya.com (5.4%). For news, the number of sites was even narrower: with 43.7% saying they most often went to QQ.com, 42.1% going to Sina.com, and just 3.2% mentioning some other site as a news source.

Word of Mouth and E-Influence

In a Confucian, communal society gaining and maintaining the approval of one's family, superiors and peers is of paramount importance. This applies to every aspect of Chinese life, from major events such as marriage, career or the purchase of an automobile, down to the minutest details of daily life, such as the choice of what music to listen to or even which toothpaste to use.

Thus, the seeking and giving of opinions is an ongoing process whereby individuals are constantly scanning those around them for what would be acceptable to say, do or purchase. Added to this is the fact that Chinese are wary of business and the media, and rely heavily on recommendations or opinions from those they trust on a personal level.

When asked about seeking advice from others when planning a purchase, 42.1% of the PCQS respondents age 18–34 said they regularly request input from others, and another 54.2% do so occasionally. Young women are even more active about seeking advice, with 44.9% replying they do so regularly. For marketers, this means it is not sufficient to simply achieve awareness and interest among a group of target customers. In China, is it critical to create a broader positive perception among a reference set, that is, those to whom a customer may turn to for advice and approval.

On the other hand, giving advice is also an important aspect of social interaction. It is an opportunity to demonstrate one's knowledge, experience and sophistication, especially when it comes to newly introduced products. Of the PCQS respondents, 41.4% report that they routinely give advice on products or services they have purchased, and another 55.1% do so occasionally. Positive word of mouth from current users can have a powerful impact on the success of a product, while negative reports are difficult to overcome in an environment in which consumers are so highly attuned to the opinions of others. For most Chinese, it would be unthinkable to purchase a product that had a negative report from, say, one's boss or one's mother-in-law.

The social importance of giving and receiving advice has been one of the driving factors shaping the Internet in China. As was noted earlier, many of the first applications to gain popularity facilitated the expression of personal opinions, often anonymously, via bulletin boards, chat rooms, user reviews and blogs.

The popularity of blogs continues unabated. As shown in Figure 6-3, young Chinese consumers are active in the blogosphere, both in passive reading as well as in active content creation. The vast majority are involved in blogging on some level, with regular or occasional participation rates reaching over 80%.

FIGURE 6-3: BLOGGING ACTIVITY ◦ CHINESE CONSUMERS

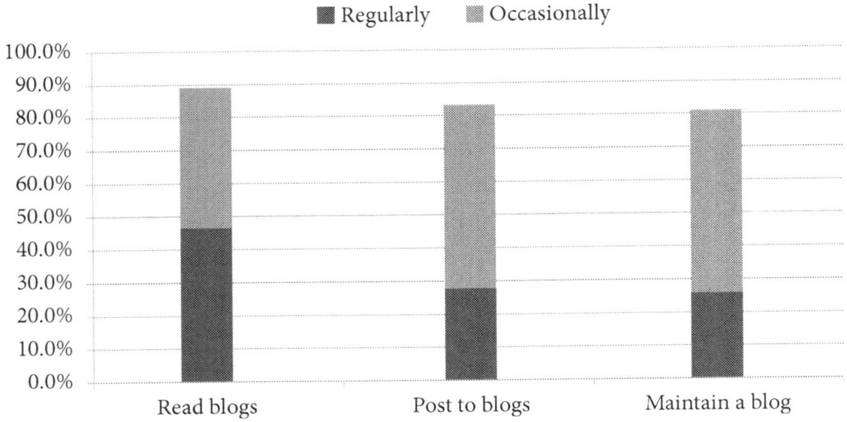

Source: ProsperChina.com

Among the PCQS respondents, 46.4% report they regularly read blogs, and another 42.6% do so occasionally. Furthermore, almost as many are active content contributors—either through posting to blogs created by others or maintaining their own blog. This is clearly an active audience anxious to express opinions on whatever matters to them personally.

Interestingly, the percentage of "regular" or "occasional" blogging activity of any sort varies little between men and women, and only slightly between tiers. Respondents in Tier 1 cities are somewhat more active in regularly posting to blogs (31.7%) than their counterparts in Tiers 2 and 3 (26.9 and 26.6% respectively). And, Tier 1 respondents more often report regularly maintaining a blog of their own (29.6% in Tier 1, 25.3% in Tier 2 and 24.9% in Tier 3). However, these differences are relatively minor and overall indicate how widespread is the desire to use the Internet as a personal forum for expression. For marketers, China's cadres of e-influencers are a potent force to be reckoned with, and can make the difference between the success and failure of a product launch, a special event or a communication campaign.

Search Behavior

If the Internet is a powerful tool to connect people to one another, it is also a highly practical mechanism to connect people with information on the products and services of interest to them. It can help them research alternatives, learn about the latest offerings, compare prices and features, educate themselves about a category and gather opinions from other customers.

Within China, Baidu is the dominant search engine, with over 80% of the Chinese respondents saying it is the one they use most often. The next closest competitor, Google, only commands about 10% of the respondent base (15.5% in Tier 1 cities), and has moved its operations to Hong Kong in order to avoid further conflict with the government over censorship. While there are a few other indigenous search engines (Qqsou.com, Sogou.com, Soso.com, Zhongsou.com), none are used by more than 2–3% of those in the 18–34 age bracket.

Among Chinese consumers, clothing and shoes are most frequently mentioned (61.7%) as a subject for search. (The figure for women is even higher, at 73.6%.) As evidenced by Figure 6-4, this is in notable contrast with US consumers, where only 37.3% say they regularly search online in the category.

In fact, Chinese respondents report more regular search in almost all categories than the Americans of the same age. The only areas where the Americans report greater regular search behavior is in areas such as restaurants, sports, and tickets for concerts or sporting events—all activities in which they are more likely to engage, as we learned in Chapter 3 (see Figure 3-2).

FIGURE 6-4: "REGULAR" ONLINE SEARCH
CHINESE AND AMERICAN CONSUMERS

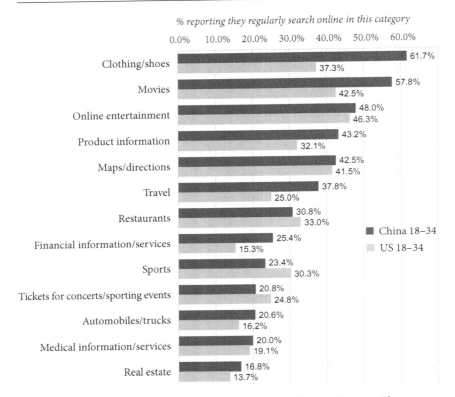

Source: ProsperChina.com

Online Search Triggers

Online search activity can be prompted by many triggers. Someone picks up a bit of information in a message from a friend, sees an ad, reads an article or sees a display in a store and then he or she becomes interested enough to begin a search for more information. It is telling that the triggers to online search are substantially different for Chinese and American consumers (see Figure 6-5), although the differences are consistent with what we have already learned about their use of various traditional and digital media.

FIGURE 6-5: TRIGGERS TO ONLINE SEARCH
◆ CHINESE AND AMERICAN CONSUMERS

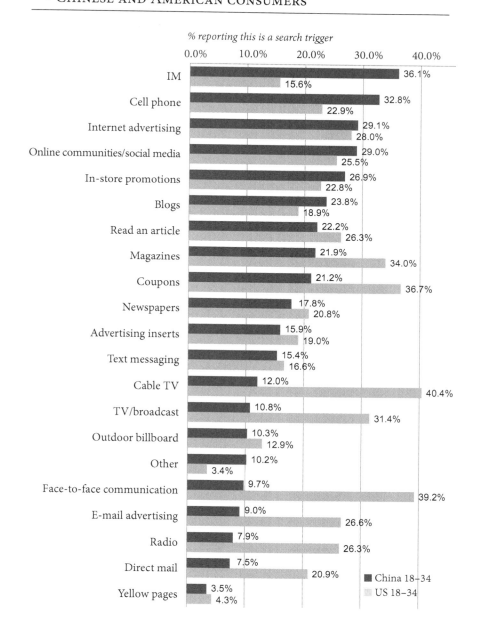

% reporting this is a search trigger

	China 18–34	US 18–34
IM	36.1%	15.6%
Cell phone	32.8%	22.9%
Internet advertising	29.1%	28.0%
Online communities/social media	29.0%	25.5%
In-store promotions	26.9%	22.8%
Blogs	23.8%	18.9%
Read an article	22.2%	26.3%
Magazines	21.9%	34.0%
Coupons	21.2%	36.7%
Newspapers	17.8%	20.8%
Advertising inserts	15.9%	19.0%
Text messaging	15.4%	16.6%
Cable TV	12.0%	40.4%
TV/broadcast	10.8%	31.4%
Outdoor billboard	10.3%	12.9%
Other	10.2%	3.4%
Face-to-face communication	9.7%	39.2%
E-mail advertising	9.0%	26.6%
Radio	7.9%	26.3%
Direct mail	7.5%	20.9%
Yellow pages	3.5%	4.3%

Source: ProsperChina.com

Here the distinguishing characteristics between the two groups are readily apparent. The two most frequent triggers for Chinese consumers—IM and cell phone—are of relatively minor importance to the Americans. The opposite is true as well. Those factors that the Americans list the most often—face-to-face communication, TV, coupons, e-mail, radio and direct mail—all play a decidedly lower role among the Chinese. Methods that marketers use to drive search traffic among American customers and prospects will need to be adapted in order to achieve success with a Chinese audience.

Online Search for Intended Purchases

The Internet has become a potent tool for consumers in China and the US to investigate and evaluate products and services prior to making a purchasing decision. Consumers in both countries now commonly go online to research big-ticket items as well as more casual purchases, and use the Internet to research the latest developments in the category, to understand product options, to educate themselves on product usage, to obtain competitive prices and to read reviews from other buyers. This is true even if they ultimately go to a store to purchase a product in person, and they expect a seamless experience between the online and offline worlds.

The categories in which Chinese and US consumers conducted such online searches before making a purchase are shown in Figure 6-6.

One of the most notable differences between the two groups is in the category of apparel. Fully 59.6% of the Chinese consumers report they research apparel online before making a purchase, compared with 44.5% in the US. Among the Chinese group, the primary searchers for pre-purchase information on apparel are young women (68.3% compared with men at 51.6%). Another point of interest is that online research for apparel is higher in Tier 3 cities (63.3%) than in Tier 1 (57.4%) or Tier 2 (59.3%). This is presumably because, while interest in fashion may be increasing, there are fewer resources available to shoppers to know about the latest styles and where to obtain the most current merchandise.

FIGURE 6-6: RESEARCH ONLINE BEFORE BUYING CHINESE AND AMERICAN CONSUMERS

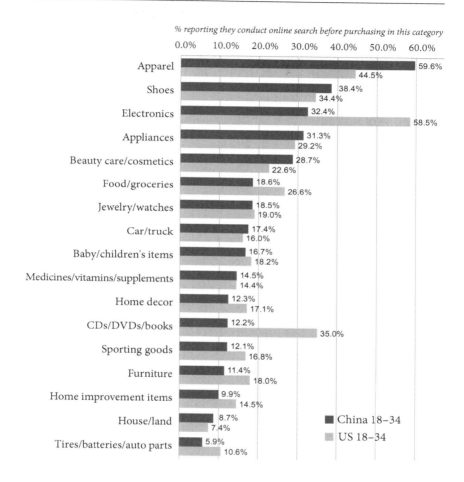

Source: ProsperChina.com

The young adult Chinese were also more likely than their US counterparts to do online research prior to making a purchase in categories such as shoes, appliances and beauty care and cosmetics. On the other hand, US consumers more often conduct pre-purchase research in areas such as food and groceries, CDs, DVDs and books, and home improvement.

Devices Used for Search Activities

A final point in this section relates to the types of devices that consumers in both countries use to conduct their search activities. A more complete discussion of the electronic and digital equipment that consumers own or intend to purchase will be covered in the following chapter. However, for now, it is useful to understand what devices are used for conducting online searches, as seen in Figure 6-7.

FIGURE 6-7: Devices used for Internet search Chinese and American consumers

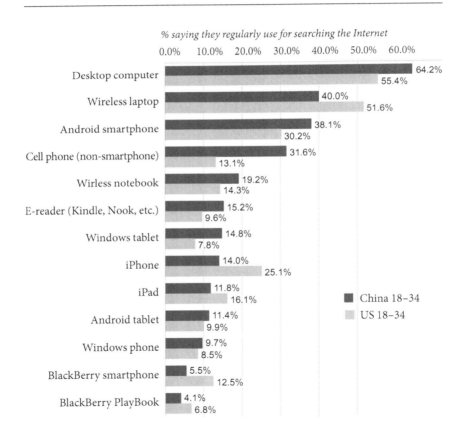

% saying they regularly use for searching the Internet

Source: ProsperChina.com

Because of the advanced nature of mobile communication in China, it is sometimes assumed that phones are the primary devices used for most online activities. While the use of mobile phones, smartphones, tablets, and so on is certainly increasing, it is interesting to note that desktop computers are still the most commonly used device for doing online search, followed by laptop computers.

Online Shopping

E-commerce had a slow and difficult birth in China, and for many years did not grow at the same phenomenal rates seen in the West. Chinese consumers were often suspicious of online merchants, fearing counterfeit goods or outright fraud (often with good reason). Payment was a barrier, as credit card penetration was low. Goods could be stolen in transit. And perhaps even more important was the fundamental, practical nature of Chinese buyers and their desire to feel, touch and experience a product before being convinced it was the best item to purchase.

Many of these issues still exist today, but the growth of large reputable merchants, the diffusion of credit cards, the introduction of secure payment system such as Alipay and improvement in logistical systems have helped to offset at least some consumer concerns. The result is the Chinese e-commerce scene is making up for lost time and now growing at breakneck pace.

According to market research firm iResearch, online shopping by consumers in China reached US$122.6 billion in 2011, up from US$73.1 billion the previous year. Looking forward, the company predicts online shopping revenue will expand by more than 50% in 2012 to US$187 billion, and will more than double to US$404.1 billion by 2015.[3]

---

3. Lin Jing and Su Zhou, "Online Shopping Gaining Popularity," *China Daily,* April 14, 2012, http://www.chinadaily.com.cn/china/2012-04/14/content_15047085.htm

The growth of online shopping is aided by the fact that sophisticated retailing is generally less developed in China than in the US, where is there is an over-saturation of shopping centers and strip malls. The lack of retail density is especially true outside major cities such as Beijing, Guangzhou and Shanghai. Thus, online shopping is particularly appealing to those outside of the mega-cities. It is estimated that by 2016, 16% of all retail trade in China will be conducted online, up from the current 3%. (Currently, online sales represent about 12% of retail trade in the US.)

For this reason, Chee Wee Gan, of A. T. Kearney, has said, "The e-commerce battle will not be fought in first-tier cities such as Beijing, Shanghai or Guangzhou. The real battle will be in second- and third-tier cities, where new middle class consumers are coming up. It is not going to be that easy for companies to expand their physical presence in these locations. Going online is the best way to ensure that they get more consumers and profits."[4]

Online Shopping Behavior

The growing interest of young consumers in online shopping is apparent in Figure 6-8. Participants were asked, "Over the next 90 days, do you plan on spending more, the same or less than you normally would spend at this time of year by Internet, catalog or TV-home shopping?"

Their response is a strong endorsement for shifting buying behavior toward the Internet, and away from catalog or TV-home shopping—a pattern that holds true for men and women, as well as across Tier 1, 2 and 3 cities.

In fact, more Chinese consumers age 18–34, who participated in the survey, indicate they shop online either regularly or occasionally than their American counterparts. Only 3.9% of the Chinese respondents said they never shop online, compared with 22.5% of the US participants (see Figure 6-9).

---

4. Lin and Su, "Online Shopping Gaining Popularity"

FIGURE 6-8: FUTURE SHOPPING INTENTIONS
CHINESE CONSUMERS

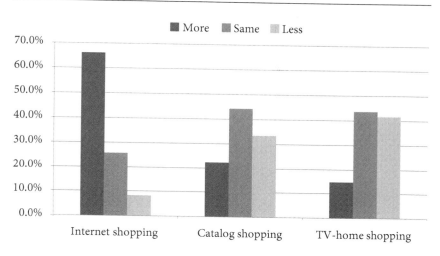

Source: ProsperChina.com

FIGURE 6-9: HOW OFTEN DO YOU PURCHASE PRODUCTS ONLINE?
CHINESE AND AMERICAN CONSUMERS

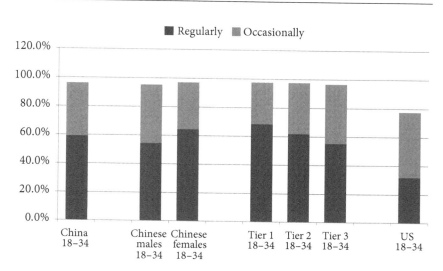

Source: ProsperChina.com

According to iResearch, the lion's share of online shopping is still consumer-to-consumer transactions. For the first quarter of 2012, iResearch reported that 72.8% of online shopping was consumer-to-consumer, with Taobao Marketplace capturing an overwhelming 95.1% of the volume.[5] Owned by B-to-B e-commerce giant the Alibaba Group, Taobao pioneered consumer-to-consumer online shopping. It enabled sellers, including small businesses, to offer new and used merchandise using fixed pricing as well as auctions, similar to eBay. The company claims to have more than 800 million product listings and more than 370 million registered users, making it a daunting presence on the Internet. The parent company also introduced Alipay, an innovative third-party escrow payment service, in which consumers can verify whether they are happy with goods they have bought before releasing money to the seller.

According to the same iResearch report, the remaining 27.2% of online shopping is divvied up among an ever-increasing number of business-to-business online retailers. However, even here Taobao dominates with its Tmall.com (formerly Taobao Mall) commanding about 51.5% of the volume in the first quarter of 2012.

The dominance of Taobao in online shopping can be seen in how respondents answered the question "Which online website do you use most often for buying products?" (see Figure 6-10).

Clearly, online retailing in China is an extremely competitive, dynamic and fragmented universe, with each company racing to achieve scale, legitimacy, trust and operational efficiency. Those selling products through online retailers will need to choose their partners carefully and work closely to develop effective offerings and promotional support.

---

5. iResearch, *China E-Commerce Report Q1 2012*, April 28, 2012, http://www.iresearchchina.com/samplereports/4148.html

FIGURE 6-10: WEBSITE USED MOST OFTEN FOR BUYING PRODUCTS • CHINESE CONSUMERS

	China 18–34	Men 18–34	Women 18–34
Taobao	73.4%	71.0%	75.9%
360buy.com	5.9%	7.1%	4.6%
Paipai	4.0%	4.7%	3.3%
Amazon China (Joyo)	3.1%	2.9%	3.2%
Dangdang	2.5%	2.2%	2.9%
1haodian	1.5%	1.3%	1.6%
Suning	0.9%	1.0%	0.8%
M18.com	0.9%	0.7%	1.1%
Newegg	0.6%	0.8%	0.4%
Gome	0.5%	0.7%	0.4%
Ctrip	0.4%	0.5%	0.4%
Eachnet (eBay)	0.4%	0.5%	0.3%
Mangocity	0.3%	0.4%	0.1%
Redbaby	0.3%	0.2%	0.3%
OK (Ihok.com)	0.2%	0.2%	0.1%
Ayhualian	0.2%	0.2%	0.1%
Carrefour	0.1%	0.2%	0.1%
SamsClub	0.1%	0.2%	0.1%

Source: ProsperChina.com

Consumer Attitudes Toward Online Shopping Services

The digital generation in China is perhaps more comfortable in conducting online transactions than the older generation, but they are nevertheless demanding in their expectations. They expect sites to have good functionality, they want top-notch customer service, they want flexibility—and they want it all at a low price and shipped for free, as seen in Figure 6-11. PCQS participants were asked to rate the importance of different online shopping services on a scale of 1 to 5, with 5 being the most important. The chart shows the average rating given to each aspect of service. Interestingly, there is very little variation in any of the average ratings either by gender or between tiers.

FIGURE 6-11: IMPORTANCE OF ONLINE SHOPPING SERVICES CHINESE CONSUMERS

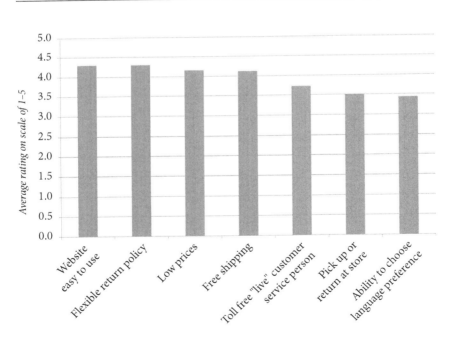

Source: ProsperChina.com

Five Key Takeaways

1. China's digital generation relies heavily on the Internet to stay in touch with friends, families and associates, and the applications they use differ substantially from those used by Americans of the same age group.

2. There is no dominant social network such as Facebook in China. The networks tend to be more fragmented and focused on special interests or audiences.

3. Chinese consumers actively search products and services before making a purchase, even if they wind up purchasing in a retail store.

4. Apparel, shoes and electronics are the categories most frequently researched online by China's digital consumers.

5. Online shopping is exploding in China, and while there are still ongoing issues with trust, payment and logistics, Chinese consumers are increasingly turning to a burgeoning number of online retailers for their shopping needs.

Moving On

This chapter has examined how the digital generation interacts with the digital world, particularly their online activities. We will next turn our attention to the devices and services they use to connect to the Internet and to one another.

Chapter 7

Digital and Mobile Devices

The marketplace for digital and mobile devices and services in China is a hyper-competitive mix of multinational and domestic brands competing on shifting dynamics of price, distribution, technological innovation and country-of-origin perceptions.

According to the global consultancy R3, two brands that are prominent in the category—Apple and China Mobile—are regarded as the number one and two most engaging brands by Chinese consumers, topping such icons as Nike, Coke and KFC. The R3 study, conducted at the end of the first quarter of 2012, is a proprietary research initiative in which urban consumers are asked to name their favorite brands, recall memorable marketing efforts and identify the values associated with each.

While these two brands are tops for engagement in the minds of Chinese consumers, each faces very different market circumstances in China. On one hand, China Mobile is the government-owned, dominant provider of mobile telecommunications services, with an overwhelming share of the market, as will be discussed later in this chapter. Apple, on the other hand, while beloved as a status symbol, faces a diverse group of international and domestic competitors in every digital device segment in which it operates. It is a testament to the strength of the brand that Apple has managed to stay clearly differentiated from these competitors, and has captured the hearts, imagination and aspirations of young Chinese consumers, who see carrying an iPad or iPhone as a clear symbol of arrival. Nevertheless, the fact remains, it is a premium brand in a highly price-conscious market. As we shall see, despite its powerful brand resonance among young Chinese consumers, Apple is often not the category leader, and often loses out to competitors such as Lenovo, Samsung, HTC and Android.

This chapter will examine how consumers make brand choices for digital and mobile devices. We will review the various devices and services that Chinese and American consumers use for online activities, for gaming and for staying connected with friends and family. Additionally, we will look at their reported plans for future purchases and the product attributes and media forms that they say influence their purchasing decisions.

Computers, Tablets and Other Digital Devices

In spite of the recent economic slowdown, the consumer electronics industry in China is continuing to grow, especially outside of Tier 1 cities. According to Business Monitor International, the broad consumer electronics devices market, including computers, mobile handsets and video, audio and gaming products, is forecast at about US$201 billion in 2012, and is expected to increase to US$289.7 billion by 2016. The key growth segments within the electronics category are computers and other types of digital and mobile devices. Approximately 40% of China's consumer electronics spending in 2011 came from computers alone (including notebooks and accessories). This is expected to grow at a compound annual rate of 10.4% through 2016, thanks in part to falling prices and the government's program to subsidize computer purchases in rural areas.[1]

From computers and tablets to cell phones and other devices, digital appliances are the central tools that enable the switched-on, always-connected lifestyles of young consumers in China and the US.

Computers

In spite of technological innovation and the introduction of tablets, smartphones and other ultra-portable devices, computers are still in wide use in the US and China. In fact, in the ProsperChina Quarterly Study (PCQS), more Chinese consumers age 18–34 report having a desktop computer than their American contemporaries. That is shown in Figure 7-1. These figures are quite consistent by gender and across Tiers 1–3, although consumers in Tier 1 cities are somewhat more likely to own a wireless netbook (10.4%) and/or a Mac (3.6%). This is most likely a reflection of their greater affluence and greater access to the most recent technologies.

FIGURE 7-1: DIGITAL DEVICES—COMPUTERS CHINESE AND AMERICAN CONSUMERS

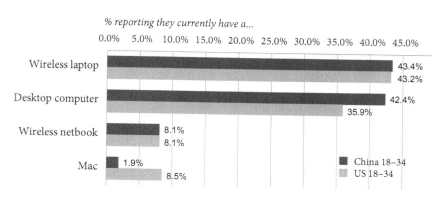

Source: ProsperChina.com

1. Business Monitor International, *China Consumer Electronics Report Q2 2012*, (2012)

While most industry experts predict continuing convergence between devices, and a slowing of growth in computer sales, the category is far from dead. To that point, 30.2% of the Chinese respondents reported that they intend to buy a computer in the coming six months, a figure that rises to 35.7% in Tier 1 cities. Even in the US, 22.4% of those in the 18–34 category said they intended to buy a computer within the same timeframe. Marketers need to be mindful of the strong established user base for computers in both countries and not get totally enamored by the hype around the new technologies.

For example, we saw in Chapter 6 that respondents in both countries report they most frequently use a desktop computer or wireless laptop for conducting online search, and this is likely to continue. Computers, which often have faster or more stable connections and the advantage of better display on a larger screen, offer consumers some important utilitarian advantages in searching and shopping. While other devices such as tablets and smartphones will no doubt gain in popularity, in many cases they will be a supplement to access via computer, not an outright replacement.

Tablets and Media Players

One of the hottest areas of the consumer electronics market is the rapid growth in tablets of all types and makes. Warc (the British publisher previously known as the World Advertising Research Center) reported that 4.9 million tablets were purchased in China in 2011, a tenfold increase over the previous year. The report also pointed out that revenues, which were in excess of US$2.9 billion, had increased only eight times over the previous year, an indication of how increasing competition is bringing prices down in the category. Globally, China accounted for just over 8% of worldwide tablet unit volume and revenue.[2]

---

2. Warc, "Tablet Sales Surge in China," March 19, 2012, http://www.warc.com/Content/News/Tablet_sales_surge_in_China.content?ID=15dd5018-592f-4e62-9d89-06ecca054761

While the iPad is the category leader in both the US and China (Figure 7-2), its advantage in China is far less than in the US. Less expensive Android and Windows tablets are providing an attractive, budget-conscious alternative for many consumers, especially in China.

FIGURE 7-2: DIGITAL DEVICES—TABLETS AND MEDIA PLAYERS
 ◆ CHINESE AND AMERICAN CONSUMERS

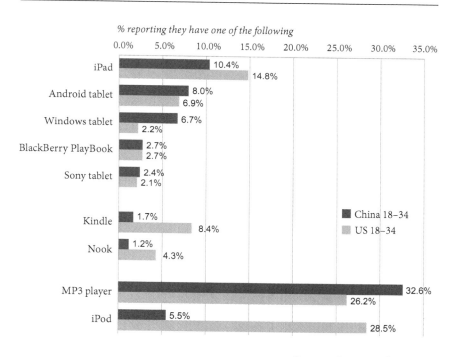

% reporting they have one of the following

Source: ProsperChina.com

E-readers such as the Kindle and Nook have not established much presence to-date in China. This is most likely a combination of price, lack of availability and the fact that both originated as single purpose (reading) devices.

Media players such as iPods are still popular devices in China and the US, and form a substantial user base for enjoying music. However, here again, this is evidence that while Chinese consumers embrace the

Apple brand, they more often than not purchase a less expensive, often domestically made, alternative.

Video Game Platforms

In earlier chapters, we addressed the popularity of video games in China, especially among young men age 18–34. We also commented that gaming often takes place not in the home, but in video game parlors. And Figure 7-3 confirms our expectation that Chinese households are less likely to have video gaming consoles compared with American households.

FIGURE 7-3: DIGITAL DEVICES—VIDEO GAME PLATFORMS CHINESE AND AMERICAN CONSUMERS

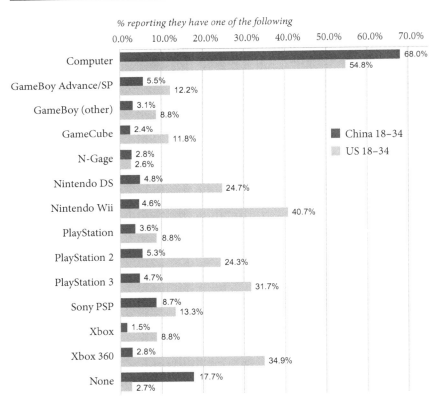

Source: ProsperChina.com

Most of the Chinese participants in the study (68%) named their computer as a video gaming platform. While 54.8% of the American also named their computer, they were much more likely to also have dedicated gaming devices, most notably a Nintendo platform, Xbox or PlayStation.

We finally note fully 17.7% of the Chinese respondents reported they did not have any digital gaming device in the home—compared with only 2.7% in the US.

Shopping for Electronics

The Chinese market for electronics is dominated by two major bricks-and-mortar retailers: Gome and Suning. When Chinese consumers are asked, "Where do you shop most often for electronics?" these two appliance and electronics specialists are by far the most frequently mentioned. And, both are strong in Tier 1, 2 and 3 cities, although Gome has a more commanding leading among PCQS respondents in Tiers 1 and 2 (see Figure 7-4).

Beyond Gome and Suning, electronics retailing in China is still highly fragmented and regionalized. Thus, Yongle is strongest in its home market of Shanghai, while Dazhong Electronics (owned by Gome) is strong in Beijing. International multi-line retailers, such as Walmart and Carrefour are not a major factor in selling electronics, even in Tier 1 cities. Walmart, with a stated global plan in 2010 to build its electronics base, has been an aggressive marketer in this area. As a result, while its overall market share is still small, it has seen its preference grow from 2.0% in 2009 to 2.7% the following year and to 3.4% by December 2011. Best Buy, which at one time operated nine locations in China, abruptly closed all of its stores in February 2011. The company's strategy is now focused on expanding its Five Star Electronics unit, which it acquired in 2009.

While Gome and Suning are currently the favorite reported destinations for shopping for electronics, the loyalty of the digital generation

FIGURE 7-4: RETAILERS SHOPPED MOST OFTEN FOR ELECTRONICS CHINESE CONSUMERS BY TIER

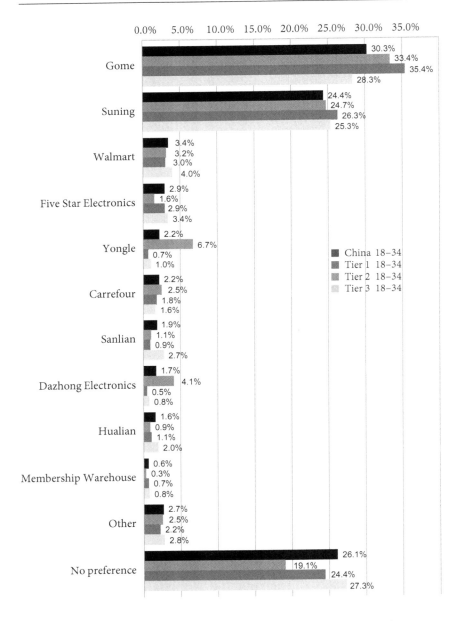

Source: ProsperChina.com

to these or any other store is not a forgone conclusion. More than one quarter (26.1%) of the PCQS respondents say they have "no preference," meaning they could be easily lured to another store by variables such as price, special promotions, availability, convenience and service.

Expenditures on Electronics

Overall, PCQS respondents report spending an average of US$273.66 per year on electronics, with men spending about 4% more than women (Figure 7-5). A more consequential spending gap is seen between respondents in different tiers. On average, respondents in Tier 1 cities spend 27% more than those in Tier 2, and 43% more than those in Tier 3.

FIGURE 7-5 : AVERAGE ANNUAL EXPENDITURES ON ELECTRONICS
⬩ CHINESE CONSUMERS BY GENDER AND TIER

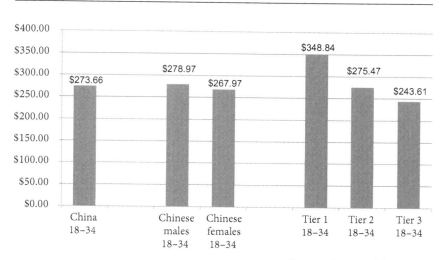

Source: ProsperChina.com

While Tier 1 may spend the most on electronics each year, consumers in Tier 2 and 3 cities spend a larger percentage of their annual income in the category, an indication of its importance to young Chinese consumers. In Chapter 2, we saw that respondents from Tier 1 had an average annual income of US$13,977, compared with US$9,891 and US$7,227 in Tiers 2 and 3 respectively. Thus, Tier 1 respondents are spending, on average, 2.5% of their income on electronics, while the percentage increases to 2.8% in Tier 2 and 3.4% in Tier 3.

Country-of-Origin Preference

The issue of country-of-origin preference is a complex question in China, with many conflicting perspectives. It is often assumed, especially by Westerners, that Chinese consumers will be drawn by the power of Western brands, with perceptions of greater reliability, better quality control, more advanced technology, or greater sophistication—all of which justify a price premium for increasingly affluent consumers.

The truth is not so easy nor so simple. The PCQS asked respondents for their country-of-origin preference in a number of different product categories. The question is purposefully non-brand specific, in order to get at respondents' basic inclinations about specific product categories without prompting for any specific brand. What we find is an interplay between a preference for things that are familiar and which play to Chinese culture and sense of identity on one hand, and on the other, concerns about safety and a desire for goods from other countries, with their perceived leadership, expertise, innovation or fashionability.

In recent years, Chinese consumers have painfully witnessed scandal after scandal dealing with tainted, counterfeit or defective products. Therefore, safety is an overwhelming concern. However, among legitimate producers, in recent years, the quality and reliability gap between China and other countries has narrowed in most categories. In many cases, the Chinese have copied, adapted and incrementally improved products to the point where they are functionally comparable or even superior to Western offerings. And, while incomes are indeed growing, most Chinese still have far less disposable income than consumers in developed markets. Therefore, they must make difficult choices regarding their spending priorities.

We have seen one example of this already. The Chinese are passionate admirers of the Apple brand, to the extent that stores are continuously jammed with young people trying out the latest gadgets. And, indeed, Apple sales have increased dramatically in the past few years. In fact, in 2011 the company achieved a milestone by surpassing Lenovo in total revenue within China for the first time.[3] Beyond quality, in many ways, the Apple products have a strong connection with Chinese consumers, as it is well known that most Apple products, from process engineering to finished product, are made in China.

However, Apple's sales are derived from multiple lines (computers, tablets, phones), whereas Lenovo's revenue is primarily from computers. On a device-by-device basis, Apple does not always have the largest share of ownership. For many, Apple remains an aspirational brand they would like to have, but, cannot afford. In many cases, they are buying not an international alternative, but a Chinese brand.

Another factor is the role of national pride and belief in the innate value of Chinese culture and civilization dating back more than 5000 years. Young Chinese consumers are immensely proud of the country's accomplishments, and often see Chinese brands as more familiar, more suited to their needs and more trustworthy. Additionally, there is still a degree of underlying fear and suspicion towards foreigners, especially in lower-tier cities, which can be fanned at times by government or competitive communication efforts. Cultural familiarity and nationalistic sentiment can be potent factors working in favor of Chinese brands. This can lead many consumers to categorically say they prefer Chinese brands over imported brands.

---

3. Robin Kwong and Paul Taylor, "Apple Overtakes Lenovo in China Sales," *Financial Times,* August 18, 2011, http://www.ft.com/intl/cms/s/2/af5dbc86-c977-11e0-9eb8-00144feabdc0.html#axzz287IeZvgd

A good example of how important culture is to the issue of country-of-origin can be seen in the music category. Among all Chinese respondents, there is a very strong preference for Chinese music well above that from any other region (Figure 7-6). This stands to reason, since Chinese music is culturally and linguistically familiar, while safety and reliability are not issues in the category. And, it is obvious that the predisposition for Chinese music increases as one moves from Tier 1 to Tier 2 and 3 cities. There is a lesson here for marketers beyond just the music category: They should not overestimate Chinese consumers' desire to embrace imported goods just because they come from the West. While there are some variations by category, there can be very strong bonds indeed between Chinese consumers and Chinese brands.

FIGURE 7-6: COUNTRY-OF-ORIGIN PREFERENCE—MUSIC CHINESE CONSUMERS BY TIER

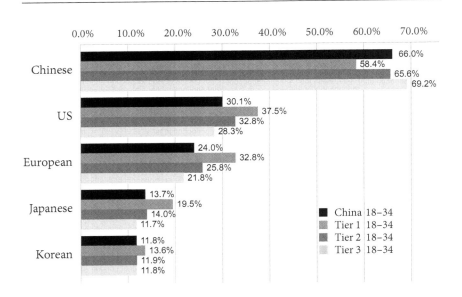

Source: ProsperChina.com

In contrast, the electronics category (which includes not just digital devices but also TV, audio equipment, cameras and so on) is one where imported products are more often preferred by Chinese consumers (see Figure 7-7).

FIGURE 7-7: COUNTRY-OF-ORIGIN PREFERENCE—ELECTRONICS CHINESE CONSUMERS BY TIER

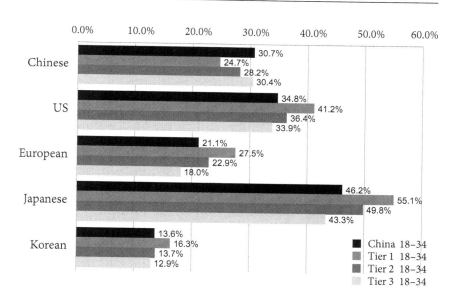

Source: ProsperChina.com

It is striking that that the most preferred country-of-origin for electronics is Japan, presumably a reflection of their ongoing strength in TVs, audio equipment and cameras. The second most popular were electronics coming from the United States. However, in both cases, note that the preference is strongest in Tier 1 cities. Again, we see that as one moves to Tier 2 and 3 cities, the preference for domestic brands grows sharply. This is a pattern we will see in a number of other categories to be discussed in coming chapters.

Media Influence in Purchasing Electronics

Of course, the country-of-origin designation is just one of many influences on purchasing decisions. Respondents in the Chinese and US studies were asked to indicate which media forms influence their purchase decision in the category. There are some striking similarities and differences between the two groups (as seen in Figure 7-8).

To a remarkable extent, the US respondents report being influenced by many more media forms than do their Chinese contemporaries. In the end, however, it is word of mouth that the Americans most often say influences their purchases in the category. The Americans report taking in and processing a wide range of media forms that influence their decision, whereas the Chinese generally say they are influenced by fewer sources.

The differences in the two countries could, at least in part, simply be a reflection of a Chinese cultural predisposition to not wanting to admit to being influenced by external media. However, we will see that this is not the case in other categories. It is important to look at the ranking that the Chinese assign to those media forms that they do say influence their decision. Paramount among them is broadcast TV, followed by in-store promotion. In classic marketing communication terms, this reflects the need to first build brand awareness through broad-based communication, followed by an incentive to facilitate an actual purchase. In China, where size and strength are important considerations to consumers, TV advertising is often seen as an indicator that a company or product has sufficient scale and stability to be worthy of consideration. However, in order to gain a customer's business, they have to offer something extra at the point of purchase. This is a pattern we will see repeated, with some variations, in other categories.

FIGURE 7-8: MEDIA INFLUENCE IN PURCHASING ELECTRONICS CHINESE AND AMERICAN CONSUMERS

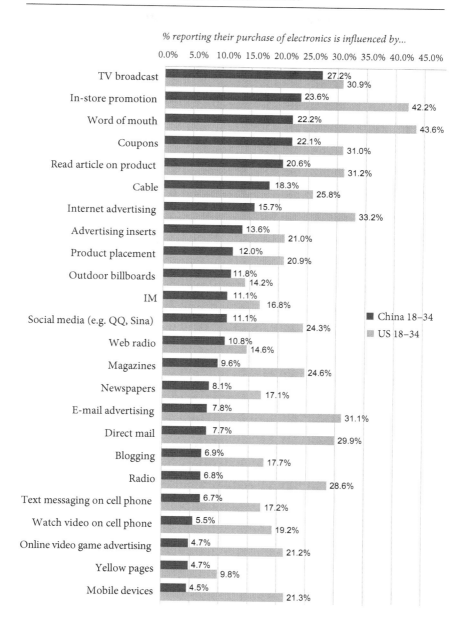

% reporting their purchase of electronics is influenced by...

Source: ProsperChina.com

Mobile Telecommunication: Handsets and Services

Perhaps no device defines the digital generation in China more than the cell phone. An astounding 97.2% of PCQS respondents state they currently own a cell phone, compared with 88.5% of the American study participants. In spite of this near universal ownership of cell phones, the Chinese are constantly on the lookout for new features, new technologies and upgrades. Thus, 44.1% say they intend to buy a new cellphone within the next 90 days. While, as would be expected, the figure is highest in Tier 1 cities (48.2%), even those in Tier 2 and 3 cities (43.4% and 41.8%) say they plan on acquiring a new cell phone in the near future.

The hottest segment in the Chinese phone market is, as elsewhere in the world, the smartphone. Gartner predicts sales in China will hit 137 million units in China in 2012, an increase of 52% over 2011, with Samsung capturing a 24.3% share of market compared with 7.5% for Apple. Samsung's strength comes, at least in part, from its lower price tag and arrangements with all three of China's major telecommunication carriers (China Mobile, China Telecom and China Unicom). Apple, on the other hand, has only partnered so far with the last two providers[4].

The growth in the smartphone category is echoed by IDC, which forecasts total smartphone unit sales in China will surpass those of the United States for the first time by the end of 2012. Within the category, IDC predicts the strongest growth will come from Android smartphones priced below US$200, the result of falling chip prices and increased competition. "Emerging domestic vendors will be another important engine of smartphone growth as giants Huawei, ZTE and Lenovo continue to ramp up with big carrier orders due to their willingness to produce customized handsets. International players such as

---

4. "iPhone Fails to Gain China Share as Samsung Lead Triples," Bloomberg.com, March 11, 2012, http://www.bloomberg.com/news/2012-03-11/iphone-fails-to-gain-china-share-as-samsung-lead-triples-tech.html

Samsung and Nokia are expected to drive volume at the low end with cheaper smartphones."[5]

More recently, in the spring of 2012 Baidu upped the ante by announcing the introduction of the Changhong H5018. This US$160 unit offers 3G connectivity, a 3-megapixel camera, a proprietary operating system, 100 gigabytes of free storage in Baidu's cloud and Mandarin voice recognition. (Apple's voice recognition system, Siri, was only available in English until late 2012, when the company introduced options for Spanish, French, German, Italian, Korean, Japanese, Mandarin and Cantonese)

FIGURE 7-9: Smartphones by operating system Chinese and American consumers

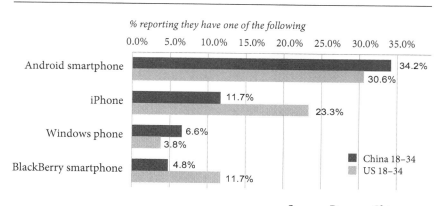

% reporting they have one of the following

- Android smartphone: 34.2% (China 18–34), 30.6% (US 18–34)
- iPhone: 11.7% (China 18–34), 23.3% (US 18–34)
- Windows phone: 6.6% (China 18–34), 3.8% (US 18–34)
- BlackBerry smartphone: 4.8% (China 18–34), 11.7% (US 18–34)

Source: ProsperChina.com

Smartphone Ownership in China and the US

The strength of Android-based phones is apparent in the PCQS and Media Behaviors & Influence Study (MBI), as seen in Figure 7-9. In both countries, Android phones have the largest share of reported

5. Terrence O'Brien, "China May Ship More Smartphones than the US This Year," Engadget.com, March 15, 2012, http://www.engadget. com/2012/03/16/china-may-surpass-us-in-smartphone-shipments/

smartphone ownership (34.2% in China and 30.6% in the US), compared with Apple's iPhone, Windows or Blackberry. There is a particularly wide gap in the share of ownership for iPhones between the two countries. Whereas 23.3% of US respondents report owning an iPhone, the share in China is about half this rate (11.7%)—a reflection of the iPhone's higher price and the fact that it is not supported by the dominant carrier, China Mobile.

Popular Smartphone and Tablet Apps

One of the drivers of interest in smartphones and tablets is the wide variety of applications (apps) that can be downloaded. Both Chinese and American respondents report downloading apps to their mobile device (smartphone or tablet). Fully 83.1% of the PCQS respondents reported downloading, considerably more than the Americans at 72.4%.

There are notable similarities in the types of apps that are popular with Chinese and American respondents. Apps related to entertainment, gaming and social networking top the list in both groups, as seen in Figure 7-10. There are some distinctive differences however. The PCQS respondents more frequently mention apps related to business, newsstand, education, utilities and retail. Respondents in the US were more likely than their Chinese counterparts to mention using apps for radio or sports.

One app of particular interest to marketers is the quick response (QR) code reader. QR codes were initially developed by a subsidiary of Toyota for tracking vehicles in the manufacturing process. Since the introduction of smartphones, they are increasingly used in marketing communication as a way to give interested customers access to special offers or more information about a product or service. They are also used to support customer loyalty programs, facilitate ticketing to sporting and entertainment events and even for transmitting money from one smartphone user to another. In early 2102, Alipay, China's biggest online payment platform, helped its customers celebrate Chinese New Year by creating virtual "red envelopes," a traditional gift to mark the holiday. Alipay enabled its users to create QR codes that could be scanned by the smartphone of another Alipay user, which then wired the cash through the ether.[6]

FIGURE 7-10: APPS USED ON SMARTPHONES OR TABLETS ⬦ CHINESE AND AMERICAN CONSUMERS

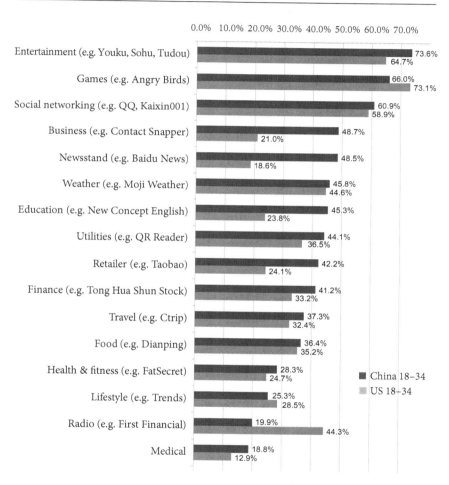

Source: ProsperChina.com

6. Steven Millward, "Alipay Enables 'Red Envelope' Gifting Via Social QR Codes for Chinese New Year," Techinasia.com, Jan 20, 2012, http://www.techinasia.com/alipay-red-envelopes-qr-codes/

The existence of QR code readers is shown in Figure 7-11. Overall, 42.4% of the PCQS respondents reported having a QR code reader on their phone, slightly lower than the 47.4% of Americans who have one. However, the presence of QR readers is higher for men (46.2%) and for those in Tier 1 cities (47.2%). As smartphones spread further across China, it would seem that QR codes will be an increasingly important tool for marketers to stay in touch and connected with customers. This will also offer up the challenge of dealing with "showrooming," an issue that US retailers have been addressing. This phenomenon is when consumers check out products in brick-and-mortar stores, compare prices using their smartphones (made easier by QR codes) and then buy the products online or at a more competitive retailer.

FIGURE 7-11: HAVE QR CODE READER APP
CHINESE AND AMERICAN CONSUMERS

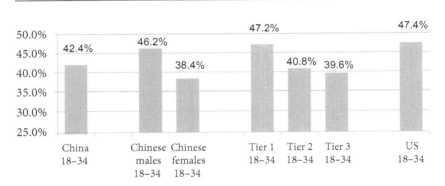

Source: ProsperChina.com

Desired Attributes in a Cell Phone

With 44.1% of PCQS respondents saying they plan to buy a cell phone of some type within the next 90 days, it is useful to consider the features and attributes most desired in a new phone (Figure 7-12). As can be seen, Chinese consumers have a long list of attributes that are important to them, including features that offer them convenience, ready access to information and entertainment options. And, of course, they want all of it at a competitive price.

FIGURE 7-12: FEATURES/ATTRIBUTES DESIRED IN A CELL PHONE — CHINESE CONSUMERS

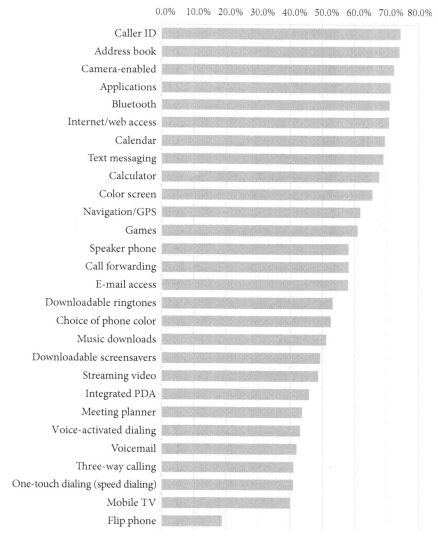

Source: ProsperChina.com

Mobile Telecommunication Service Providers

China is the world's biggest market for mobile telecommunications and in early 2012 became the first country to have over 1 billion cell phone subscribers. Of these, approximately 135 million subscribe to one of China's 3G networks, a number that is expected to increase dramatically as more and more users adopt smartphones.[7]

The job of servicing this enormous user base falls to three state-owned companies: China Mobile, China Unicom and China Telecom. As mentioned earlier, China Mobile is by far the dominant mobile carrier in the country, with 83.2% of PCQS respondents saying the company is their cell phone service provider (Figure 7-13).

FIGURE 7-13: CELL PHONE SERVICE PROVIDER
CHINESE CONSUMERS BY TIER

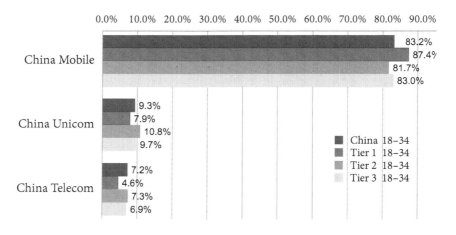

Source: ProsperChina.com

---

7. Goutama Bachtiar, "China World's Biggest Mobile Subscriber Population, But Still Has Plenty of Room to Grow," Techwireasia.com, Feb 29, 2012, http://www.techwireasia.com/2118/china-worlds-biggest -mobile-phone-population-but-still-has-plenty-of-room-to-grow/

Cell Phone Expenditures and Usage

On average, PCQS respondents report they spend US$20.96 per month on their cell phone services. As shown in Figure 7-14, this amount rises for men, and for those in Tier 1 cities. However, once again, those in Tiers 2 and 3 are spending a higher proportion of their income on telecommunications than those in Tier 1. As smartphones gain in popularity, it is likely that these monthly expenditures will increase as consumers utilize the extended functionality of Internet-enabled phones. With budgets already tight for many Chinese households, this could mean they will need to consume less of some goods or trade down in some categories, or otherwise shift their spending priorities.

FIGURE 7-14: Average monthly cell phone bill
Chinese consumers by gender and tier

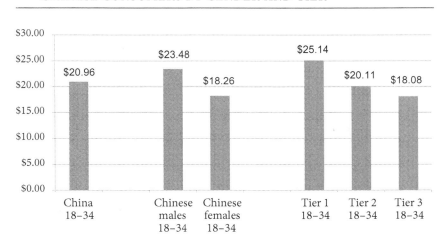

Source: ProsperChina.com

Cell phones in China are used for a mix of personal and business purposes. While 64.1% say their phone is primarily for personal use, slightly over one third say it is used mainly for business. This is particularly true among men, where 43.2% state the phone is used primarily for business, and in Tier 1 cities (39.8%). Nevertheless, the cost of using a phone is generally considered a personal responsibility. Most PCQS respondents (84.2%) say they pay their own cell phone bill, with only 8.1% saying it is paid for by their employer and 7.0% saying it is paid by someone else in their family.

Switching Carriers

A marketplace with only three competitors—one of which is overwhelmingly dominant—does not leave much room for consumer choice. However, 21.2% of the PCQS respondents indicated they were considering switching cell phone service providers in the next six months, a figure that varied little by gender or by tier. Of those who did indicate they were considering switching, the most commonly cited reasons had to do either with improved coverage, getting free minutes or achieving a better price-to-value relationship. Figure 7-15 shows the various reasons for a potential switch reported by men and women.

FIGURE 7-15: Reasons for switching cell phone providers
◆ Chinese consumers by gender

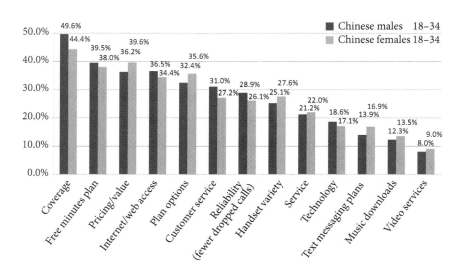

Source: ProsperChina.com

FIGURE 7-16: Media influence in purchasing telecommunications • Chinese and American consumers

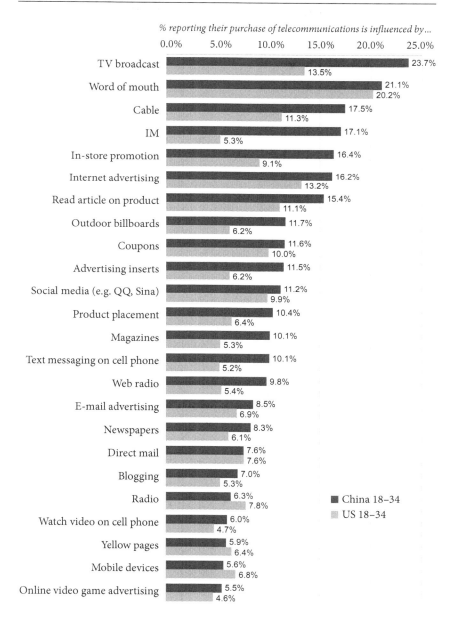

% reporting their purchase of telecommunications is influenced by...

	China 18–34	US 18–34
TV broadcast	23.7%	13.5%
Word of mouth	21.1%	20.2%
Cable	17.5%	11.3%
IM	17.1%	5.3%
In-store promotion	16.4%	9.1%
Internet advertising	16.2%	13.2%
Read article on product	15.4%	11.1%
Outdoor billboards	11.7%	6.2%
Coupons	11.6%	10.0%
Advertising inserts	11.5%	6.2%
Social media (e.g. QQ, Sina)	11.2%	9.9%
Product placement	10.4%	6.4%
Magazines	10.1%	5.3%
Text messaging on cell phone	10.1%	5.2%
Web radio	9.8%	5.4%
E-mail advertising	8.5%	6.9%
Newspapers	8.3%	6.1%
Direct mail	7.6%	7.6%
Blogging	7.0%	5.3%
Radio	6.3%	7.8%
Watch video on cell phone	6.0%	4.7%
Yellow pages	5.9%	6.4%
Mobile devices	5.6%	6.8%
Online video game advertising	5.5%	4.6%

Source: ProsperChina.com

Media Influence in Purchasing Telecommunications and Wireless Services

With so much at stake in the highly competitive and rapidly expanding telecommunication sector, most handset manufacturers and service providers invest heavily in all forms of marketing communication. So, which forms do consumers say have the greatest impact on their decision to purchase a given handset, or subscribe to a given carrier? The responses of Chinese respondents are quite different from those of their American counterparts, as depicted in Figure 7-16.

When we examined the media forms that influence purchase decisions in the electronics category earlier in this chapter (Figure 7-8), we noted that the Americans reported far more media forms influence their decision than did the Chinese. In the telecommunications category, the opposite is true. Here we see far greater gaps between the influence the Chinese assign to media such as TV, IM, in-store promotion, "read an article," outdoor and advertising inserts than that which the Americans report. While word of mouth is the most frequently reported influence for the American respondents, it ranked third among the Chinese participants. Clearly, this is a category in which telecommunications marketers must pull out all of the stops and use a rich mix of mass media, promotion, PR and online communication to gain attention and incent purchases.

Five Key Takeaways

1. Digital appliances—computers, tablets, smartphones—are the key tools enabling the switched-on, always-connected lifestyles of the digital generation in China and the US.

2. Chinese consumers in Tier 2 and 3 cities spend a disproportionate share of their income on digital devices and mobile services compared with those in Tier 1.

3. Chinese consumers have a strong, built-in preference for Chinese brands, but will consider imported brands where there are demonstrable advantages in areas such as safety, reliability, innovation, fashion or status.

4. Consumers weigh intricate issues of brand recognition, status associations, functionality, reliability, country of origin and price when considering which brand to purchase in the telecommunications area.

5. TV, in-store promotion, word of mouth and coupons are the media forms Chinese consumers most often say influence their purchases in the electronics and telecommunications category.

Moving On

To young consumers, the digital and mobile devices discussed in this chapter are essential necessities in a modern lifestyle. Life simply could not function smoothly without them.

We will now turn our attention to the other goods and services that compete for their discretionary funds. With incomes rising, young Chinese consumers now have greater ability to buy the products they see advertised all around them. What shapes their spending priorities, and how do they balance the desire to spend against the need to save for the future? This will be the focus of our next three chapters.

Chapter 8

Discretionary Spending and Conspicuous Consumption: Big-Ticket Purchases, Apparel and Automobiles

Much has been written in recent years about the rapid growth of the moneyed classes in China. In fact, China can now boast more than a million millionaires, and around a hundred billionaires. Much of the increase in wealth has been fuelled by the non-stop rush to urbanization and modernization—with fortunes made in real estate, construction, material handling, high tech and related industries. At the same time, the emergence of the middle class, now estimated to be approximately 50% of urban households, has increased dramatically.[1]

1. Tami Luhby, "China's Growing Middle Class," CNNMoney, April 25, 2012, http://money.cnn.com/2012/04/25/news/economy/china -middle-class/index.htm

Along with the growth in income there has been a steady stream of press reports on the growing demand for ultra-high-end products—from Ferraris and Maseratis, to magnums of vintage Bordeaux (red, of course) and diamond-encrusted, handmade Swiss watches.

Reports of such conspicuous consumption, however, are more indicative of the press's fascination with excess than they are representative of true consumer behavior among wealthy and middle-class Chinese. And while the sales of premium designer brands have, indeed, skyrocketed, the reality is that it is not only the very wealthy who buy them, nor is it the flashiest brands that are the most popular. To understand how Chinese spend their discretionary income (that is, funds above those needed to pay for daily necessities such as food, shelter, utilities and so on) we need to look more closely at Chinese consumers' income levels and the cultural drivers shaping their acquisition of major goods and services.

It is essential to remember that the majority of Chinese consumers still have very limited incomes by US standards. There are varying definitions of what constitutes the middle class in China, but China's National Bureau of Statistics officially categorizes the middle class as households with an annual income ranging from RMB 60,000 to 500,000 (US$7,250–62,500). In her book *The Chinese Dream: The Rise of the World's Largest Middle Class and What It Means To You*, Helen Wang says that income alone is deceiving, as the cost of living in China is very different. A more useful rule of thumb, she feels, is to define a household as middle class if at least a third of its income is available for discretionary spending.

Among the 18–34-year-old respondents to the ProsperChina Quarterly Study (PCQS), the average household income is US$9,348. While this would put most respondents squarely within the middle class, their income is less than one fifth of their US counterparts. On the upper end, only 5.3% of the PCQS respondents reported an income above US$31,000, which is, according to McKinsey, roughly equivalent to an American income of around US$100,000 in terms of spending power. While the percentage of PCQS respondents making more than US$31,000 increases to 11.3% in Tier 1 cities, clearly, this is still a relatively small proportion of the digital generation. The truth is most Chinese consumers must choose very carefully how to spend their money, and make crucial trade-offs between spending and saving.

Embracing "the Good Life"

The increase in the proportion of income available for discretionary purchases has given Chinese consumers the power to enjoy material goods on a broad scale. In that, they have much in common with the generations before them who moved into the middle class as a result of the Industrial Revolution (in Europe) or the post-WWI economy (the US and Japan). Like these earlier generations, they want the material accoutrements of the "good life," and often seek to display their newfound wealth and status through the goods they acquire. In particular, like Americans in the 1950s and 1960s, many Chinese have come to see owning a home and a car as the "twin pillars" of middle-class lifestyle.

However, while there are similarities between the emergent middle class of today's China and that of mid-century Americans, there are key differences in how the Chinese use their newfound purchasing power. The communal, Confucian culture in which they have grown up, and still live, deeply influences their marketplace behavior. The traditional teachings of Confucianism stress how the individual should live harmoniously with others, with great emphasis on qualities such as loyalty, righteousness, benevolence, altruism and frugality. Whereas Western society seeks individual growth and self-actualization as ends unto themselves, for the Chinese an individual strives for excellence in order to win the respect of others.

Another crucial motivational factor shaping Chinese shopping habits is *mianzi*, the multi-faceted concept of "face." There is no direct English equivalent for this concept, but face broadly means a person's perceived dignity, prestige, reputation and respect both within one's self and the surrounding society. It is extremely valued in Asian cultures and fundamentally shapes complex and highly nuanced social and business interactions. Face can be given, gained, lost or saved. That is, face is *given* when one displays respect toward another by granting them a compliment, showing deference or otherwise according them honor such as giving them an expensive gift. Face is *gained* by demonstrating achievement, status, skill or virtuous behavior consistent with Confucianism. Face is *lost* through anything that smacks of failure, such as the inability to accomplish or complete a task, having a lack of knowledge or skill, making an unwise decision or behaving in an inappropriate manner. Face is *saved* when an unpleasant or potentially embarrassing situation is avoided, thereby sidestepping a situation in which someone could lose face. It is this mix of very complicated social mores which often puzzles Western observers.

Characteristics of Chinese Discretionary Spending

Confucian values, and the need to gain and preserve face, have important implications for how Chinese consumers spend their discretionary income. They must constantly balance the need for self-projection and status seeking against the need to do so in a manner consistent with traditional Confucian sensibilities of modesty, humility and frugality. It is socially acceptable, even expected, to demonstrate one's position and status by dressing in style, carrying fine accessories or driving a new automobile. Such goods signal accomplishment, modernity and being "on the way up." On the other hand, ostentation, flashiness and excessive displays of wealth are generally considered to be vulgar and contrary to Confucian values. While lavish, over-the-top consumption certainly does occur in China, just as it has among generations of *nouveau riche* in the West, it is more the exception than the rule among affluent Chinese.

There are five broad characteristics of how middle-class Chinese utilize their discretionary income:

- *Spending to impress*—consuming famous brands in a manner that is visible to others is an important means for gaining face, that is, signaling one's sophistication, status and achievement. Hence, the young office worker who spends a month's salary (or more) on an imported designer handbag to show off her stylish worldliness is one well-known example. The more famous the brand, the better. However, such displays of fashion are rarely of the avant-garde, "break-the-mold" type, and tend towards brands that are already established, recognized and accepted. Even among the young, who are generally more adventurous and self-expressive, fashion tends toward "hip" brands that are already popular and embraced by one's peers or vetted by the fashion media.

- *Spending to facilitate advancement*—Chinese consumers favor goods or services that will equip them for advancement, and they are willing to make sacrifices today to gain advantages tomorrow. Thus, designer business suits, prestigious writing instruments, logoed briefcases and joining a health club are seen as the essentials for preparing oneself to move up the ladder. Even for children, brands that are seen as having an educational component will have greater favor with mothers than those that simply promise a "fun" experience.

- *Spending to avoid risk*—Chinese consumers are highly value con-scious, and will go to considerable lengths to comparison shop on price and features. However, they see almost daily examples of food contamination, shoddy construction, inferior cleanliness standards in public places and a numerous other risks to their health, safety and well-being. They will trade up for goods that can offer functional, protective benefits or that can reinforce a sense of security, harmony or risk avoidance. Additionally, since they are often unsure of their knowledge in some categories, they turn to well-known brands because they represent authority and leadership, and therefore lessen the risk of making a bad, potentially face-losing, purchase decision.

- *Scrimping on private consumption*—while Chinese consumers will spend, sometimes lavishly, for goods on public display, the opposite is generally true for goods that are consumed in private. There is little room in their tight budgets for "private luxuries" that cannot be seen by others. Thus, they are likely to look for the least costly option when it comes to items such as underwear, household goods, personal care products, snacks and other items for personal, private consumption.

- *Save, save, save*—the penchant to save is a deeply engrained, traditional value in China. The Confucian virtue of frugality in daily living means that Chinese consumers have a compelling desire to strive for the lowest price, the advantageous deal, the best value. And the current economic realities mean that they must set aside significant portions of their income for healthcare and retirement. Thus, Chinese consumers are constantly balancing the desire to save money against the desire to acquire goods that help fulfill their dreams of the good life.

We will examine Chinese discretionary spending in three specific categories: big-ticket items for the home and personal use, apparel and automobiles.

Purchase Plans for Big-Ticket Items

The differences in how young Chinese and American consumers choose to spend discretionary funds for major purchases are illustrated in Figure 8-1. When asked what major purchases (big-ticket items) they anticipate making in the following 6 months, the Chinese strongly favor those items that are visibly used in public, and are less inclined to invest in goods for private comfort or entertainment.

FIGURE 8-1: Major purchases planned in next 6 months Chinese and American consumers

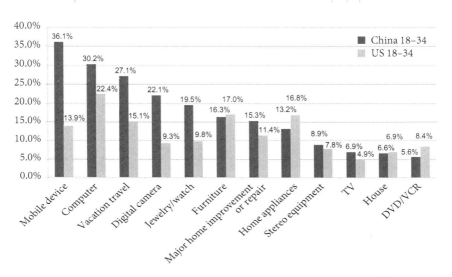

Source: ProsperChina.com

Top of the shopping lists for China's digital generation are items we have discussed in earlier chapters: mobile devices (cell phones, smartphones, and so on), computers and vacation travel. The percentage of respondents indicating they anticipate purchasing one of these within 6 months far exceeds the proportion of Americans with similar intentions. This is, of course, consistent with our earlier discussions of Chinese interests in digital devices and the high priority they put on vacation travel.

Cameras

The next most frequently mentioned category is digital cameras. Almost a quarter of the Chinese respondents indicate they plan on purchasing a camera within 6 months, compared with fewer than 10% of American respondents. Given that most digital devices now come with a built-in camera, it is interesting to note the great desire Chinese consumers still have for buying cameras, presumably to have greater flexibility and advanced photo-taking options. Photography is extremely popular in China, especially taking group photos of friends and colleagues. Any important business meeting, seminar or other group activity would not be complete without a round of photo taking, and having the coolest, newest camera in the group is a good way to gain face by displaying one's seriousness and knowledge about photography.

Jewelry and Watches

Twice as many PCQS respondents (19.5%) report that they intend to buy jewelry or a watch in the coming six months than do their American contemporaries (9.8%). Investment in jewelry has become particularly appealing to Chinese consumers in recent years, as it provides two highly sought-after benefits.

First, it meets their desire for visible consumption, with chains, rings and watches worn by both men and women. Particularly popular are designs that incorporate traditional Chinese symbolism for good luck, prosperity and long life, as well as jewelry made with jade, pearls and colored gemstones.

Second, an investment in fine jewelry is seen as a hedge to preserve value in the face of rising prices for gold and platinum. China is now the largest market in the world for platinum jewelry (a whopping 68.3% of the global market), the second-largest market for gold jewelry (after India) and the second-largest market for diamonds (after the US).[2] According to China's National Bureau of Statistics, jewelry sales increased by 42% in 2011, more than any other consumer goods category tracked by the organization.[3] Part of this impressive growth

---

2. Research and Markets, *China Jewelry Industry Report 2011-2012*, (March 2012), http://www.researchandmarkets.com/reports/2103297/china_jewelry_industry_report_2011_2012 (summary only)

3. "Jewelry Sales Rise by More than 40 Percent in China," National Jeweler, March 6, 2012, http://www.nationaljeweler.com/nj/majors/a/~27995-Jewelry-sales-rise-more-than

is attributable to the fact that major jewelry domestic chains such as Chow Tai Fook are spreading beyond Shanghai and Beijing to reach the expanding middle class in lower-tier regions.

House and Home

One of the most important purchases consumers can make is a home. It is perhaps the ultimate symbol of middle-class life, both in China and in the US, and in recent years each country has experienced roller-coaster rides of property price inflation and deflation.

A significant aspect of China's economic reform has been the government initiative to encourage home ownership among urban citizens. Between 1998 and 2003, rental housing stock belonging to the public sector and state-owned companies, was sold to those with permanent residency permits at heavily subsidized prices. During the same period, there was a shift in the home construction industry from the state to for-profit enterprises, opening the door to the growing ranks of entrepreneurs such as real estate developers, property agents and construction magnates.[4]

Given the massive influx of residents to urban areas, rising demand for more and better housing and increasing household income, China underwent a period of extraordinary expansion in the residential real estate market, as well as dramatic inflation of housing prices. For example, according to the Urban Land Institute, in Shanghai "commodity" level housing is currently estimated to be about US$221 per square foot for private existing housing and US$354 per square foot for new construction. Thus, an "average" new, two-bedroom, one-bath unit with 900 square feet would be priced above US$310,000—and it most likely would not include appliances. Top-end luxury units in cities such as Shanghai and Beijing run substantially higher: US$1,475 per square foot, or more.

---

4. Ken Rhee and Chen Jie, "Anticipating the Correction of China's Housing Bubble," Urban Land Institute, April 20, 2012, http://urbanland.uli.org/Articles/2012/April/ul/RheeChinaBubble

Steep as these prices may be, they actually represent a decrease in average prices over the past few years. Beginning in 2010 the government stepped in with a number of policies to cool off the real estate market, with measures to increase required down payments, discourage speculation, and in particular, to stem overdevelopment in the luxury sector. The result has been a decline in the number of residential real estate transactions, as well as a decrease in the average price per square foot.

While housing prices have been dropping, the downshift in the real estate market has not had the same devastating impact on the economy as was experienced in the United States. The primary reason is that Chinese consumers are far less dependent on mortgages to make real estate purchases. In spite of high prices, the natural frugality and financial conservatism of the Chinese means that most real estate purchases are either fully paid, or have down payments substantially higher than the required minimums (currently 30% for first-time buyers and 50% for second homes).

Among the PCQS respondents, 8.9% indicate they anticipate purchasing a house or apartment within the next 6 months, compared with 7.8% of the Americans. The percentage is highest among young Chinese consumers in Tier 1 cities (10.8%) and Tier 3 (9.4%), and dips to 7.9% in Tier 2 cities.

While purchasing a home is of great importance to Chinese people, and there is great "face" associated with home ownership, thus, as a rule, Chinese consumers are less concerned with what goes inside the home than the simple fact of owning one. According to the DIY retailer B&Q, which operates 39 stores in China, the average middle-class family spends only US$15,000 to fully fit out a completely bare 1,000-square foot apartment.[5]

---

5. Tom Doctoroff, "What the Chinese Want," *Wall Street Journal*, May 18, 2012, http://online.wsj.com/article/SB10001424052702303360 504577408493723814210.html

The consequences of this can be seen in Figure 8-1: Chinese consumers place relatively low priority on furniture, appliances and at-home entertainment (TV, stereos, DVD players). Since most apartments and houses come without installed appliances, new homebuyers have little choice but to purchase the basic necessities such as a refrigerator, cooktop, air conditioning units and maybe even a washing machine. However, Chinese household funds are limited, and therefore, trade-offs must be made. Since Chinese do little entertaining in their homes, there is little face to be gained from owning high-end appliances, stylish furniture or entertainment equipment. Thus, they shop very frugally for necessities for the home and then put their other funds to use in ways they deem more valuable—either in the bank or in goods and services that are more conspicuous. Chief among those more conspicuous alternatives are categories such as apparel or automobiles.

Shopping for Apparel

According to the Boston Consulting Group (BCG), the fashion industry in China has tripled in market size over the past decade, and is estimated to triple again to more than RMB 1.3 trillion (US$206 billion) by 2020.[6] However, to date. most Western clothing brands have concentrated primarily in Tier 1 cities, and with only a few exceptions, have not yet established a broad footprint. For instance, according to BCG, Zara had roughly 70 stores in China in 2011, Benetton about 25 and Gap 5 stores. By contrast Nike and Adidas, both early entrants into the market, could claim approximately 6,000 stores each. Chinese sportswear brands Li-Ning and Anta each have roughly 7,000 stores, while local clothing brands Meters/bonwe and Semir have more than 3,000 stores each.

---

6. Vincent Lui, Yunling Zhou, Hubert Hsu, Waldemar Jap, Carol Liao and Yan Lou, *Dressing Up: Capturing the Dynamic Growth of China's Fashion Market*, Boston Consulting Group, (July 2011)

BCG predicts robust growth in the fashion sector, but sees it becoming increasingly competitive as companies fight to establish a share of mind among consumers, as well as for prime retail real estate. BCG estimates that it currently requires a presence in 462 cities to reach 80% of the market for mid- to high-priced priced fashion, but predicts that by 2020 companies will have to expand into the top 568 cities to sustain the same market coverage.

Euromonitor International echoes the bullish outlook for clothing and footwear, reporting that annual per capita expenditure on clothing in China has surged 71% since 2006. Euromonitor also notes the huge increase in apparel sold online, with a 168% increase in 2011 alone. While online purchases are still a relatively small portion of the apparel market—approximately 2% of sales—it is expected to keep expanding and challenging traditional retailers. This move is driven largely by China's digital generation. According to the report, "That apparel has registered the strongest growth of all online retailing should come as no surprise, given that those fastest to switch to online shopping are younger people ... Diversity of choice, lower prices, and convenience in terms of payments means that younger customers have been quick to spend their extra money buying clothes online and will continue to do so in continuing numbers." [7]

Label Consciousness Among Chinese Consumers

In shopping for apparel, Chinese consumers show their interest in well-known brands as well as their fundamental practicality and conservative nature.

All segments of the Chinese respondents are more likely to state that familiar labels are important to them when shopping for apparel than the American respondents, as shown in Figure 8-2. Overall,

7. Warc, "Apparel Sales Surge Online in China," July 5, 2012, http://www.warc.com/LatestNews/News/Apparel_sales_surge_online_in_China.news?ID=30066

66.1% of the Chinese respondents said familiar labels are important, compared with 56% of the Americans. The figure is highest among Chinese consumers in Tier 1 cities (74.2%), but even those in Tier 3 (63.4%) attach greater importance to buying known brands than do those in the US.

FIGURE 8-2: RESPONDENTS WHO SAY, "WHEN BUYING APPAREL, FAMILIAR LABELS ARE IMPORTANT TO ME" CHINESE AND AMERICAN CONSUMERS

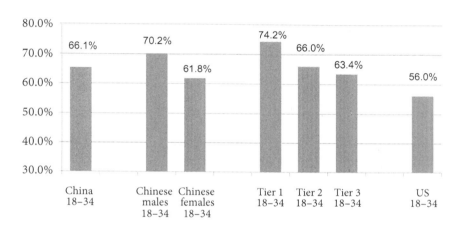

Source: ProsperChina.com

The issue of purchasing familiar labels does not necessarily equate to designer or high-fashion brands. It does, however, refer to brands that are known, understood and recognized by the consumer and presumably his or her reference set. In this context, familiarity may also mean that the consumer can buy with a degree of confidence in the quality and appropriateness of the merchandise. Men appear to be even more label conscious than women, with 70.2% of males stating they desire familiar labels compared with 61.8% of the female respondents. For men, buying a well-known or familiar brand simplifies the decision-making process. They are generally less interested in fashion than women, thus, buying a familiar brand reduces the risk of losing face by purchasing apparel that is not recognized or respected by others. Chinese women respondents, on the other hand, attach slightly less importance to purchasing a familiar brand, perhaps because they shop more frequently, have a wider range of references to draw upon and may be more willing to try an unknown brand that looks good on them.

Feelings about Fashion

For Chinese consumers, the interest in labels is balanced against practical considerations. While it is important to buy known labels, for the majority of PCQS respondents, fashion takes a back seat to value and comfort (Figure 8-3). The respondents from the US, on the other hand, are more likely to place importance on the newest trends and styles, yet, they are also more likely to say they prefer a traditional, conservative look.

FIGURE 8-3: FEELINGS ABOUT FASHION
CHINESE CONSUMERS BY GENDER AND TIER

	China 18–34	Chinese males 18–34	Chinese females 18–34	Tier 1 18–34	Tier 2 18–34	Tier 3 18–34	US 18–34
Newest trends and style are important to me	25.7%	24.4%	27.1%	32.8%	24.3%	23.3%	34.0%
I prefer a traditional, conservative look	13.3%	17.9%	8.4%	11.0%	13.6%	12.7%	29.8%
Fashion less important than value and comfort to me	61.0%	57.7%	64.5%	56.2%	62.1%	64.0%	36.2%

Source: ProsperChina.com

Among the PCQS respondents, value and comfort trump style among each of the groups measured: men, women and respondents in Tier 1, 2 and 3 cities. Somewhat unexpectedly, the preference for value and comfort is higher for women (64.5%) than for men (57.7%). While young Chinese women definitely eschew a traditional, conservative look, their desire to appear modern and fashionable must be done in comfort and, at a price they perceive as fair.

Shopping Strategies

Another fascinating aspect of Chinese consumers' purchasing of apparel concerns their reported shopping strategies. Figure 8-4 shows the differences between men and women and their attitudes about purchasing apparel on sale.

FIGURE 8-4: SHOPPING STRATEGY FOR CLOTHING CHINESE CONSUMERS BY GENDER

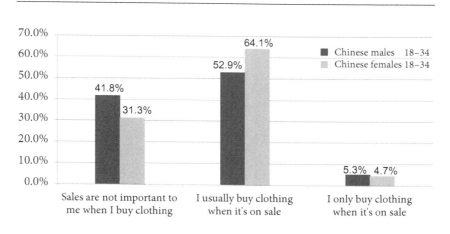

Source: ProsperChina.com

Although they are highly price and value conscious, Chinese consumers have a flexible shopping strategy when it comes to apparel. Over half of the men and women respondents agree that they usually buy their apparel on sale, although the figure is quite a bit higher for women (64.1%) than for males (52.9%). Of course, as we learned in Chapter 3, young Chinese women embrace shopping as a leisure-time activity, so they are often on the hunt for bargains. Men, on the other hand, are more likely to report that sales are not important when buying clothing: 41.8% compared with about a third of the women respondents. Young Chinese men do not particularly care for shopping in general, do not devote a great deal of time to shopping for apparel and most likely do it primarily when they have a specific need. For them, the task is to find a familiar label, make sure the garment is comfortable and at a reasonable price, and then get on with it, regardless of whether there is a promotion or sale going on.

Country-of-Origin Issues

With Chinese consumers putting high importance on familiar labels, value and comfort, it is no surprise that they overwhelmingly express a preference for Chinese brands when it comes to apparel. As we have seen in other categories, the preference for Chinese brands increases the further one gets from Tier 1 cities (Figure 8-5). While individuals in all tiers express affinity for Chinese brands, there are important differences on how various imported brands are perceived. US and European brands have their strongest following among respondents in Tier 1 cities, but Japanese and Korean brands are nearly as popular in these areas. Interest in US, European and Japanese brands falls off sharply in Tier 2 and 3 cities, however, while Korean brands maintain higher levels of popularity in lower-tier regions.

Since apparel is a category highly influenced by gender differences, it is useful to examine how attitudes on the country-of-origin issue vary between men and women. Figure 8-6 shows young men and women respondents have a strong preference for Chinese apparel brands, although this preference is more pronounced among men (75.1%) than among women (61.0%). However, it is not the imported brands from the US and Europe that young Chinese women turn to next, it is apparel from Korea. While the US and European brands may be desirable for designer goods and related accessories, for day-to-day apparel Asian brands, particularly those from Korea, are deemed preferable.

FIGURE 8-5: COUNTRY-OF-ORIGIN PREFERENCE—APPAREL CHINESE CONSUMERS BY TIER

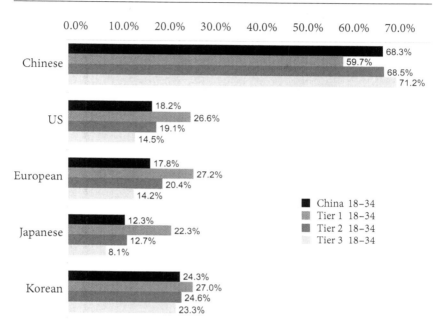

Source: ProsperChina.com

FIGURE 8-6: COUNTRY-OF-ORIGIN PREFERENCE—APPAREL CHINESE CONSUMERS BY GENDER

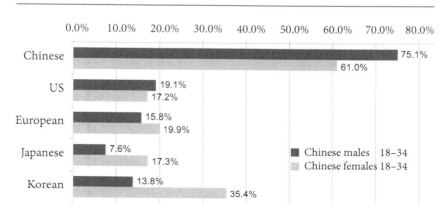

Source: ProsperChina.com

There is logic behind this preference: Korean clothing would be more suitable than standard Western clothes for Asian body types, the color palette is developed with Asian skin tones in mind and designs are rooted in an understanding of Asian women's preference for clothing that is fashionable, yet modest.

Retailers Shopped Most Often for Apparel

In Chapter 6, we learned that apparel and shoes are the two categories that Chinese consumers age 18–34 are most likely to research online before making a purchase. And, we also learned that Taobao.com is the website they most frequently use for buying products of any sort. It should be no surprise, then, to learn that Taobao is the retailer both men and women turn to most often for purchasing apparel (Figure 8-7).

The apparel retailing industry in China is highly regionalized, with few multi-brand chains having anything close to a national footprint. The bricks-and-mortar retailers that shoppers turn to most often for apparel shopping are the Malaysian-owned department store chain Parkson, local retailers such as Yi Chun, Hualian and Sen Ma (particularly in Tier 3) and general merchandise operations such as Walmart and Carrefour. Single brand retailing has been a common business model in China, as can be seen by the mentions of stores such as Li-Ning, Jeanswest, Nike, Giordano and Baleno. (Two of the other notable categories in Figure 8-7 are Xidan, a shopping and business district in Beijing near Tiananmen Square, and Pacific Shopping Plaza, a chain of large department stores in many cities.)

As we have noted in previous chapters, the high incidence of "No Preference" is both a cautionary point, as well as a potential opportunity. It would indicate that Chinese consumers do not have strong emotional attachments to established retailers, making them vulnerable to brand switching. Given the dynamic nature of the fashion business, a clothing retailer that can distinguish itself through factors such as location, online or offline accessibility, selection, merchandising, customer education, value and customer service could likely capture the loyalty of China's digital generation.

FIGURE 8-7: RETAILERS SHOPPED MOST OFTEN FOR APPAREL CHINESE CONSUMERS BY GENDER

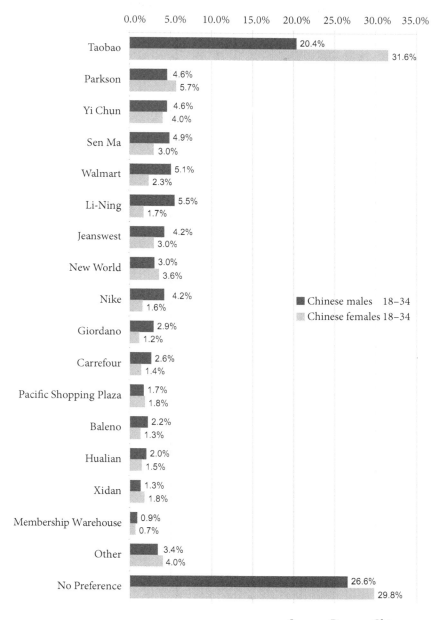

Source: ProsperChina.com

Monthly Expenditures on Apparel

The average PCQS respondent typically spends US$56.23 per month on apparel, a figure that increases to US$68.40 in Tier 1 cities (Figure 8-8).

FIGURE 8-8: AVERAGE MONTHLY EXPENDITURE ON APPAREL
⬩ CHINESE CONSUMERS BY GENDER AND TIER

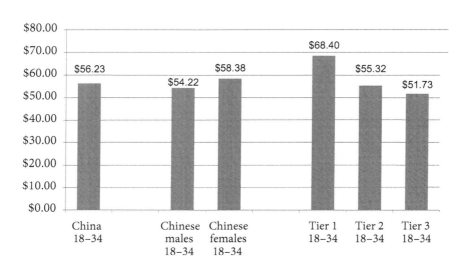

Source: ProsperChina.com

Young Chinese women spend, on average, more than their male counterparts, but the difference is not great (US$58.38 compared with US$54.22). BCG reports that up until now, Chinese men and woman have spent close to equal on apparel, and that the category has been dominated by sportswear for both genders. However, it predicts that as women's incomes increase, as there are more opportunities for dressing-up, and as their tastes and interests in fashion become more sophisticated, the sector will skew more prominently toward women's fashion.

Additionally, BCG sees the sector shifting more toward Tier 2 and 3 cities as incomes rise, retailers expand their footprint and consumers learn more about fashion. Given the enormous scale required, this is a category where the race for share of market among Tier 2 and 3 consumers will likely require a multi-faceted strategy involving online, e-commerce capabilities along with building out bricks-and-mortar locations to establish the necessary presence in the minds of young Chinese consumers.

Media Influence in Purchasing Apparel

In-store promotion is the media form that both young Chinese and American respondents most often say influences their decision to purchase apparel. The Chinese also frequently mention TV, advertising inserts, product placement, word of mouth and coupons as influential media forms in this category. The American respondents, on the other hand, strongly lean toward coupons, word of mouth, e-mail advertising and magazines as key influences (Figure 8-9).

Women respondents to the PCQS survey particularly cite in-store promotion, word of mouth and coupons at a rate well above that of the young Chinese males. As we saw earlier in this section, women apparel buyers place great importance on value and usually buy their apparel when it is on sale. They also are highly conscious of the opinion of others regarding fashion choices, so it is not surprising that they respond well to in-store incentives or coupons to trigger and complete a purchase.

FIGURE 8-9: Media influence in purchasing apparel
Chinese and American consumers

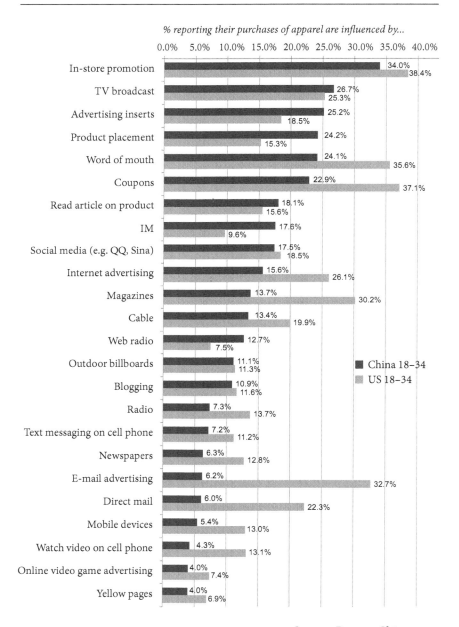

% reporting their purchases of apparel are influenced by...

Source: ProsperChina.com

Shopping for Automobiles

Automobile ownership is the second great pillar associated with middle-class life in China, along with home ownership. In spite of high costs for gasoline, air pollution and unbearably heavy congestion in cities such as Beijing, Shanghai and Guangzhou, owning a car remains a powerful status symbol to Chinese consumers.

For much of the past few years, automotive sales have been nothing short of dizzying: surging 54% in 2009 alone, and another 33% in 2010.[8] This rapid expansion was due, at least in part, to government incentives to encourage car sales, especially for smaller, energy-efficient cars. By the beginning of 2011, however, those incentives were eliminated, and a cap was put on new car sales in Beijing, both of which contributed to a marked slowdown in car sales. These actions and the recent economic slowdown have brought the growth rate in passenger vehicles sales down to a modest 2.5% in 2011. However, most economists and industry experts remain very bullish for the long-term outlook. In fact, according to *Advertising Age*, the next "sweet zone" for new car sales will be Tier 2 and 3 cities. Many of these cities do not even have car dealerships yet, so there is a rush by automotive companies to build out their sales and service infrastructure to meet the rapidly growing demand in these areas. It has been predicted that by 2020 the total volume of new passenger vehicles will hit 30 million per year—twice the forecast size of the US market.

Current Automobile Ownership

While this is a market of astounding dimensions, it must be kept in mind that compared with the Chinese, a much higher proportion of Americans already own an automobile. China may now be the world's

---

8. Hans Greimel, "China's Car-Industry Slowdown Blip Before Next Boom," *Advertising Age,* April 30, 2012, http://adage.com/article/global-news/china-s-car-industry-slowdown-blip-boom/234469/

largest passenger car market, yet the total number of cars sold *per capita* is 13 times smaller than in the United States—and most car buyers are first-time purchasers.[9]

Among American respondents age 18–34, 91% report that they own a car, compared with only 31.9% of Chinese of the same age. Figure 8-10 details car ownership in China by gender and tier.

FIGURE 8-10: CAR OWNERSHIP
CHINESE CONSUMERS BY GENDER AND TIER

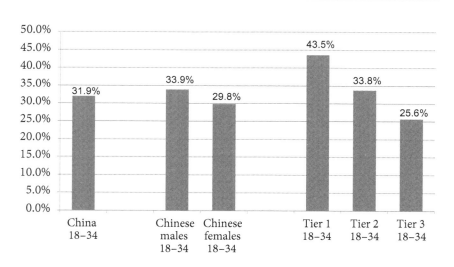

Source: ProsperChina.com

Among the young Chinese respondents who reported owning some type of vehicle, 80.9% state they own a standard car, while 6.2% currently own an SUV and 5.4% have a minivan. All-electric and hybrid cars have had only a minimal impact on the market so far, with

9. Yuval Atsmon, Max Magni, Molly Liu and Lihua Li, *The New Frontiers of Growth*, McKinsey Insights China, (October 2011), http://www.mckinseychina.com/wp-content/uploads/2011/11/ McKinsey-2011-Chinese-Consumer-Report-English.pdf

only about 1.1% of the PCQS respondent saying they own either of these more environmentally friendly models.

There are literally dozens of domestic and international automotive brands available in China. The top 15 brands that PCQS respondents say they drive the most often are shown in Figure 8-11. Clearly, there are distinctive preferences by gender and by tier. Of the top 15 marques, 4 are domestic brands (BYD, Chery, FAW and Changan), 3 are from Japan or Korea (Hyundai, Toyota, Nissan) and 8 are American or European.

FIGURE 8-11: TOP 15 BRANDS DRIVEN MOST OFTEN
CHINESE CONSUMERS BY GENDER AND TIER

Rank		China 18–34	Chinese males 18–34	Chinese females 18–34	Tier 1 18–34	Tier 2 18–34	Tier 3 18–34
1	Audi	9.6%	10.3%	8.9%	13.7%	7.9%	7.1%
2	Volkswagen	8.5%	9.0%	8.0%	8.5%	10.7%	8.6%
3	Honda	8.5%	6.7%	10.4%	9.3%	5.5%	9.8%
4	Buick	7.1%	7.8%	6.4%	9.3%	7.6%	6.6%
5	Chevrolet	6.8%	6.2%	7.6%	7.3%	7.4%	6.1%
6	Hyundai	4.8%	4.1%	5.6%	4.3%	4.6%	6.7%
7	BYD	4.8%	5.3%	4.2%	4.8%	3.7%	4.6%
8	Chery	4.7%	4.7%	4.7%	3.3%	4.7%	3.9%
9	Toyota	4.6%	4.0%	5.1%	4.5%	6.1%	4.4%
10	BMW	4.2%	5.3%	3.1%	4.7%	3.1%	3.6%
11	FAW	3.5%	3.3%	3.7%	2.6%	5.3%	2.7%
12	Nissan	2.7%	2.3%	3.1%	2.9%	3.1%	1.6%
13	Changan	2.6%	2.9%	2.2%	1.5%	1.9%	3.3%
14	Citroen	2.4%	2.2%	2.6%	2.6%	2.3%	3.0%
15	Ford	2.2%	2.0%	2.4%	2.7%	2.6%	1.6%

Source: ProsperChina.com

By contrast, among the American respondents age 18–34, the most frequently driven brands are Ford (10.4%), Honda (9.8%), Toyota (9.7%), Chevrolet (9.1%) and Dodge (4.5%).

There are a number of automotive brands that have become extremely popular in China, but, which have a far smaller following in the US. For example, the number-one car among Chinese age 18–34, Audi, is the most often driven car of only 1% of the American respondents. Similar gaps exist for Volkswagen (driven by 1.5% of US respondents), and Buick (1.3% of US respondents).

For many young Chinese, car ownership will for now remain a dream deferred. Most who do not currently own a car report that they are not planning on purchasing one within the coming six months, as shown in Figure 8-12. A similar percentage of PCQS and MBI respondents said they do not plan on buying a car within the time-frame (65.1% of the Chinese and 65.6% of the Americans), however, as noted above, most of the Americans already own a car whereas the majority of the Chinese do not.

FIGURE 8-12: PLANS TO BUY OR LEASE A CAR/TRUCK WITHIN 6 MONTHS ⋅ CHINESE AND AMERICAN CONSUMERS

	China 18–34	Chinese males 18–34	Chinese females 18–34	Tier 1 18–34	Tier 2 18–34	Tier 3 18–34	US 18–34
Yes	20.8%	22.4%	19.0%	27.4%	20.8%	18.1%	17.3%
No, I bought/leased within the past 6 months	14.1%	15.6%	12.5%	14.2%	13.8%	13.5%	17.1%
No	65.1%	62.1%	68.4%	58.4%	65.3%	68.5%	65.6%

Source: ProsperChina.com

Recent Automobile Purchases

Among the 14.1% of PCQS respondents who completed a purchase or lease within the previous six months, the majority (73.5%) acquired new (as opposed to used) vehicles. The percentage of new car buyers goes up to 77.5% for women and 84.9% in Tier 1.

The 15 brands most frequently purchased or leased in the past six months are shown in Figure 8-13.

FIGURE 8-13: WHAT BRAND DID YOU BUY?
CHINESE CONSUMERS BY GENDER AND TIER

Rank		China 18–34	Chinese males 18–34	Chinese females 18–34	Tier 1 18–34	Tier 2 18–34	Tier 3 18–34
1	Chevrolet	8.1%	8.1%	8.1%	7.4%	9.3%	10.5%
2	Honda	8.1%	6.2%	10.1%	9.3%	7.3%	8.2%
3	Audi	7.1%	6.9%	7.3%	8.2%	8.9%	4.9%
4	Buick	6.9%	6.8%	7.1%	10.0%	6.3%	5.5%
5	Volkswagen	6.9%	6.3%	7.5%	8.2%	11.1%	3.6%
6	BYD	6.1%	6.7%	5.6%	6.7%	5.8%	7.1%
7	Chery	4.6%	4.5%	4.7%	3.1%	3.6%	6.4%
8	Hyundai	4.4%	4.0%	4.9%	3.6%	3.3%	7.0%
9	FAW	3.9%	3.9%	3.8%	3.0%	3.6%	4.9%
10	Toyota	3.5%	3.5%	3.5%	3.2%	4.8%	1.8%
11	Changan	3.4%	4.0%	2.8%	1.6%	3.8%	3.2%
12	BMW	3.3%	3.6%	3.0%	2.6%	2.1%	2.3%
13	Citroen	3.1%	2.8%	3.5%	4.1%	3.0%	1.5%
14	Dongfeng	2.8%	2.2%	3.5%	1.9%	3.4%	3.2%
15	Ford	2.7%	2.3%	3.1%	3.6%	3.1%	3.5%

Source: ProsperChina.com

This shows some switching in brand preferences from the Top 15 listed in Figure 8-11. Chevrolet and Honda topped the list for recent purchases, while higher-end brands such as Audi, Buick, Toyota and BMW are further down the rankings. Additionally, Nissan, which ranked 12 in the brands most often driven, does not appear in the top 15 brands recently purchased (it ranked 18). In contrast, Dongfeng, a domestic Chinese marque that didn't feature in the top 15 most driven, was at 14 among most popular newly acquired vehicles.

Overall, the Chinese respondents who recently purchased an automobile paid on average US$18,570 (see Figure 8-14). The average for Tier 1 is higher (US$21,489), which is not surprising given the greater number of higher-end brands reportedly purchased in those cities.

FIGURE 8-14: PRICE PAID FOR VEHICLE PURCHASED IN PAST 6 MONTHS ◈ CHINESE CONSUMERS BY GENDER AND TIER

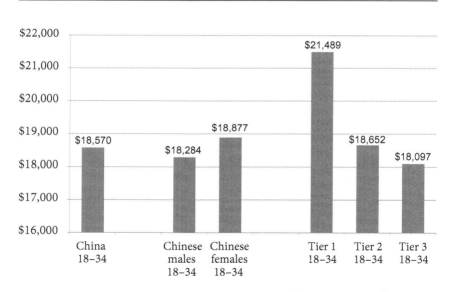

Source: ProsperChina.com

While most Chinese consumers have yet to acquire their first car, many of the PCQS respondents who purchased a car in the past six months were replacing an existing car. When asked about the motivations for their recent car purchase, many indicated they were looking for some type of upgrade in mileage or features (Figure 8-15). Among women the most common response was that they needed another car for their family—an indication that China's affluent drivers may be moving into the age of the two-car family.

FIGURE 8-15: MOTIVATIONS FOR PURCHASING A NEW VEHICLE CHINESE CONSUMERS BY GENDER

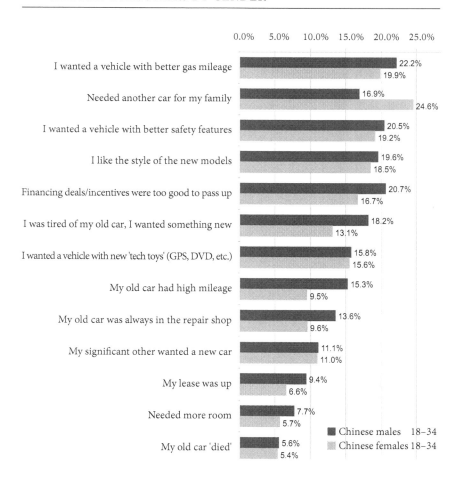

Source: ProsperChina.com

Plans for Future Automobile Purchase

So far we have discussed respondents who acquired a car within the past six months. What about the 20.8% of the respondents who say they are planning on buying a car within the coming six months? To what extent, if any, are they different from those who recently completed a car purchase?

For one thing, there is a noticeable shift in the types of vehicle they intend to purchase. Figure 8-16 compares the types of vehicles acquired within the past six months against those respondents say they are planning on purchasing or leasing in the next six months. While standard cars are still the norm, there is markedly greater interest in larger vehicles, such as SUVs, minivans and crossovers (a combination of an SUV and a minivan). Also, PCQS respondents who are planning to purchase a car are more likely to mention hybrid (and even all-electric) models than those who completed a purchase in the past six months.

FIGURE 8-16: TYPES OF VEHICLE ACQUIRED OR UNDER CONSIDERATION • CHINESE CONSUMERS

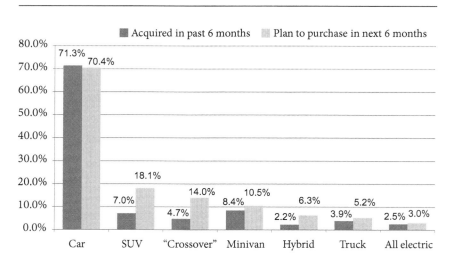

Source: ProsperChina.com

PCQS respondents who indicate they plan to purchase a car in the next six months indicate they are planning on spending somewhat more than those who recently completed acquisitions. Overall, those who are planning a purchase within six months have an average target price of US$20,652, 11.5% higher than the average price paid US$18,570 in the last six-month period. The average target price for anticipated purchases is shown in Figure 8-17. The most notable increases are among men (target prices are 16.4% higher than among men who reported a recently completed purchase), and in Tier 1 (12.9% higher). Part of the increase is due to the greater reported interest in purchasing an SUV, minivan or crossover car by both of these groups.

FIGURE 8-17: TARGET PRICE RANGE FOR A NEW VEHICLE CHINESE CONSUMERS BY GENDER AND TIER

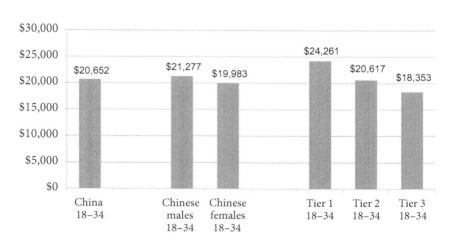

Source: ProsperChina.com

Another factor driving target purchase price is the brand consumers report they are considering purchasing. When respondents are asked which vehicles are under consideration high-end brands are generally more often mentioned than their ranking on the list of recently completed purchases would seem to suggest. Figure 8-18 ranks the 15 most frequently mentioned nameplates consumers are considering. Audi is at 2, but it is ranked 1 by men and by respondents in Tier 1 cities. Similarly, BMW and Buick rank highly in consumers' consideration sets.

FIGURE 8-18: BRANDS UNDER CONSIDERATION FOR PURCHASE WITHIN 6 MONTHS ◈ CHINESE CONSUMERS BY GENDER AND TIER

Rank		China 18–34	Chinese males 18–34	Chinese females 18–34	Tier 1 18–34	Tier 2 18–34	Tier 3 18–34
1	Honda	10.2%	10.8%	9.5%	11.9%	9.3%	7.5%
2	Audi	9.8%	10.3%	9.3%	11.6%	9.5%	8.4%
3	Volkswagen	8.4%	7.8%	9.0%	8.5%	8.2%	9.1%
4	Chevrolet	8.2%	7.8%	8.5%	6.9%	9.3%	9.4%
5	Buick	6.8%	6.7%	7.0%	8.0%	6.4%	4.9%
6	BMW	5.3%	5.7%	4.9%	7.3%	4.8%	3.1%
7	Hyundai	4.9%	4.3%	5.5%	3.4%	5.6%	7.5%
8	BYD	4.3%	4.2%	4.3%	4.1%	3.5%	6.1%
9	FAW	3.8%	3.4%	4.2%	3.3%	3.6%	4.4%
10	Ford	2.9%	2.4%	3.5%	2.7%	3.7%	2.7%
11	Chery	2.7%	2.7%	2.8%	1.7%	1.5%	4.0%
12	Dongfeng	2.7%	2.7%	2.7%	2.0%	1.7%	2.0%
13	Toyota	2.4%	2.7%	2.1%	3.5%	1.5%	0.7%
14	Changan	2.3%	3.0%	1.5%	1.2%	3.0%	2.2%
15	Citroen	2.0%	2.0%	1.9%	1.6%	2.9%	3.3%

Source: ProsperChina.com

New versus Used Car Purchases

One important way in which the Chinese automotive market differs from the US is the relatively low proportion of used car purchases. Whereas Americans are roughly split fifty-fifty on new versus used, Chinese consumers lean strongly to buying a new car (75.4%), with 15.4% saying they will buy a used car, and 9.2% are "not sure."

The Chinese automotive market is so new that a true infrastructure for reselling used cars has yet to develop. The market for pre-owned cars consists largely of open-air markets in major cities where buyers and sellers meet face-to-face to negotiate a mutually acceptable price. So far, the market has little organization and limited representation from the automotive manufacturers.

According to the *Wall Street Journal*, that is about to undergo dramatic change.[10] Western manufacturers understand that a healthy market for used cars serves their long-term purposes. For one, it establishes a car's residual value, which helps justify the price and support new car sales and build brand loyalty. It facilitates new car sales by enabling trade-ins. It is a way to attract a first-time buyer, who hopefully will trade up to a new car on their next purchase. Finally, it is a way to increase dealerships' revenues through expanding the number of customers to whom they can offer ongoing maintenance services.

As a result, automakers such as Nissan, Mercedes-Benz and Toyota are actively assisting dealers in setting up used car operations, and in training them to properly assess the value of used cars.

Over the past several years, the percentage of PCQS respondents willing to consider a used car has been clearly on the rise, and there is little doubt that this is a trend that will continue to grow.

---

10. Norihiko Shirouzu, "China's Next Milepost: Used Cars," *Wall Street Journal*, Nov 21, 2011, http://online.wsj.com/article/SB1000142405 29702035373045770319531455053334.html

Media Influence in Shopping for Automobiles

The automotive category is perhaps one of the most brand image-driven consumer product categories—price, functional attributes, self-projection needs and risk avoidance issues come together to influence the decision-making process. It is a category in which most consumers will actively research the brands under consideration, solicit input from friends and associates and seek information from manufacturers and the media.

The media forms which Chinese and US consumers report are the most influential when it comes to purchasing a car are shown in Figure 8-19. Once again, we see significant differences in how these Chinese and Americans of the same age say the different media forms influence their decision-making.

Young Chinese consumers consider broadcast TV and articles in the press to be the most influential media forms when it comes to the automotive category. Interestingly, the next highest rated media form is outdoor billboards. This would speak to the immense awareness-building capabilities of outdoor, especially in a market where many of the brands have been newly introduced.

Young American consumers, on the other hand, having more overall marketplace experience, rely more heavily on personal, word-of-mouth recommendation, and then often turn to the newspaper to find the dealers with the best offers of the weekend. While newspaper readership is high among Chinese, automotive marketers have not had to rely as heavily on rebates, discounts and other incentives in order to move cars. Thus, promotional media appears to have less influence in China in this category than in the US.

FIGURE 8-19: MEDIA INFLUENCE IN PURCHASING AUTOMOBILE CHINESE AND AMERICAN CONSUMERS

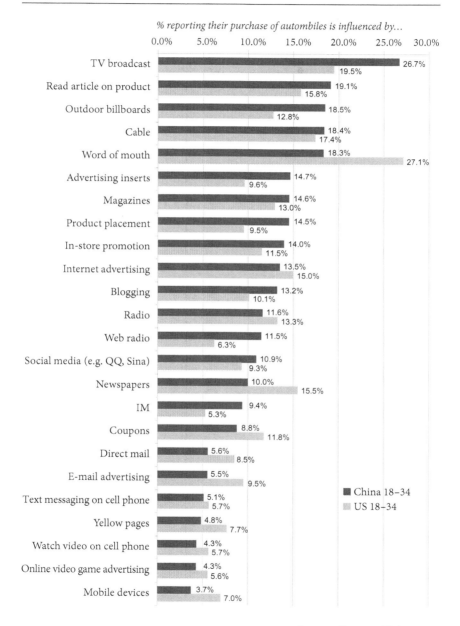

% reporting their purchase of autombiles is influenced by...

Media	China 18–34	US 18–34
TV broadcast	26.7%	19.5%
Read article on product	19.1%	15.8%
Outdoor billboards	18.5%	12.8%
Cable	18.4%	17.4%
Word of mouth	18.3%	27.1%
Advertising inserts	14.7%	9.6%
Magazines	14.6%	13.0%
Product placement	14.5%	9.5%
In-store promotion	14.0%	11.5%
Internet advertising	13.5%	15.0%
Blogging	13.2%	10.1%
Radio	11.6%	13.3%
Web radio	11.5%	6.3%
Social media (e.g. QQ, Sina)	10.9%	9.3%
Newspapers	10.0%	15.5%
IM	9.4%	5.3%
Coupons	8.8%	11.8%
Direct mail	5.6%	8.5%
E-mail advertising	5.5%	9.5%
Text messaging on cell phone	5.1%	5.7%
Yellow pages	4.8%	7.7%
Watch video on cell phone	4.3%	5.7%
Online video game advertising	4.3%	5.6%
Mobile devices	3.7%	7.0%

Source: ProsperChina.com

Five Key Takeaways

1. Rising income has given Chinese consumers greater ability to purchase the goods and services they desire, but their spending is deeply influenced by present economic realities as well as traditional Chinese values. Their discretionary purchases are shaped by five overarching characteristics: spending to impress, spending to facilitate advancement, spending to avoid risk, scrimping on private consumption, and a pervasive desire to save money.

2. Chinese consumers generally attach greater importance to goods or services that are on public display than do their American counterparts. Privately used goods and individual indulgences are a low priority for Chinese consumers unless they can be seen as either helping them to prepare for a challenge, to be seen as competent, skilled or successful, to achieve greater respect or to avoid a risk.

3. While much has been written in the press about the huge growth in luxury goods in China, most affluent Chinese remain highly conscious of value and look to established, familiar names for reassurance and status, rather than breakthrough, revolutionary or cutting-edge brands.

4. The recent downturn in the global economy, as well as in China, has brought down the once-torrid growth rates in categories such as housing and automobile purchases. However, most economists see high long-term potential, especially as the emergent middle class in Tiers 2 and 3 seek the goods and services previously only available in major metropolitan areas. Developers, retailers and automotive dealers are racing to expand their footprints to meet the demands of increasingly sophisticated and discerning consumers in these markets.

5. While consumers in Tiers 2 and 3 are enjoying greater disposable income, and becoming more knowledgeable about the goods they intend to buy, they are nevertheless conservative in their tastes and have a strong preference for Chinese brands. This is an issue that goes beyond low price, as Chinese consumers often will see Chinese brands as more suited to their lifestyle, more emotionally satisfying, more comfortable and in tune with their personal values.

Moving On

With the exception of a few mega-wealthy at the very top, most Chinese of the digital generation have incomes considerably lower than their US counterparts. Although the cost of living is lower in China, in many product categories, Chinese consumers are faced with steeply rising prices especially for housing, energy, food and healthcare, and have few government-provided safety nets in the event of a disaster. It was a theme of the chapter that, in spite of rising discretionary incomes, young Chinese consumers must choose carefully between consuming and saving. In the next chapter, we will examine how this influences their purchases of the necessities of day-to-life—medicines, groceries and various other types of packaged goods.

Chapter 9

Shopping for Daily Needs: Health, Beauty, Groceries

One of the greatest challenges for Western marketers is the mental conversion that must be made to understand Chinese consumers, that is, how and why they purchase and consume the wide variety of products and services used in their daily lives. In an abundant marketplace, which is what most developed markets have been for the past sixty or so years, consumers are offered a wide and continuously expanding cornucopia of consumer products such as foodstuffs, cosmetics, small appliances and health and beauty aids, all easily available and generally at reasonable or competitive prices. While this type of expansive marketplace is increasingly prevalent in China, it is still a relatively recent development.

It was not until the mid to late 1980s that a true consumer marketplace began to develop in China. And, for the most part, it initially occurred primarily in the Tier 1, coastal cities. While Beijing, Shanghai, Guangzhou and others quickly developed into retail and consumer product meccas, up until the mid-1990s, the bulk of Chinese citizens generally struggled with a subsistence level economy. Thus, a majority of today's Chinese consumers have been effectively parachuted into the twenty-first-century marketplace with little background, training or experience in how to operate in a marketplace of abundance—one of plentiful products, continuously expanding retail alternatives, imports from around the world supported with a broad array of brands and increasingly promoted with Western-style marketing communication.

At the same time, they have seen their personal discretionary incomes grow, making purchase of those products and services increasingly possible. Generally, today, a large portion of the Chinese population has access to, as well as the economic capability to purchase and enjoy, many of the things consumers in more advanced economies have long taken for granted.

So, a key element in understanding the Chinese consumer market is simply to recognize and appreciate the astounding speed with which it has developed, and, the speed with which it continues to change. While Chinese consumers may not have been all that ready for the momentous changes they have experienced, those changes have occurred and Chinese consumers have simply learned to cope.

The other critical factor in understanding the Chinese consumer marketplace is the massive population migration that has occurred in China over the past thirty years. Millions have experienced the shock of moving from a rural location with no running water, electricity or sewage to a very cosmopolitan city such as Shanghai or Guangzhou, where luxury goods abound and wealth is on display everywhere.

These two major changes, compounded by the almost unbelievable development of the new digital and mobile communication marketplace, where information and content is available 24/7 to most urban dwellers, makes it quite difficult for most traditional marketers entering the Chinese marketplace to understand the cultural and economic factors which seemingly drive these new consumers. Even those organizations and brands which have had substantial experience in emerging market economies often find it difficult to understand China and Chinese consumers and how, why and in what ways they must change their traditional marketing and communication views. These challenges are beginning to take their toll on non-native marketers who came to China with the idea of millions and millions of potential customers in their plans, but, are now finding it difficult to cope with the challenges. Many well-known and otherwise successful global brands are starting to withdraw or severely cut back their expansion plans in China.

To succeed today in the Chinese consumer goods arena means taking off the lens of developed marketplace experiences and trying to understand the Chinese consumers as they exist and are evolving today. That is a challenging assignment for Western managers who, because of the sheer size and scope of the market, are often confounded by what to do.

What follows is an overview of what Chinese consumers do within the framework of their continuously evolving economic system. That which will lay the foundation for a discussion of their purchase and consumption of consumer package goods and other items needed for day-to-day life.

Pragmatically Practical

If two words could summarize Chinese consumers today, we would choose practical and pragmatic. Given their sometimes tumultuous 5000-year history, the Chinese have mastered practicality and pragmatism as basic survival skills and social virtues. Yet, while these two factors have long been the mainstay of Chinese culture, today, they are playing out in new and different ways.

When consumers come from what was essentially a subsistence economic system, such as China was prior to economic reform, individuals and groups must be eminently practical. Each person had to wring all the value from everything available. That is the practicality that shows through even today in the products Chinese consumers buy and how they use and adapt them to fit their needs.

Having had very limited economic resources in the recent past, means Chinese often spend what seems like an inordinate amount of time determining the absolute best value for themselves and their situation. That is often driven by trying to find the lowest possible cost. But cost is not just the retail price. It commonly includes acquisition expense judged against the value they believe will be delivered over the long term. That, in turn, is often influenced by the acceptance of the product, service or brand among their reference group. As discussed in the last chapter, the Chinese view of "face" or acceptance by their peers, family and associates is critically important in all purchase decisions.

Chinese consumers search prodigiously for value. They compare and haggle over price. Impulse purchasing is still generally a foreign or easily resisted concept. They buy from friends, associates, vendors and others whom they trust, and who meet both their needs and their price points. Since many of the new products and concepts introduced into the Chinese market have failed to deliver the value they promised, this is a marketplace of relatively low consumer trust for new or unknown brands—and consequently relatively low consumer brand loyalty. Either the products offered did not perform or they have been quickly supplanted by alternatives. That is part of the reason why well-known luxury goods, with their established market acceptance and value, are one of the few areas where brand loyalty seems to be important. Not only is there "badge" value in carrying a Louis Vuitton handbag, there is also the trust the brand brings to the purchaser. So, while the Chinese value brands, they view them more as symbols of status, achievement, safety and reliability in a marketplace of uncertainty. However, though the brand may add value today, it does not mean another brand cannot create greater value for Chinese consumers tomorrow.

That is where pragmatism comes in. With a wealth of possibilities being presented to them through a blizzard of marketplace communications, yet with relatively limited incomes and increasing inflation, the Chinese are continuously looking for the best solution for themselves.

Part of this marketplace pragmatism doubtless comes from the long history of Chinese experience with feast and famine. Being historically an agricultural society, the Chinese have a built-in concern for the future. Abundant crops for a few years, followed by droughts and failures, have been the history of those whose living came from the soil. That, clearly, has influenced the Chinese views of the world and their future views over the centuries. There is an underlying concern about economic security. Therefore, it is not as much a lack of economic capability to buy consumer products, as it is a lack of perceived need that marketers, and now the government, are continually trying to unlock. With the governmental focus on moving from a manufacturing- and export-based economy to one in which consumer consumption plays an important role, the ordinary Chinese are caught in the middle. The government is saying "spend and consume" while their culture and experience is saying "save and retain." This is not a matter that will be resolved quickly.

Comparable Consumption

One issue that often confuses external-to-China marketers is the importance of the family, the clan, the community and national pride to the Chinese population. Much of what drives every Chinese is their deep connection to their culture and heritage. China, like so many Asian countries, is a communal society. Rather than the individualistic societies of the West, where personal freedom is paramount, in China, it is the family or group or clan that matters most. In a communal society, individual wants and needs come second to the needs of the community and the desire to maintain harmony within the group. Consequently, much Chinese purchase behavior is driven not by the individual's desire to have a unique look or style, but to gain acceptance and respect within the group. True, there is considerable self-expression among younger Chinese buyers, but that self-expression is guided by group beliefs, norms and practices which are always in play. Here again is the ongoing balancing act that young Chinese must perform. While individual achievement is admired and deeply sought, even the most successful individual must observe the strictures and norms of the communal society. There is an ancient Chinese saying that sums up this situation quite well: The lead nail that sticks up always gets pounded down. That simply means that ostentation, standing out, being outside the norm is not accepted. Chinese must conform, and that is a major challenge today for the restless youth. There are, of course exceptions. A limited number of individuals, families and companies are accepted and revered for their accomplishments, but those are the exception, rather than the rule.

The result of this "comparable consumption" is that individuals buy what is acceptable to the group, not just what they themselves desire. Products, including personal products, are purchased to signify being part of the group, and to gain acceptance and admiration. We will see this recurring theme as we investigate three primary areas of Chinese consumer goods: health products, beauty products and groceries.

Trading Up, Trading Down

Nowhere do the traits of practicality, pragmatism and comparable consumption become more evident than in what Chinese consumers do by trading up or trading down in various product categories. Because of the economic realities of an expanding, yet less than stable marketplace, the Chinese consumer must continuously adjust, adapt and rationalize what they buy, where they buy it and how they use it. This is a big factor in all product categories.

For example, a study by McKinsey in 2010 found that among the 15,000 Chinese consumers surveyed 75% of the respondents said that in the past year, they had "traded up," that is, moved up to a more expensive or better quality product in at least one category. Two-thirds of those same people said they had offset this increased spending by purchasing less expensive goods in other, less important categories. To quote the report:

These emerging trade-off behavior patterns underline our as-
sertion that Chinese consumers have today become some of
the most pragmatic in the world, willing to make very explicit
choices about spending their growing income. This is a key insight for marketers seeking to capture growth. In particular, we
found significant trade-off activity in seven different areas. Our
survey showed, for example, that more than 70% of trade-up
demand for dining and 50% for alcohol is driven by white-collar
males who are willing to sacrifice spending on personal care and
packaged food products in order to improve their standing with
clients or colleagues. In addition, we found that some 80% of
trading up to high quality clothing, shoes and accessories was
due to wardrobe upgrades. Surprisingly, this trend applies not so
much to "fashionistas" as it does to lower-middle income consumers looking either to impress in job interviews or otherwise
advertise their graduation from the "working" to the "consumer"
class. In each case, the increased spending was balanced by trade
down decisions in three or four other product categories.[1]

Thus we see the yin and yang of Chinese consumption, the continual
weighing and balancing. Trading up and down is a fact of life in the Chinese
economy and has an impact on the concept of brand loyalty. While Chinese
consumers may like your product and your brand, the marketer is often
caught in the vise of disciplined consumer saving and the importance of
the product in the consumer's overall lifestyle. Traditional Western-trained
brand managers are generally not accustomed to this new type of impact
on brand preference, use and purchase. They will have to learn, and learn
quickly, if they are to be relevant in the Chinese marketplace.

---

1.   Yuval Atsmon, Vinay Dixit, Max Magni and Ian St-Maurice, *2010 An-
     nual Chinese Consumer Study*, McKinsey Insights China, (August 2010),
     http://csi.mckinsey.com/~/media/Extranets/Consumer%20Shopper
     %20Insights/Reports/2010_annual_Chinese_consumer _study.ashx

Lifestyle Changes

One of the best ways to track changing attitudes and behaviors of Chinese consumers is through the sections in the ProsperChina Quarterly Study (PCQS) that report on changes respondents say they have made in the past six months. Following those changes on an ongoing basis can provide not just clues, but, often specific direction, on how the Chinese consumer is changing.

Figure 9-1 illustrates the changes reported by male and female respondents. The "practicality" of the Chinese consumer comes through loud and clear in the PCQS. Well over 50% of males and females say they have become more "practical and realistic" in their purchases over the past six months. Women are perhaps slightly more pragmatic (60.4% report this trait) than men (53.4%) in these areas. There is not much difference between consumers in Tier 1, 2 or 3 cities—this practicality and realism seems to permeate the entire respondent population.

This is further reflected in the responses to the question about "needs versus wants" and how spending resources are allocated. Over one-third of all respondents report they are focusing more on their absolute needs rather than marketer-initiated or inspired wants. This fits with the trading up and trading down phenomenon described earlier. It is further supported by the fact that a third of respondents endorse the statement "I have become more budget conscious" in the past six months. Again, this holds true for both men and women and there are only slight variations between Tiers 1, 2 and 3.

In terms of specific activities being undertaken to support these changes, two seem to be most relevant. Reflecting the ongoing concern for health and wellness (likely the result of recent high-profile food contamination issues in the country), 43.6% of the respondents report they are more conscious about food safety. In many instances, press reports suggest this is, at least in part, what is behind the surge in sales for McDonald's, KFC and Pizza Hut in China. Chinese consumers believe that while the food at these foreign-owned chains may not be as culturally relevant to them, as tasty or even as healthy, they are likely much safer to consume simply because of the quality controls the parent organizations have developed and maintained over time. Safety and savings are also reflected in the growth of the "home-cooked meals" response in the PCQS study where nearly a quarter of all respondents say they are doing this more than in the past.

FIGURE 9-1: LIFESTYLE CHANGES MADE IN PAST 6 MONTHS CHINESE CONSUMERS BY GENDER

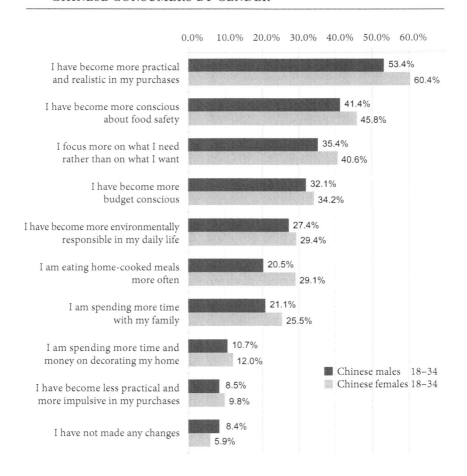

Source: ProsperChina.com

On the other side of the coin, however, only about 11% of respondents report they are spending "more time and money on decorating [their] home." Given the large number of household formations occurring in China, this is bad news for those firms which rely on marriages, new home purchases, upgrading of housing and the like to drive their business. It is clear a substantial number of Chinese consumers are focusing on purchases that have external observable value rather than those things that are more personal and private, such as home-related products for "nesting." This simply supports the points made earlier that Chinese consumers give priority to items which have public, that is, peer group, value rather than private consumption value.

This view of China's digital generation consumer is put in perspective when we compare (see Figure 9-2) Chinese consumers in the 18–34 age cohort with a similar group in the US Media Behaviors & Influence Study (MBI).

That safety issues dominate many Chinese purchasing decisions becomes quite evident in this comparison. For example, food safety, a high-ranking concern for the Chinese, is not nearly as prevalent in the US, where only 14.9% of all respondents express concern. Additionally, Chinese consumers are beset by polluted air and water and other evidence of environmental degradation wherever they turn. Thus, 28.4% are responding to the issue by trying to be more environmentally responsible in their daily lives. By contrast, only a small proportion of the American respondents (10.7%) make the same statement.

There are only three areas where US respondents outdistance their Chinese cohorts in terms of lifestyle changes. Those are focusing "more on needs than wants," becoming "more budget conscious" and having more home-cooked meals. All three are likely directly related to the economic concerns of US consumers.

These views of lifestyle changes in China lead directly to the next related area: health, well-being and medicine in China.

FIGURE 9-2: LIFESTYLE CHANGES MADE IN PAST 6 MONTHS CHINESE AND AMERICAN CONSUMERS

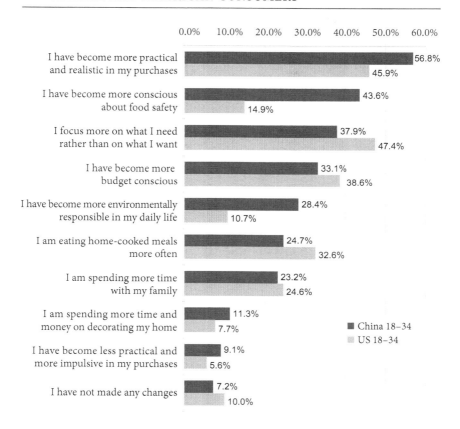

Source: ProsperChina.com

Health, Well-Being and Medicine

Concern for health and well-being has a long history in China. But, as in other areas, Chinese health formularies have developed unique ways of providing solutions. In contrast to the West, Chinese medicine is heavily dependent on methodologies and approaches developed over the centuries. Thus, it relies more on personal evaluation and herbal remedies than on diagnosis and chemical intervention. All that is driven by the basic

Chinese belief that ill health comes as a result of "disharmony patterns" that occur in the body. Those come as a result of external and internal interactions and are unique for each and every individual. Thus, by "inspection of the person," the Chinese medical approach tries to bring these disharmonies into alignment through the use of herbal medicine, acupuncture, massage, exercise and dietary therapy.

A survey conducted in 2010 by the Horizon Research Group found almost 90% of Chinese consumers report using traditional Chinese medicine (TCM). Of these, nearly 50% said they chose it over Western medicine because "it costs less and has fewer side effects."[2] Even where Western medicine is being introduced, it is often done in a way that incorporates traditional remedies, so that the overall approach is seen to combine and integrate the best of both.

As a result of the dominance of TCM practices, the market for chemically based, Western patent medicines and prescription pharmaceuticals is developing, but, slowly, compared with the high growth rates in other areas of consumer products. Part of the reason is the difference in the types of medical complaints that Chinese and American respondents report having.

Because of the complexity of the Chinese healthcare systems, the number of questions posed in the PCQS reports is necessarily limited. The data that have been gathered, however, are quite revealing. For the most part, PCQS data focus on broad health categories and questions that can be quite helpful to marketers in developing general strategies. The greatest value, of course, is that these data come directly from Chinese respondents and are not filtered by consultants or health advocates. Three broad categories make up the bulk of the PCQS data: reported health conditions, steps taken to manage personal health, and the influence of media in purchasing medicines and treating illnesses.

---

2. "Traditional Chinese Medicine Hopes for Global Approval," *China Daily*, Oct 10, 2010, http://www.chinadaily.com.cn/business/2010-10/25/content_11453741.htm

Reported Health Conditions

Figure 9-3 compares the health conditions and maladies that the PCQS and MBI respondents report having. The differences in complaints and illnesses are quite striking.

FIGURE 9-3: REPORTED HEALTH CONDITIONS CHINESE AND AMERICAN CONSUMERS

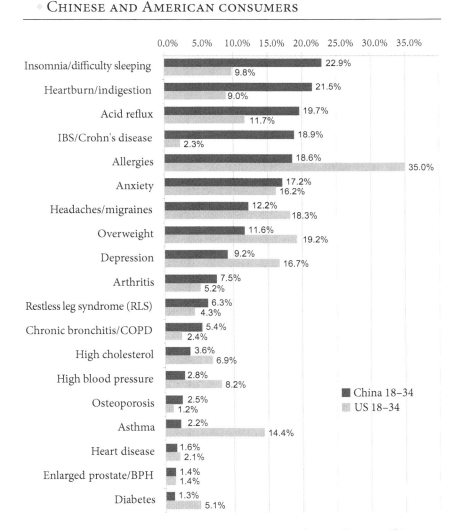

Source: ProsperChina.com

Keep in mind that all the conditions listed are self-reported, thus, they may simply be the opinion of the respondent or they may be conditions diagnosed by a healthcare provider. In either case, they are disorders or ailments the respondent believes are impacting his or her health.

What is most striking about the reported health conditions shown above is the difference between the maladies suffered by Chinese and American respondents. Chinese respondents report a much higher incidence of conditions, generally believed in the West to be connected to external and internal stress such as insomnia, heartburn, acid reflux, IBS (irritable bowel syndrome), Crohn's disease (an inflammatory disorder of the digestive tract) and anxiety. It may well be that the dramatic changes in lifestyle, the pressure to succeed and the movement from small towns and villages to major urban areas are leading to conditions symptomatic of stress.

That said, however, it is notable that the incidence of depression, also commonly associated with high levels of stress, is far lower among Chinese respondents (9.2%) than the Americans (16.7%). Mental and emotional health are, unfortunately, still considered taboo subjects in China, and are more often considered to be the result of personal moral failure than a treatable medical condition. Hence, Chinese respondents' probable reluctance to report suffering from depression, even though there is a relatively high incidence of related symptoms and conditions.

Alternatively, US consumers report much higher incidences of allergies, headaches, obesity and depression, all which could logically be related to diet and exercise (or lack thereof). One of the largest anomalies in the data is the high incidence of asthma in the US, which is relatively uncommon in China. General wisdom would suggest that the higher levels of pollution in China would exacerbate bronchial and breathing conditions, but the data do not support that supposition. The other chief difference is the high incidence of allergies in the US. It may well be that diet has much to do with these reported allergic situations as US respondents likely consume more chemically treated, processed foods than do the Chinese. Diet may well also be part of the reason for the much higher reported incidence of diabetes among the US sample than among the Chinese.

A final note on health conditions is the very low number reporting heart disease and prostate problems in both groups. This is to be expected, as these are health complaints normally associated with age, whereas this discussion is limited to individuals who are 18–34 years old.

There are a number of notable differences between the men and women respondents in China. For example, women report higher incidences of heartburn, indigestion, IBS, Crohn's disease and allergies than men. Alternatively, more men report high cholesterol and high blood pressure than women. Again, while asthma is an infrequent complaint of the Chinese respondents, the proportion of those that do suffer from this ailment is twice as great among male respondents as females.

When we look at the incidence of medical conditions by tier, there appear to be only a few differences. There are some indications that respondents living in Tier 1 cities suffer more frequently from complaints traditionally associated with a fast-paced, urban lifestyle such as anxiety, chronic bronchitis, high cholesterol and high blood pressure. Beyond these, the distribution of various complaints is relatively similar across all three tiers.

What Chinese Consumers Are Doing About Their Health

Having learned what conditions Chinese respondents report on the PCQS questionnaires, we now review how they are managing these health issues (Figure 9-4).

There is evidence that at least some young Chinese consumers are taking steps to maintain a healthy lifestyle. For example, 58.4% of the men report that they exercise at least three times a week, although considerably fewer say they are watching their intake of fat, salt or sodium, calories or carbohydrates. Chinese women, on the other hand, are most likely to watch their fat intake (48.6). Only 11.9% of the men and 13.0% of the women say that they do not engage in any of the listed health-related practices.

FIGURE 9-4: REGARDING YOUR HEALTH, WHICH OF THE FOL-LOWING ARE YOU DOING...? ◆ CHINESE CONSUMERS BY GENDER

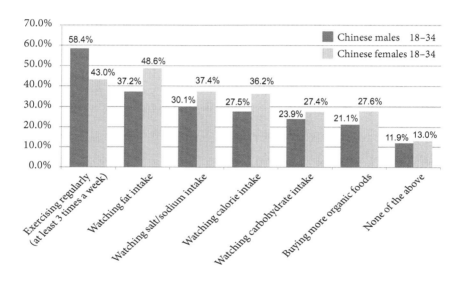

Source: ProsperChina.com

Exercise and watching dietary elements are much more commonly mentioned in Tier 1 cities than in Tier 2 or 3. In fact, to even think about the need limit intake of food is a luxury of the affluent classes and a sign of how Chinese eating habits have changed.

Media Influence in Purchasing Medicines

The final area found in the PCQS data related to healthcare is the question of what media forms most influence the purchase of medicines to deal with health issues. Figure 9-5 shows the influence of various media forms reported by Chinese and American study participants.

FIGURE 9-5: MEDIA INFLUENCES IN PURCHASING MEDICINES CHINESE AND AMERICAN CONSUMERS

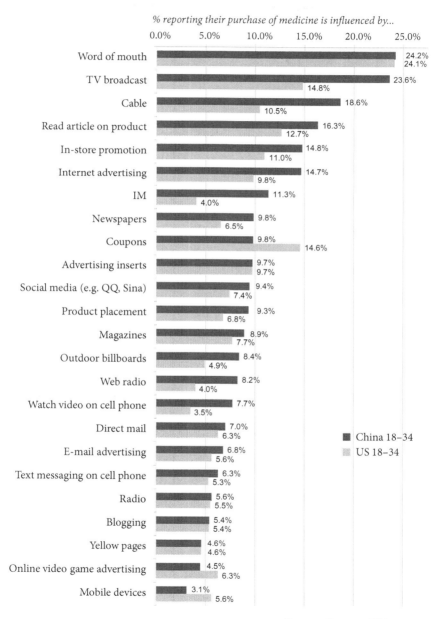

% reporting their purchase of medicine is influenced by...

China 18–34
US 18–34

Source: ProsperChina.com

When it comes to buying and using medicine, word of mouth and television are the two media forms that dominate consumer responses for both groups. Close to one quarter of Chinese and Americans indicate word of mouth is a frequent influence in the category. Beyond that, however, there are some noteworthy differences between the two cohorts. The Chinese respondents frequently report broadcast and cable TV as an influence, whereas television is far less important in the US. In more direct media, nearly 15% of the Chinese report the Internet influences their purchasing of medicines and over 10% say instant messaging has an influence. Those figures illustrate the impact of digital media in China.

In contrast, in the US, one of the more influential media forms is couponing, reflecting the advanced development of American pharmaceuticals and their marketing programs. What is also interesting in this category is the wide diversity of media influences consumers report. Multiple media forms have an influence and doubtless each one has a specific impact on a specific group of consumers and for a particular malady. It is this widespread number of media forms that requires specific attention for a marketer operating in the medical area in China.

Shopping for Health and Beauty Aids

The market for health and beauty aids (HBAs) has seen tremendous growth in China since the inception of market reforms. Rising incomes, urbanization, greater concern for personal well-being and increasing desire to look one's best have all contributed to the steady growth in demand for over the counter remedies, personal care products, toiletries, skincare and cosmetics. And the market is expected to continue expanding rapidly, especially in lower-tier regions. Euromonitor International estimates China's personal care and beauty products sales will grow a whopping 58% between 2010 and 2015 to reach US$40 billion.[3]

While the health and beauty segments each have their own unique characteristics and dynamics, which we will discuss separately, it is useful to look first at the overall retail environment in which these products are sold.

In our discussion of the electronics category in Chapter 7, we commented that the segment is dominated by two major chains, Gome and Suning, and that the rest of the market is highly fragmented. In the case of health and beauty product retailing, the situation is even more localized and diffused. Establishments that sell health and beauty products range from small, traditional storefront shops to drugstores, specialty stores, salons, department stores, supermarkets and hypermarkets.

While there are no truly national chains in the HBA category, there are a number of retailers that are expanding aggressively into Tiers 2 and 3 and beyond. For example, Watsons, the Hong Kong HBA specialty chain, announced in December 2011 that it had opened its 1000th store and that it aims to have 3,000 in the mainland by 2016.[4] This dwarfs the combined total of fewer than 400 outlets for all of Walmart's Chinese operations (334 Walmart Supercenters, 29 Trust Mart Hypermarkets, 6 Sam's Clubs, 2 Neighborhood Markets and 3 Discount Compact Hyper stores) or the 208 hypermarkets operated by Carrefour.

---

3. "Mary Kay to Invest $25 Million in China, Soon Its Largest Market," Bloomberg.com, Sept 19, 2011, http://www.bloomberg.com/news/2011-09-19/mary-kay-to-invest-25-million-in-china-soon-its-largest-market.html

4. "Watsons Aims 3,000 Mainland China Stores in Five Years," chinaretailnews.com, Dec 23, 2011, http://www.chinaretailnews.com/2011/12/23/5321-watsons-aims-3000-mainland-china-stores-in-five-years/

In addition to these foreign bricks-and-mortar retailers, Chinese consumers increasingly buy health and beauty products through Western direct sellers such as Avon, Mary Kay and Amway. Direct selling in China has a checkered history. American direct sellers entered the market in the 1980s, only to be banned by the Chinese government in 1998 after accusations of pyramid schemes, overpromising by the sellers, high-pressure selling tactics and other controversial practices. After considerable lobbying, in 2006 the direct sales ban was lifted, and direct selling was reinstated with limitations on agent's compensation and the size of sales meetings. That has not hampered growth, however, as most direct sellers now report rapidly increasing sales, and the industry has grown to over US$8 billion in annual sales.[5] The prospects for growth are so great that in 2011 Avon opened an R&D center in China (its largest outside the US)[6] and May Kay announced plans to invest US$25 million to build is first overseas plant and distribution center to support the work of its 600,000 sales representatives in China. While direct sellers represent a relatively small portion of the overall market for HBAs, they are a growing, competitive presence that must be reckoned with by domestic and international retailers and brand marketers.

Retailers Shopped Most Often for Health Product Shopping

Health products in China consist of a mix of TCM, Western-style pharmaceuticals, as well as products for dental care, eye care, analgesics, bandages, lotions, baby care, toothpaste and the like.

Retailing of prescription and non-prescription drugs is substantially different in China than in the US. Traditionally, the sale of

---

5. David Barboza, "Direct Selling Flourishes in China," *New York Times*, Dec 25, 2009, http://www.nytimes.com/2009/12/26/business/global/26marykay.html

6. *China's Cosmetics Market, 2011*, Li & Fung Research Centre, (Feb 2012), http://www.funggroup.com/eng/knowledge/research/industry_series20.pdf

prescription drugs in China has been restricted primarily to hospital dispensaries, and Chinese hospitals make the majority of their earnings from drug dispensing rather than patient care. In the US, 74% of prescriptions are filled at retail pharmacies, leading to the development of large, profitable drug store chains, which have generally replaced small mom-and-pop pharmacies around the country.

By contrast, in China the retail drug store market is highly fragmented and most operations are on a very small scale. While there are an estimated 360,000 drug retailers in urban China, only 492 had annual sales of more than US$7.3 million.[7] The Research Partnership, a market research firm specializing in healthcare, predicts the industry will undergo a wave of consolidation as larger operators seek greater economies of scale in order to better serve an increasingly affluent, but aging, population. Retail pharmacists have already seen large general mass merchandisers and grocery chains encroaching on their turf by selling OTC drugs and other health products and devices, and small or weak retailers are at risk of being squeezed out of the market.

Walmart, Carrefour and Da Run Fa (known in English as RT-Mart) are the retailers most frequently mentioned by the PCQS respondents for health products. Watsons runs closely behind in preference, and beats out Da Run Fa in Tier 1 for number of mentions (see Figure 9-6).

The fragmented nature of the category is apparent. No retail outlet, with the exception of Walmart and Carrefour, is mentioned by more than 14% of the survey respondents as the store visited most often for health products, and that is only in the higher tier cities. The majority of health product outlets are the large number of homegrown operators, plus a limited number of American and European retailers. Many of the retailers visited most often for health products are, in fact,

---

7. Marc Yates, *The Rise of the Retail Pharmacy in China*, PBIRG Perspectives, the Research Partnership, (Fall 2010), http://www.researchpartnership.com/uploadFiles/files/PBIRG-Perspectives-Fall-2010.pdf

FIGURE 9-6: RETAILERS SHOPPED MOST OFTEN FOR HEALTH PRODUCTS ◆ CHINESE CONSUMERS BY TIER

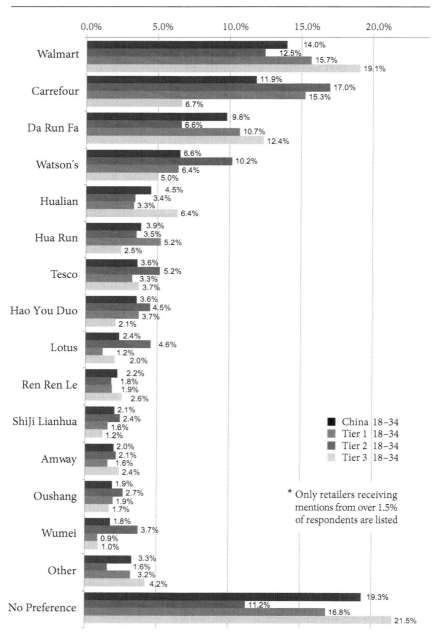

Source: ProsperChina.com

supermarkets, hypermarkets and general merchandisers, reflecting the presence these types of stores have achieved in the health products category.

As we saw earlier in the electronics and apparel retailing categories, there is a significant proportion of Chinese consumers who report "no preference" when asked about retailers they visit most often for health products, particularly in Tiers 2 and 3. In part this reflects the limited presence of most major chains in these tiers, as well as the general lack of shopper loyalty that typifies Chinese consumers. In this category, however, it also reflects the continuing popularity of traditional Chinese herbal remedies and other TCM approaches.

Monthly Expenditures on Health Products

PCQS survey participants spend, on average, US$16.80 per month on health products such as OTC medicines, toothpaste, and lotions. The averages by gender and tiers are shown in Figure 9-7.

FIGURE 9-7: AVERAGE MONTHLY EXPENDITURE ON HEALTH PRODUCTS ⬦ CHINESE CONSUMERS BY GENDER AND TIER

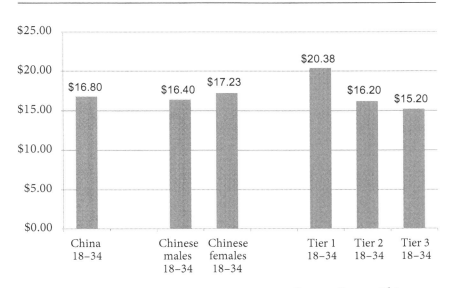

Source: ProsperChina.com

There is little variation between the sexes on the amount spent each month on health products. However, those in Tier 1 spend, on average, 25.8% more than those in Tier 2, and 34.3% more than those in Tier 3. This not only reflects the income differences between the different regions, but also the differing product assortments available in each locale. Many marketers offer lower-priced goods in Tier 2 and 3 cities—products with reduced features, less expensive ingredients or less elaborate packaging—in order to appeal to the more limited budgets in these areas.

Retailers Shopped Most Often for Beauty Products

Until the 1980s, the Chinese government banned the use of cosmetics in the country. Since the restrictions have been removed, the growth of beauty, skincare and cosmetics in China has been spectacular. Euromonitor International estimates China's beauty business at approximately US$23.6 billion, making it the fourth-largest market behind the US, Japan and Brazil.[8]

There are significant social and cultural differences in how Chinese and American women buy and use beauty products. For one, in the US, the market is rather evenly divided between skincare, color cosmetics (makeup) and fragrance. In China, however, the segment is dominated by skincare, especially anti-aging and whitening products, which account for approximately 70% of beauty consumption.

Chinese women value a radiant, glowing complexion, and begin to use skincare products at a much earlier age than their American counterparts. And, since skincare is deemed essential to creating an attractive, professional look, women will often justify paying for premium brands because they feel it is an investment in their future success.

---

8. Kathleen E. McLaughlin, "China in Development," *Women's Wear Daily* (WWD.com), June 17, 2011, http://www.wwd.com/beauty-industry-news/marketing-trends/china-in-development-3662310?full=true

In the US, young women often learn skincare and beauty routines from their mothers, aunts or sisters. Given the "one child policy" under which Chinese young women have grown up, this reservoir of knowledge and brand preference for young women to draw on is much more limited. Thus, the challenges of introducing and expanding and extending beauty brands is more challenging in China than in the US.

Beauty marketers have stepped up to fill the void by launching extensive in-store education programs, counter demonstrations, workshops, seminars and online forums. These initiatives have paid off handsomely, sometimes in unexpected ways. For one thing, Chinese women are more likely than their American sisters to use the full suite of products offered by a line, greatly increasing the value of each acquired customer. And, in a country where brand loyalty is otherwise generally low, Chinese woman tend to stay with a beauty product or brand that they feel works well for them.[9]

Another difference between the two countries is the age at which young girls begin to use cosmetics and fragrances. In the US, it is common for cosmetics use to start in high school or even junior high. In China, however, young women do not usually begin to use color cosmetics until their late teens or early twenties, as it is often considered unseemly for a younger girls to be seen wearing make-up.

Digital communication and e-commerce are having a profound impact on the future shape of the cosmetics and beauty category. According to iResearch, online turnover on cosmetics products increased 66.6% between 2010 and 2011. This encompasses sales not only through the giant Taobao.com and its sister site Tmall.com, but also, the small, but growing dedicated cosmetics sites, such as Lefeng.com (previously Lafaso.com),

9. Patricia Pao, "Engaging Affluent Chinese Through Beauty Products," MediaPost.com, Feb 1, 2012, http://www.mediapost.com/publications/article/166553/engaging-affluent-chinese-through-beauty-products.html

Jumei.com and Tiantian.com.[10] Furthermore, brand marketers are beginning to go around intermediaries by establishing their own e-commerce
sites, with Shiseido, Clinique, Lancôme and others now selling directly to
consumers. Additionally, brand marketers are placing increasing emphasis
on social media as a means to connect and engage with their customers.
According to Thindov, a market researcher in China, 80% of the top 100
cosmetics brands promote their lines on Sina Weibo.[11]

Among the PCQS respondents, the most frequently visited
retailer for beauty products is Watsons, the HBA retailing giant, which
is mentioned by over one-fifth of the participants. Other retailers
include Taobao (the online shopping platform of retailers and entrepreneurs developed by Alibaba, see Chapter 6), followed by Walmart
and Carrefour. Other distribution channels are shown in Figure 9-8
including the presence of the direct sellers.

Watsons greatest strength lies in Tier 1 cities, where shoppers are more
likely to be affluent and more engaged in the beauty category. However,
Watsons is also the most visited store in Tiers 2 and 3, a testament to the
company's expansion effort and effective marketing in these areas.

As might be expected, both Watsons and Taobao are extremely
popular with woman, being mentioned by 26.8% and 19.1% respectively
as the retailer visited most often for beauty products. The third-most
popular retailer among woman is Avon, being mentioned by 4.2% of
the respondents.

So far we have only discussed women shoppers in the beauty category. However, this is increasingly a category in which men participate
as well, particularly for skincare products. Among the male respondents, 18% say they have shopped at Watsons for beauty products, and
another 11.6% report shopping at Taobao. This is another example of
the continuously evolving nature of the Chinese consumer.

---

10. "Online Makeup Market Prime to Grow," *Global Times*, July 5, 2012,
    http://www.globaltimes.cn/content/719326.shtml
11. *China's Cosmetics Market*, Li & Fung Research Centre

FIGURE 9-8: RETAILERS SHOPPED MOST OFTEN FOR BEAUTY
PRODUCTS* ◆ CHINESE CONSUMERS BY TIER

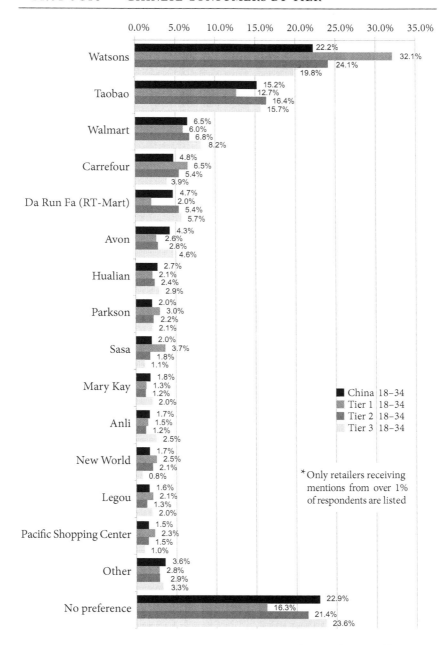

Source: ProsperChina.com

Monthly Expenditures on Beauty Products

On average, members of the Chinese digital generation spend US$20.77 per month on beauty products. As seen in Figure 9-9, spending is highest among women (US$24.15 per month) and among residents in Tier 1 (US$27.53).

FIGURE 9-9: MONTHLY EXPENDITURES ON BEAUTY PRODUCTS
❖ CHINESE CONSUMERS BY GENDER AND TIER

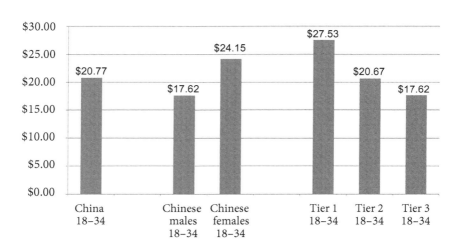

Source: ProsperChina.com

The differences in spending levels between tiers naturally reflect basic income disparities. However, it is also attributable to the fact that the premium, imported brands popular in Tier 1 have very limited distribution in lower-tier cities at this point. While Chanel, Shiseido, Estée Lauder, Clinique, Lancôme and other premium international brands are well represented in department stores in Tier 1, they have had little presence to date in lower-tier cities. However, these brands are working on expansion plans to gain greater distribution across the country, in the belief that there is now a sizeable base of consumers who follow fashion and who have sufficient disposable income to trade up in their beauty purchases. For example, L'Oréal has announced it intends to expand to 600 Tier 2 cities to reach this market with its high- and mid-priced brands, and Shiseido and Estée Lauder have similar initiatives to extend their reach. To date, the Tier 2 and 3 cities have been served primarily by domestic companies with value-for-money products. Clearly, they will begin to face increasing competition from imported brands.[12]

Shopping for Groceries

Food retailing in China, like many other retail categories, is changing quite rapidly. Historically, in Chinese families, the female (mother or grandmother) commonly did most of the food shopping on a daily basis. Since Chinese prize freshness in all food categories, "wet markets" are still quite common and many modern retailers incorporate this pattern by slaughtering chickens in their stores or displaying live fish in tanks. When this desire for freshness is combined with the fact that most families have limited home storage facilities, particularly refrigeration, daily food shopping continues to be a ritual for Chinese families.

Grocery retailing is big business in China, accounting for 41% of all retail sales in China in 2011, up 10% over the previous year.[13] According to IDG, the UK-based global research agency, China became the world's largest grocery market in 2011, with total grocery sales of US$972 billion compared with US$913.5 billion in the US, (although on a per capita basis the market in China is still far behind the US). The researchers say this growth in grocery retail revenue has been fuelled by three main factors: rapid economic growth, population expansion and increasing inflation of food prices.[14]

---

12. *China's Cosmetics Market*, Li & Fung Research Centre
13. Euromonitor International, *Grocery Retailers in China*, (Dec 2011), http://www.euromonitor.com/grocery-retailers-in-china/report (overview only)
14. "China Surpasses US as World's Biggest Grocery Market," BBC.co.uk, April 4, 2012, http://www.bbc.co.uk/news/business-17595963

As with other sectors, grocery retailing is still quite fragmented. For example, according to a study conducted by CTR Market Research and Kantar Worldpanel, modern trade (hypermarkets and supermarkets) only accounted for 46% of total grocery sales in 2010.[15] Walmart Group (which includes the Trust-Mart stores) was the largest grocery retail brand in China, yet it represented only 3.6% of total retail grocery sales and only had a usage penetration rate of 21.3% of the total national market. Traditional grocery stores, open-air markets and direct sales still make up a large portion of consumer food purchases in China, particularly in lower-tier and rural areas.

Where large-scale retailing has developed in China, in the form of enormous hypermarkets and giant supermarkets, food has predominated in terms of store assortments. Part of this is reflected in the lower level of interest in home improvements and enhancements, categories that are key revenue generators in US hypermarkets. Large format stores in China are not used as weekly stock-up destinations as they are in the US. Rather, they are shopped in the same way as smaller stores and are used on a daily basis. This tendency toward frequent shopping for daily needs, a strong emphasis on foods and low purchase rates for home goods lead to average check-out amounts in Chinese hypermarkets that are much lower than those found in the West. In a report prepared by Planet Retail, Chinese hypermarkets average US$2,161 in sales per square meter—40% of the US average and one-ninth of that in Britain.[16]

---

15. InfoseekChina, "Chinese Grocery Market Sector Is Highly Fragmented: CTR, Kantar Worldpanel," *China Beverage News* (blog), Nov 7, 2010, http://www.chinabevnews.com/2010/11/chinese-grocery-market-sector-is-highly.html

16. Louise Herring, Daniel Hui, Paul Morgan and Caroline Tufft, *Inside China's Hypermarkets: Past and Prospects,* McKinsey & Company, (May 2012), http://www.mckinseychina.com/wp-content/uploads/2012/05/Inside_Chinas_Hypermarkets.pdf

One of the great attractions of hypermarkets and large super-markets to the Chinese consumer is the vast array of brands they have available. Chinese consumers are highly brand conscious, with a strong belief that well-known or expensive brands are of better quality. That does not make them brand loyal, however. There may be times that they are willing to trade down to lower quality if a category is not important to them. Additionally, research by Bain & Co and Kantar Worldpanel found that Chinese shoppers typically rotate purchases through a repertoire of brands in a given category. The study tracked purchasing in 40,000 Chinese households in categories such as beverages, packaged food, personal care and home care. The study found there is considerable brand loyalty in certain narrow areas, specifically infant formula, diapers, milk, beer, soft drinks and chewing gum. Beyond these, Chinese typically have 3–4 favorite brands in any given category. Furthermore, as usage in a particular category increases, so does the number of brands purchased. This indicates that Chinese consumers are experimenting more with different brands, perhaps trading up and trading down according to circumstances and opportunities. The study has important implications for marketers. For one thing, they must ensure their brand is part of the shopper's consideration set, and use in-store activation to recruit and capture shoppers. Additionally, new customer acquisition and achieving distribution scale are critical, especially in categories where the marketer cannot depend on a high rate of repeat purchases to sustain sales levels.[17]

Retailers Shopped Most Often for Groceries

The PCQS tracks approximately three dozen grocery retailers, asking consumers where they shop most often. Figure 9-10 shows those

---

17. *China Shopper Report 2012*, Bain & Company and Kantar World-panel, (June 2012), http://www.kantarworldpanel.com/dwl.php?sn= news_downloads&id=69

retailers that were mentioned by at least 1% of the respondents age 18–34.

Walmart and Carrefour clearly dominate the preferences of PCQS respondents, having been mentioned by 16.0% and 12.7% of respondents respectively. However, there are some geographic differences: Walmart is strongest in the Tier 2 and 3 cities, while Carrefour is preferred in Tier 1.

Da Run Fa, is a strong third in the PCQS findings, followed by Hualian, Hao You Duo, CRC, Lianhua. Because of the highly localized nature of the marketplace, the balance of the mentions are spread across a large number of indigenous regional players such as Lotus, Ren Ren Le and Yinzuo, as well as a few Western retailers such as the UK's Tesco and France's Auchan.

It is interesting to note that in this category there is a higher level of mentions for "other" than we have seen in the various retail segments discussed so far. Overall, 4.1% report they shop most frequently at a retailer not listed among the study's choices, a figure that increases to 5.6% in Tier 3. This attests to the continuing popularity of small, independent local shops and open markets, especially in less developed areas.

Another point to be noted is the 10.7% of PCQS respondents who indicate they have no preference in their choice of grocery retailer. The proportion of no preference is lowest in Tier 1 (5.7%) and increases in Tier 2 (8.6%) and Tier 3 (10.5%). This is a departure from the generally low level of shopper loyalty that we have noted in other retail categories. Furthermore, it is dramatically different from comparable research in the US where 35.6% of American respondents (of the same age group) state they have no preference in their choice of grocery retailer. Thus, grocery retailers in China seem to have forged stronger bonds with their customers than have other types of retailers in the country, and they definitely have achieved higher customer preference than grocery retailers in the US.

FIGURE 9-10: RETAILERS SHOPPED MOST OFTEN FOR GROCERIES*
CHINESE CONSUMERS BY TIER

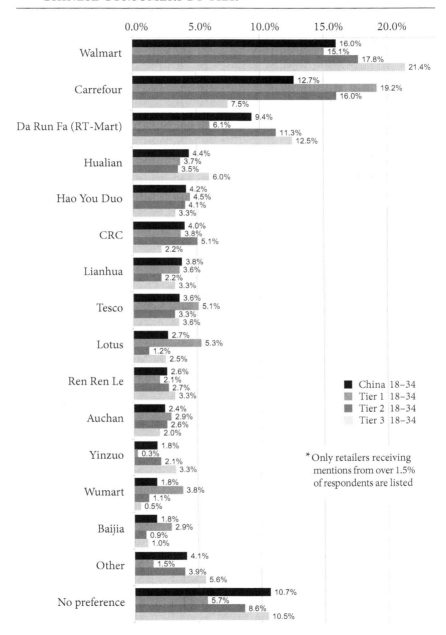

*Only retailers receiving mentions from over 1.5% of respondents are listed

■ China 18–34
▨ Tier 1 18–34
▨ Tier 2 18–34
▨ Tier 3 18–34

Source: ProsperChina.com

Reasons for Shopping at Chosen Retailer

The reasons for the high level of store preferences may be seen in Figure 9-11, in which PCQS respondents were asked to indicate the reasons why they buy groceries at the store they visit most often.

As might be expected, in a marketplace where daily shopping for food and groceries is the norm, where automobile ownership is limited and traffic congestion overwhelming, location is by far the greatest driver of consumer store choice. More than 60% of women respondents and over 50% of male respondents say location is why they choose the retail store they do. Close behind, for men and women, is price. Both reasons demonstrating the Chinese focus on practicality and pragmatism. Selection and quality are the next most frequently mentioned reasons, reflecting the Chinese concern for food safety discussed in an earlier section. Service and one-stop shopping are also key decision points for Chinese shoppers. And, a truly Western concept, the frequent shopper card, promising rewards and prizes for store loyalty, is starting to emerge as well although data is still quite limited in this area.

Many of the traditional Western food store differentiators have yet to impact the Chinese market such as wide aisles, store layout and other internal factors. And, advertising and coupons, mainstays of most food retailing in the US, are not prevailing factors in Chinese store choices.

Average Monthly Expenditures on Groceries

Figure 9-12 shows average monthly expenditures for grocery items by gender and tier.

As can be seen, the average spend is approximately US$74.38 per month, which is fairly even between the genders, with women spending slightly more. However, as would be expected, there are considerable differences between Tier 1–3 cities. Tier 1 residents spend 14.4% more per month than those in Tier 2, and 27.5% more than those in

FIGURE 9-11: REASONS FOR CHOICE OF GROCERY RETAILER CHINESE CONSUMERS BY GENDER

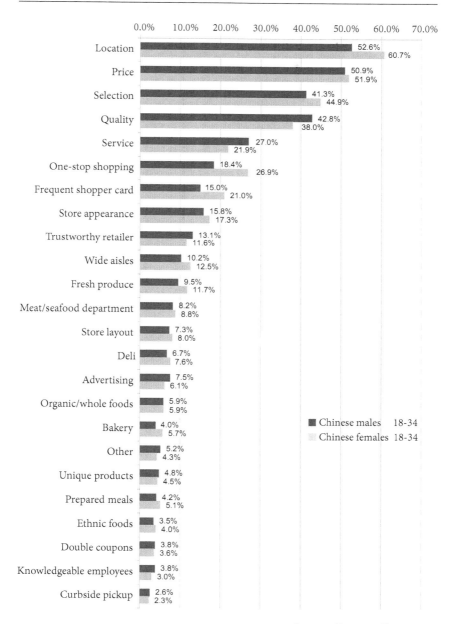

Source: ProsperChina.com

Tier 3. Part of this difference may be the purchasing of more expensive products by residents in Tier 1. However, it also reflects the overall higher cost of living and higher prices for products in all areas in the larger cities.

FIGURE 9-12: AVERAGE MONTHLY EXPENDITURE ON GROCERIES
⬧ CHINESE CONSUMERS BY GENDER AND TIER

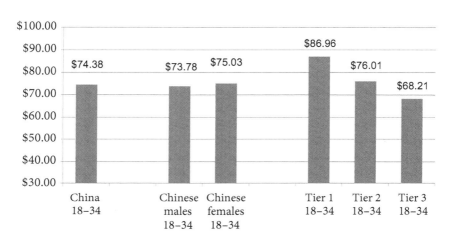

Source: ProsperChina.com

Country-of-Origin Preferences for Consumer Packaged Goods

In earlier chapters, we examined country-of-origin preferences in China across categories such as music, electronics and apparel. Now we investigate two more categories: health and beauty products (Figure 9-13) and soft drinks (Figure 9-14).

The health and beauty category includes a mixed bag of products ranging from traditional medicines, OTC drugs and toiletries to skin-care and cosmetics. Thus, we need be cautious in how the responses to the country of origin question are interpreted in this category.

FIGURE 9-13: COUNTRY-OF-ORIGIN PREFERENCE—HEALTH
AND BEAUTY PRODUCTS · CHINESE CONSUMERS BY TIER

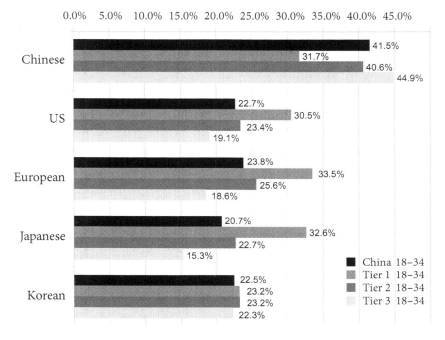

Source: ProsperChina.com

Overall, PCQS respondents said they preferred Chinese health and beauty brands. This would certainly be built on a foundation of preference for TCM, and similar health-related products, but would also include Chinese brands that have developed in the beauty, shampoo and cosmetics sectors.

The strong showing of US, European and Japanese brands, especially in Tier 1, is most likely a reflection of interest in global skincare, cosmetic and fragrance brands. P&G's Olay brand is the market leader in China, and dominates the mid-priced segment. In the higher-priced segments, Japan's Shiseido, France's L'Oréal and the American company Estée Lauder all have attracted strong followings. Additionally, P&G and Unilever have both been very adept in marketing personal care products in China, another contributing factor to the strong showing of American and European brands in Tier 1 and, to a lesser extent, in Tier 2.

There are striking differences between men and women in their country-of-origin preferences in the health and beauty category. Men show a more pronounced preference for Chinese brands (43.7% for men versus 39.2% for women), and away from Japanese brands (15.8%). Among women, there are overall stronger levels of preference for imported brands: Korea (28.6%), Japan (26.1%), Europe (23.9%) and the US (22.3%).

FIGURE 9-14: COUNTRY-OF-ORIGIN PREFERENCE—SOFT DRINKS
♦ CHINESE CONSUMERS BY TIER

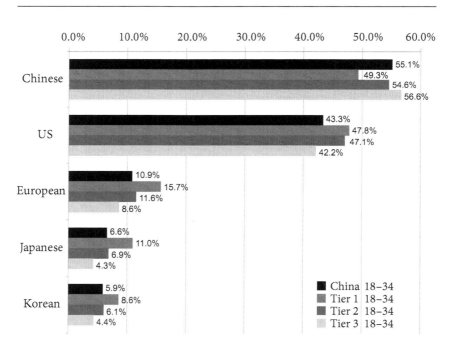

Source: ProsperChina.com

Quite a different picture emerges in the soft drinks category. While again there is strong preference for Chinese soft drink brands,

American brands (predominantly Coca-Cola and, more recently, Pepsi) are right behind. Interestingly, there is relatively little fall-off from Tier 1 to Tiers 2 and 3, a reflection of the strong marketing and distribution practices that have made American soft drinks popular across large portions of the country. US brands rank second, behind Chinese brands, among both men (48.6%) and women (37.7%). Soft drinks from Europe, Japan and Korea have yet to attract much of a following in China, although they are mentioned somewhat more often by women than by men.

Media Influence on Purchase of Grocery Products

Finally, we look at what media Chinese shoppers report influence their grocery (food, cleaning and beauty products) purchase decisions, as shown in Figure 9-15.

As we have seen in most of the other product categories discussed in this text, Chinese respondents report that word of mouth has a powerful influence on their purchase decisions. Over 26% of all Chinese respondents say that is the primary influence in their grocery purchasing decisions. As can be seen from the chart, however, that is far less than US respondents report, at nearly 35%.

In China, the second most important influence is broadcast TV, which is mirrored by a similar percentage of the US respondents. The third and fourth most important factors for the Chinese are in-store promotions and coupons, but here we see major differences with the US. For US respondents these two are cited as the most significant influences on their grocery purchasing decisions. Coupons are the most frequently mentioned—by over half the US consumers (57.2%) compared with 22.2% of Chinese. The sales promotion industry, and the infrastructure required to redeem and process coupons, is not yet as developed in China as in the US. It may be that the necessary capabilities will eventually develop in China, but for now marketers who are dependent upon couponing

FIGURE 9-15: MEDIA INFLUENCE IN PURCHASING GROCERIES (FOOD, CLEANING, BEAUTY) ◆ CHINESE AND AMERICAN CONSUMERS

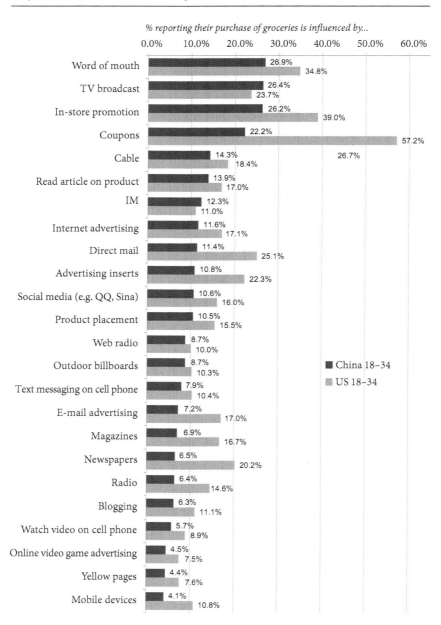

% reporting their purchase of groceries is influenced by...

Source: ProsperChina.com

in the developed markets must learn different approaches to incenting Chinese consumers.

When we look at media influence by gender, females are much more influenced by the top four activities (word of mouth, television, in-store promotions and coupons) than men. There are, however, only minor differences between tiers.

Recapping Monthly Expenditures for Daily Needs

We end this chapter with one final view of Chinese consumer behaviors: a comparison of the amount spent monthly in the three consumer purchasing categories—groceries, beauty and health products. The consolidated average expenditures for these three categories are depicted in Figure 9-16.

FIGURE 9-16: AVERAGE MONTHLY EXPENDITURES ON GROCERIES, BEAUTY AND HEALTH PRODUCTS CHINESE CONSUMERS BY GENDER AND TIER

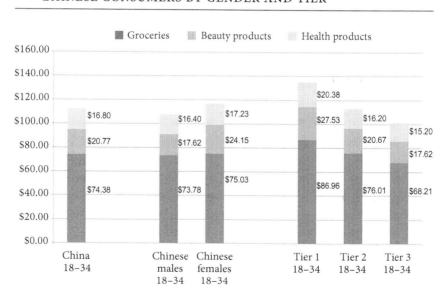

Source: ProsperChina.com

As a whole, China's digital generation spends slightly over US$100 per month in these three categories, with food claiming almost two-thirds of the outlay. Purchases are about the same by gender for groceries and health, while women spend more on cosmetics each month than men of the same age.

It is in the tier data we see significant differences. As would be expected, PCQS respondents residing in Tier 1 cities spend substantially more on all three categories than those in Tiers 2 or 3. However, their expenditures represent a lower proportion of their overall average monthly income. For Tier 1 residents purchases of health, beauty and grocery products take up 11.6% of their average income. In Tier 2 these items are 13.7% of monthly income, and in Tier 3 consumers must devote 16.8% of average income to these necessities

As income increases in lower-tier cities, and as marketers distribute a broader assortment of products at a wider range of price points, we will likely see spending on groceries and HBAs approach the level in Tier 1 cities. Marketers, however, must carefully synchronize their plans and the introduction of higher-priced goods with the incremental changes in income. Additionally, they must link benefits for higher-priced goods to desired outcomes valued by Chinese consumers—namely, the need for self-projection, gaining face, facilitating advancement or avoiding risk. Chinese consumers have shown they are willing and even anxious to trade up for products that help them achieve their goals. However, products that are used primarily in the home for personal use are at risk of losing out if the marketer cannot clearly communicate the value of trading up.

Five Key Takeaways

1. Members of China's digital generation are showing signs of the strains of their fast-paced, high achievement-oriented lifestyle, with

troubling incidences of insomnia, indigestion, anxiety, acid reflux and other conditions associated with stress. However, the reported incidence of depression is low, reflecting the cultural biases against any form of mental or emotional illness.

2. Retailing in China is still highly fragmented, and shopper loyalty is relatively low, leaving the door open for consumers to find alternative means of acquiring products such as direct selling and e-commerce.

3. Safety and trust are big factors in influencing the purchase of consumer products, particularly health, beauty and food products. The widely publicized drug and food contamination problems that have occurred over the past several years have encouraged Chinese consumers to move toward the purchase of imported brands simply because they are often considered to be safer, with more stringent quality-control systems than those practiced by Chinese manufacturers.

4. Brand loyalty for fast-moving consumer goods is generally low in China, with consumers rotating purchases among a consideration set of 3–4 brands. The exceptions are certain high involvement categories where there are special concerns about safety, purity or suitability. Beyond categories such as baby care, milk, skincare and the like, Chinese consumers freely trade up and down for reasons of price, availability or variety.

5. Daily shopping is a common practice for most Chinese consumers. Culturally, Chinese prefer "fresh products," meaning those that have not traveled long distances to market. The lack of home storage space, particularly refrigeration, is another contributing factor. Thus, "stocking up" promotions meet with little acceptance. For the most part, Chinese consumers practice the habit of buying no more than they can carry on each shopping trip.

Moving On

In this chapter, we have emphasized the practical and pragmatic nature of China's consumers. They carefully weigh their purchase choices, trading up in categories that are important to them, and trading down in those that are not. How does what we have learned about Chinese consumers translate to their financial planning? In the next chapter, we will look more closely at Chinese attitudes towards the economy, and the steps they are taking to plan for their financial futures.

Chapter 10

Personal Finance and Planning For The Future

China's digital generation has known almost nothing but dramatic economic growth and increasing affluence during their lifetime. In less than four decades, China has seen an elevenfold increase in per capita income, and has lifted more people out of poverty in a shorter time than any country in the history of the world.[1] Yes, poverty still exists on a massive scale in China, but the young, post-revolution adults profiled in this text do not represent the broad population of mainland China. Rather, they are an elite group—the most educated, the most pampered, the most connected generation in the country's history. As such, they have ridden the crest of China's phenomenal growth, and are central to the country's attempt to transition to a more consumption-based economy.

---

1. Keisuke Nakashima, Neil Howe and Richard Jackson, *China's Long March to Retirement Reform,* Center for Strategic & International Studies, (2009), http://csis.org/files/media/csis/pubs/090422_gai _chinareport_en.pdf

Yet, China's young adults are still greatly influenced by history and the experiences of their parents, relatives and other elders. While the digital generation did not have to "eat bitterness" as their parents did during periods of natural and manmade disaster in the twentieth century, the collective memory of hardship and deprivation remains and influences their approaches to planning for the future. They are clearly optimistic about their future, but, as we will see, their optimism is tempered, in true Chinese style, by belief that luck works in both directions. Good luck (and hard work) bring prosperity, but bad luck is never far away. Thus, it is important to not take one's good luck for granted, to be cautious and set aside funds for that inevitable rainy day.

The digital generation, like their elders, are keenly aware that China's economic transformation, however brilliant, has not always been a smooth ride. A financial crisis in the late 1990s brought many banks and state-owned companies to the edge of bankruptcy, and triggered the lay-offs of millions of workers. The government stepped in with a number of initiatives to shore up failing banks, including sharply lowering the interest rates paid to depositors. During this time the government began to discard the "iron rice bowl" of social programs—that is, the commitment to lifelong employment, state-supported education, medical care and retirement. This period marked a step forward to the managed-market system, sometimes referred to as state capitalism, which continues to evolve today. These initiatives clearly helped spur growth in the early 2000s, particularly infrastructure development, real estate and export manufacturing. However, they also left a double-barreled, negative legacy in the form of low interest rates paid to savers and placing greater responsibility on households to provide for their own financial future.[2]

2. David Barboza, "As Its Economy Sprints Ahead, China's People Are Left Behind," *New York Times*, Oct 9, 2011, http://www.nytimes.com/2011/10/10/business/global/households-pay-a-price-for-chinas-growth.html?ref=endangereddragon

The current Five-Year Plan attempts to address some of the underlying issues that discourage domestic consumption, particularly improving the social welfare network, instituting reforms in the equity and bond markets and opening the doors to allow consumers a wider choice of investment vehicles with potentially higher rates than traditional saving accounts. These initiatives are designed to encourage consumers to spend more and save less. However, the long-term success will depend on many factors, including how consumers feel about the economic prospects for China, as well as their own personal needs for financial security.

Brief Overview of the Chinese Economy

There was a time when China could largely do what it wanted, with relatively little regard for the rest of the world. This isolation enabled the country to move forward by "feeling the stones," that is, making careful, gradual, incremental change in its economic, legal, industrial, political and judicial systems. Now, however, it finds itself inexorably linked economically and diplomatically to nations around the world. What happens in Berlin, Madrid, Paris, London or Washington has an impact in Beijing, Guangzhou and Chengdu. And whatever steps the Chinese government takes to manage its internal affairs increasingly have an impact on its international relations.

Nowhere has this new world interdependency been more apparent than on the economic front. With the EU struggling under a sovereign debt crisis, rapidly increasing unemployment rates in Spain, Greece and Italy and no solution in sight on the debate between austerity and stimulus, China has seen a significant fall-off in its exports to Europe, its largest trading partner.[3] Furthermore, ongoing weakness in the US economy raises questions about China's ability to sustain its economic

3. Matthew Philips, "China's Big Trade Deficit May Kill Yuan Appreciation," *Bloomberg Businessweek*, March 12, 2012, http://www.businessweek.com/articles/2012-03-12/chinas-big -trade-deficit-may-kill-yuan-appreciation

expansion. Meanwhile, a possible slowdown in China's economy is seen as bad news for the US and European exporters, who have come to view the country as one of the few bright areas for potential growth.

The days of annual growth rates in excess of 12% in China's economy are probably now history, unlikely to return. As the economy expands and matures, it is natural that the rate of increase would moderate. The consensus among most economists is China will continue to grow probably at an inflation adjusted rate of about 7–8% a year.

However, even at this level, there are many challenges facing the Chinese economy. Among the key factors that will shape China's economic performance over the next few years are inflation, the value of the yuan, the housing market, employment and corruption. These are complex and often interrelated issues, so the following is but a brief and necessarily superficial view of each.

Inflation

In July 2011, the official inflation rate peaked at 6.5%, although the actual rate of increase was much higher in certain sectors that impact consumer's daily lives, notably housing and food. Government initiatives have since brought the official rate down under the historical average of around 4%, but concern for inflation is a top policy issue and influences activities on many fronts. Inflation is eroding the cost advantages that have been central to China's business model as a low-cost exporter. At the same time as the government is attempting to address inflation, it is also encouraging enterprises to raise wages in order to boost domestic consumption—a policy dichotomy that will require deft balancing to be sustainable.[4]

---

4. Bill Conerly, "China's Economic Forecast, 2012-2013: A Business Perspective," *Forbes*, Dec 19, 2011, http://www.forbes.com/sites/billconerly/2011/12/19/chinas-economic-forecast-2012-2013-a-business-perspective/

Value of the Yuan

While American politicians harp on about what they perceive to be the undervalued exchange rate for Chinese currency, the fact is that on an inflation-adjusted basis the yuan has been allowed to appreciate by approximately 3% since 2005.[5] This makes imported goods relatively less expensive and more attractive for China's consumers. However, it also makes China's exports relatively more expensive in international markets. This presents a problem coming at a time when the global economy is softening and China is losing some of its cost competitiveness due to inflation. Writing for *Forbes*, economist Bill Conerly commented, "Allowing the yuan to rise to market levels is a good inflation-fighting technique and also relieves some political pressure. Don't expect China to go too far in this direction, however, especially if economic growth slows."

Housing Market

Home prices have been in a steep decline for the past couple of years, the result, at least in part, of an overly heated, speculative real estate market, especially at the high end of the spectrum. To an extent, this adjustment was necessary to curb some of the excess and bring the market back to normalcy and stability. The fact remains that overall China's cities are not overbuilt, and there is plenty of sub-standard housing that needs to be upgraded or replaced in order to adequately house both workers and the middle class. The short-term impact of the housing "bust" will probably be to redirect investment among some speculators, but in the long run, demand for new housing is likely to continue to grow.

---

5. Larry MacDonald, "Global Economy Weakening, Say Experts," CanadianBusiness.com, April 19, 2012, http://www.canadianbusiness.com/blog/investing/80360--global-economy-weakening-say-experts

Employment

It is estimated that about 25 million people will join the workforce in China in 2012, half of whom will be college graduates. And, about 10 million rural residents will seek jobs away from home.[6] While China's official unemployment rate hovers around 4%, far lower than Europe (at over 10%) or the US (at approximately 8%), the figure only represent China's registered urban unemployed. The actual rate of unemployment is most likely significantly higher, especially for workers in the manufacturing sector. The soft global economy poses further threats to the employment picture, as demand weakens in Europe and America for low-cost goods imported from China. Perhaps nothing presents a greater challenge to social stability and harmony than the specter of increased unemployment, a fact well recognized by the central government. Among all possible economic policies and initiatives, those that will foster employment will be the highest priority, even at the cost of inefficiency or slowing the pace of market reforms.

Corruption

The Chinese economy is rife with corruption at all levels, from government bureaucrats and state-run enterprises to small and mid-size entrepreneurs. The effect is to burden the system with enormous inefficiencies, to undermine trust, to thwart true progress and create barriers for legitimate operators. There have been ongoing reform efforts, yet bribery, abuses of power, violations of building and safety codes, counterfeiting and cover-ups still occur all too often. These are a key source of social unrest, especially at the local level where consumers are most likely to see the impact on their daily lives.

---

6. Maria Siow, "China's Unemployment Rate Expected to Rise Further," ChannelNewsAsia.com, May 9, 2012, http://www.channelnewsasia. com/stories/economicnews/view/1200186/1/.html

There is another socio-economic factor that will have an impact on China's digital generation: the long-term impact of the one-child policy and increased life expectancy are profoundly altering the demographic make-up of the society. In 2005, there were just 16 elderly Chinese for every 100 working adults, whereas, by 2050 there will be 61. By the time the digital generation reaches retirement age, a much smaller proportion of working adults will be supporting a growing proportion of retirees. Currently there is mandatory "basic pension system" for urban workers, which consists of a first tier of pay-as-you-go benefits and a second tier of largely notional personal retirement accounts. However, most experts consider the system inadequate to accommodate the expected demands. According to a report by the Center for Strategic International Studies and the Prudential Foundation, "Unless China prepares for the challenge, a retirement crisis of immense proportions looms just over the horizon." The report goes on to warn that China's public pension system leaves large gaps in coverage and that its private pension system is still in its infancy. Strengthening both systems will require ongoing financial and legal reforms, including greater accounting transparency, enhanced protection of shareholder rights, expert regulatory administration of financial markets, greater investor protection against deception and fraud and similar steps to strengthen the operation of capital markets.[7] This concern is echoed by the World Bank, which has predicted that by 2075 the country's pension fund could face a shortfall in excess of US$1.4 trillion.[8]

Against this brief overview of the Chinese economy, we now look more closely at how members of the digital generation feel about the economy and how they approach managing their personal financial situation.

---

7. Nakashima, Howe and Jackson, *China's Long March to Retirement Reform*
8. Danielle Andrus, "China Considers 401(k)-Style Retirement Plan," AdvisorOne.com, July 29, 2011, http://www.advisorone.com/2011/07/29/china-considers-401k-style-retirement-plan

How China's Digital Generation Regards the Economy

Since China's digital generation has generally had a front row seat to their country's astounding growth, there is a natural optimism in their views of the future. However, that is tempered by an understanding that not everyone benefits, at least not at the same time. Figure 10-1 details those who feel they are better off, the same or worse off than they were a year ago.

FIGURE 10-1: REGARDING YOUR PERSONAL FINANCIAL SITUATION, COMPARED WITH THIS TIME LAST YEAR ARE YOU...? ◆ CHINESE CONSUMERS BY GENDER AND TIER

	China 18–34	Chinese males 18–34	Chinese females 18–34	Tier 1 18–34	Tier 2 18–34	Tier 3 18–34
Better off	40.1%	41.8%	38.2%	43.4%	39.8%	39.4%
Same	45.0%	43.4%	46.8%	45.0%	46.1%	44.7%
Worse off	14.9%	14.7%	15.0%	11.7%	14.2%	15.8%

Source: ProsperChina.com

Overall, 45% say their personal financial situation is the same as a year ago, and there is little variation between the demographic segments. Relatively few of the PCQS respondents feel they are worse off than a year ago—overall only 14.9%. The remaining respondents are those who feel their personal financial circumstances have improved (40.1%). Chinese men feel somewhat better off than do their female counterparts, and those in Tier 1 also are more likely to feel their situation has improved. In the latter case, this could be the result of having moved to a Tier 1 city in search of better career prospects.

For comparison, a study from BIGinsight in late 2011 asked Americans the same question. Among those age 18–34, 46.2% feel their personal financial situation is the same as a year ago, close to the proportion of Chinese respondents. Beyond this, however, the US respondents exhibit a much more negative outlook. Nearly a third (29.8%) reported their personal financial situation was worse than a year earlier, twice the number of Chinese who felt their situation had deteriorated. While only 23.9% of the Americans reported feeling better off financially, far less than the 40.1% of Chinese respondents who thought their situation had improved.

Confidence in the Economy

Among PCQS respondents, the majority express confidence in China's chances for a strong economy during the next six months. Whether due to faith in government planners, patriotic sentiments or natural optimism, young Chinese adults perceive that their country's economy is on the right track (Figure 10-2).

FIGURE 10-2: FEELINGS ABOUT CHANCES FOR A STRONG ECONOMY DURING THE NEXT 6 MONTHS ◦ CHINESE CONSUMERS BY GENDER

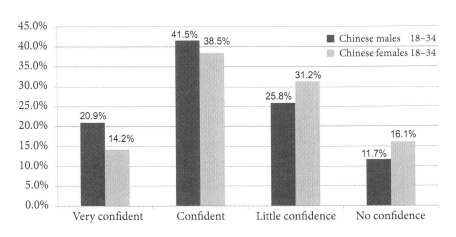

Source: ProsperChina.com

Overall, almost two-thirds (62.4%) of the male respondents say they are confident or very confident of a strong economy in the next six months. This is somewhat higher than the women respondents, where 52.7% responded they are confident or very confident.

In spite of this relatively optimistic outlook, PCQS respondents' confidence in the economy appears to be moderated by their views on the outlook for unemployment and the possibility of additional lay-offs in the coming six-month period. In this regard, men are generally more pessimistic than women, as seen in Figure 10-3.

FIGURE 10-3: REGARDING THE CHINESE EMPLOYMENT ENVIRON-MENT OVER THE NEXT 6 MONTHS, DO YOU THINK THERE WILL BE MORE, THE SAME, OR FEWER LAY-OFFS THAN AT PRESENT? ⬧ CHINESE CONSUMERS BY GENDER

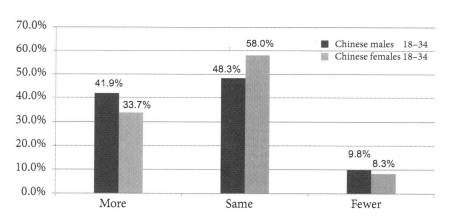

Source: ProsperChina.com

Almost half of the male PCQS respondents (48.3%) feel unemployment will stay about the same, while 41.9% believe that lay-offs will increase over the next six months. The majority of woman, on the other hand, believe lay-offs will remain at about the current level, while a third feel they will increase. This is consistent with trends over the past few years, which have shown a growing concern about the level of anticipated lay-offs (and a consequent decline in those who predict fewer future lay-offs).

Attitudes Towards Personal Spending and Saving

Chinese consumers show a number of conflicting attitudes when it comes to their personal financial situation. In general, we see a fair amount of doubt, uncertainty and ambivalence in many of their answers to questions about spending, saving and personal financial management.

For example, PCQS respondents were asked their feelings about the statement "My philosophy on spending is to live for today, because tomorrow is so uncertain." Figure 10-4 depicts the differing responses between young men and women.

FIGURE 10-4: AGREE WITH STATEMENT: "MY PHILOSPHY ON SPENDING IS TO LIVE FOR TODAY BECAUSE TOMORROW IS SO UNCERTAIN" • CHINESE CONSUMERS BY GENDER AND TIER

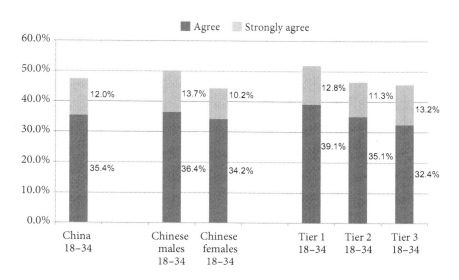

Source: ProsperChina.com

Slightly over one half of all male respondents (50.2%) either agreed or strongly agreed with the statement compared with only 44.4% of the women. The level of agreement with the statement tends to correlate with income. Thus, men, who generally make more than women, are more likely to feel they can "live for today." Likewise, those in Tier 1 cities are more likely to agree or strongly agree with the statement (51.9%) than those in less affluent Tier 2 (46.5%) and 3 (45.6%) cities. Clearly, having greater income allows one greater freedom to spend as one wishes.

Here is where respondents' doubts become apparent: 26.3% of the men and 30.2% of the women expressed uncertainty on the question. This ambivalence is normal for consumers during a period of rapid economic change, especially when there has been a dramatic run-up in prices. Some may feel they might as well buy what they want today, because the price will only be higher tomorrow, while for others the opposite is true. In such periods the result often is confusion and hesitation on the part of consumers.

Thus, we begin to see the yin and yang of savings and consumption among young Chinese adults, that is, their desire to take advantage of their rising economic situation by purchasing today, facing off with the built-in cultural belief that saving is important precisely because tomorrow is so uncertain. This is, in essence, the continuing financial balancing act facing China's digital generation.

Saving for the Future

The Chinese penchant for saving is a virtue born of historical necessity—to guard against famine and shield their families from the vagaries of wars, natural disasters and political upheavals. Today, that tradition continues, as most Chinese citizens must now pay for their own higher education, healthcare and retirement. Combined with concerns about unemployment or a potential downturn in the economy, this has led China to having one of the highest savings rates in the world.

The participants in the PCQS do not represent the "average" Chinese, however. They are younger, better educated and certainly more affluent than the average citizen. They are central to the government's plan to expand domestic consumption, and they are a key target demographic group for marketers. Therefore, the feelings these young adults have about saving and spending will have an important impact on their purchasing habits and how they choose to handle their personal finances.

Two questions are quite revealing: first, whether or not the respondents feel they are setting aside an adequate amount to meet their future needs; and then how much of their income they actually are saving.

Am I Saving Enough?

Overall, PCQS respondents show a pronounced level of discomfort with their current level of savings. In spite of wanting to "live for today," as we saw in the previous question, they know they must set aside funds for tomorrow. However, few are in agreement with the statement "I am setting aside enough to meet my future needs." Since men and women have similar attitudes on this question, Figure 10-5 illustrates the different responses by tier.

FIGURE 10-5: AGREEMENT WITH: "I AM SAVING ENOUGH TO MEET MY FUTURE NEEDS" ◆ CHINESE CONSUMERS BY TIER

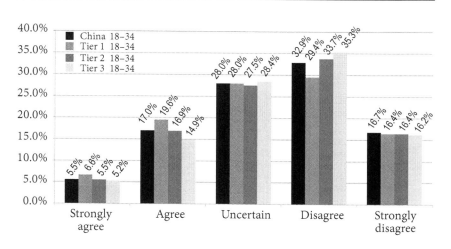

Source: ProsperChina.com

Nearly one half of all respondents (49.6%) either disagree or even strongly disagree that they are saving enough. Additionally, another 28% are uncertain. Thus, only a quarter of the PCQS respondents feel a degree of comfort with the rate at which they are building their nest egg for the future. Consumers in Tier 1 are only slightly more comfortable with their savings rate, so it is fair to say that overall most respondents do not believe they are saving enough for future needs— a feeling shared across the board with little difference by gender or geography.

To put this in perspective, consider the difference between how Chinese and Americans view the sufficiency of their savings rates (Figure 10-6).

FIGURE 10-6: Agreement with: "I am saving enough to meet my future needs" ◆ Chinese and American consumers

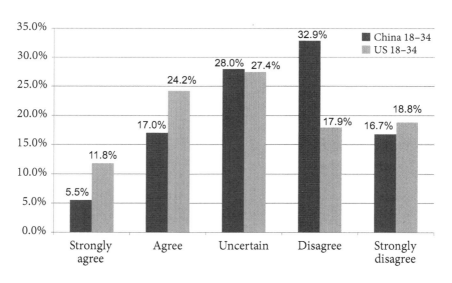

Source: ProsperChina.com

Rightly or wrongly, American respondents are much more confident that they are saving adequately for their future. This is in spite of continuing economic uncertainty and the lower overall level of employment among the American group, as discussed in Chapter 2. Perhaps most striking is the fact fully twice as many American agree strongly with the statement than their Chinese counterparts: 11.8% in the US compared with only 5.5% in China. Overall, 36% of Americans either agree or strongly agree with the statement, compared with only 22.5% of the Chinese participants.

From these comparisons, it is clear that the Chinese are much more pessimistic about what they are accomplishing with their savings plans than those in the US. It may well be that the numerous government and corporate social support plans in America—Social Security, corporate retirement plans, group health insurance and the like—make the US respondents more confident that they are saving a sufficient amount for their future.

A different picture emerges when we look at the actual rate of savings that each group reports.

Proportion of Income Saved Last Year

Figure 10-7 shows the proportion of income saved last year by Chinese and American study participants. Although the level of income is significantly higher among US participants, the general rate of savings is substantially lower. Overall, 53.8% of Chinese respondents report setting aside 11% or more of their income compared with only 34.8% of the Americans. Furthermore, over one quarter of the American reported zero savings last year, well above the 17.8% of Chinese respondents who also failed to set aside any income during the period.

Within China, there are important differences by gender and geography. For example, 57.9% of men report saving 11% or more, compared with 49.4% of women. Additionally, almost one-fifth of the female respondents admit to not having saved anything in the past year, while 16% of male participants also reported that they did not manage to set aside any funds for their future.

FIGURE 10-7: PROPORTION OF INCOME SAVED LAST YEAR
CHINESE AND AMERICAN CONSUMERS

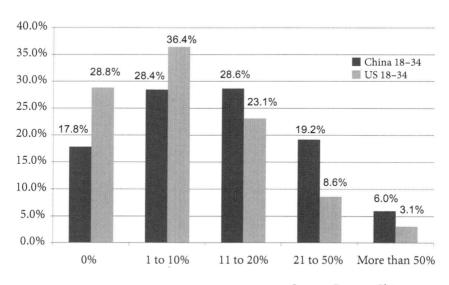

Source: ProsperChina.com

Of course, saving is a function of income, especially the level of disposable income. At the lowest income levels there is little ability to save a large percentage of one's earnings. Thus, we would expect the highest saving rates to be in Tier 1, where 64.5% report saving 11% or more of their income, and almost a third report saving more than 21% of their earnings (Figure 10-8).

The particularly higher rate of savings in Tier 1 is naturally attributable to the higher level of income in these cities. However, it is also partially a reflection of the fact that many young workers and professionals in Tier 1 must save in order to send money home to their families in less economically developed areas.

That said, even a majority of respondents in far less affluent Tiers 2 and 3 report saving at least 11% of their income (54.8 and 46.9% respectively). Clearly, all segments of China's digital generation out-save their US counterparts by a wide margin.

FIGURE 10-8: PROPORTION OF INCOME SAVED LAST YEAR ✦ CHINESE CONSUMERS BY TIER

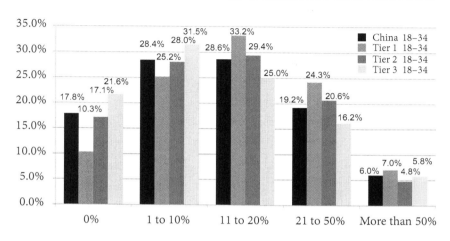

Source: ProsperChina.com

Plans for Future Savings

Yet another perspective emerges when Chinese consumers discuss their future savings plans. Most plan on saving at least the same amount as last year, and a sizable percentage say they intend to save more, as seen in Figure 10-9.

FIGURE 10-9: DO YOU PLAN TO SAVE MORE, LESS OR ABOUT THE SAME AS LAST YEAR? ✦ CHINESE CONSUMERS BY GENDER AND TIER

	China 18–34	Chinese males 18–34	Chinese females 18–34	Tier 1 18–34	Tier 2 18–34	Tier 3 18–34
Plan to save more	43.9%	43.1%	44.7%	42.6%	44.8%	44.8%
Plan to save about the same	35.5%	36.7%	34.2%	42.3%	36.6%	33.6%
Plan to save less	12.1%	12.3%	11.8%	10.1%	11.2%	12.7%
Not sure	8.5%	7.8%	9.2%	6.0%	7.5%	8.9%

Source: ProsperChina.com

The segments that saved less than the average last year show the highest reported intention of increasing their saving in the coming year. Thus, women are more likely to report they intend on saving more, as are those in Tiers 2 and 3.

However, it is noteworthy that a sizeable segment is not sure of the best way to plan for the future. Whether this is because of concerns about the economy, a possible change in employment situation or general lack of planning or financial knowledge, 8.5% of the PCQS respondents could not say if their saving would go up, down or stay the same.

With this view of the savings patterns of the digital generation, we can now turn to examining where those savings are held and what investments are being made with the money.

Managing Personal Finances and Investments

In the previous section, we noted the distinct uncertainty and discomfort PCQS respondents express about their level of saving and their plans for the future. To a certain extent, young Chinese consumers are groping their way forward when it comes to their personal financial planning. While saving is a deeply embedded characteristic in the Chinese culture, modern-day personal finance and investment, as it is known in developed economies, is a relatively recent development within China. Consumers have few established guidelines upon which to draw, and even fewer independent, trained advisors they can turn to for objective financial planning assistance.

Until recently banks had a virtual monopoly on consumers' savings. With little competition, China's retail banks could offer abysmally low interest rates and notoriously poor levels of customer service. In recent years, however, continuing economic reforms and concern about inflation have led to allowing further competition in the financial services marketplace. For example, insurance companies now offer not only life and health insurance, but also annuities, securities and wealth management services. Likewise, mutual funds and security brokerage firms have attracted savers seeking higher returns via instruments such as stock, options and bonds.

Banks have responded by developing more competitive products, introducing wealth management services and stepping up their marketing campaigns.[9] Even with new competition, banks are still the institution that PCQS respondents turn to most often for banking and financial services. However, as seen in Figure 10-10, respondents now often diversify their holdings across multiple institutions.

FIGURE 10-10: INSTITUTIONS USED FOR BANKING AND FINANCIAL SERVICES ⬩ CHINESE CONSUMERS BY GENDER

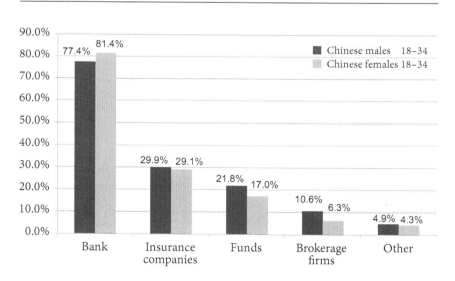

Source: ProsperChina.com

Banks are most popular with women respondents, who generally tend to be more conservative in financial matters. While 77.4% of the men also report using a bank, they are more likely to also deal with a

9. Bloomberg News, "China's Savers Wise Up to Above-Market Rates," *Bloomberg Businessweek*, Feb 23, 2012, http://www.businessweek.com/articles/2012-02-23/chinas-savers-wise-up-to-above-market-rates

fund or a brokerage firm. Men and women turn to insurance companies in about equal proportions.

Types of Investment Vehicles

With inflation a pressing concern for most households, and a desire to build wealth, PCQS respondents increasingly are using a diverse range of investment instruments (Figure 10-11).

FIGURE 10-11: CURRENT FINANCIAL INVESTMENTS
◆ CHINESE CONSUMERS BY GENDER

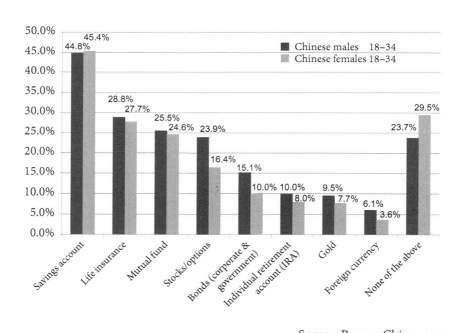

Source: ProsperChina.com

For many PCQS respondents, safety appears to be the watchword for their investments, with a strong emphasis on relatively secure vehicles such as savings accounts and life insurance. Almost half of the men and women questioned report having a savings account, over a quarter hold life insurance and a quarter hold mutual funds.

On the other hand, there are a significant number of respondents, especially males, attracted by the potential for higher returns from vehicles such as stocks and options, bonds, gold and foreign currency.

A word should be said about the growing interest in holding gold and foreign currency. These were both forbidden by the central government until a few years ago. However, with inflation increasing and consumers' search for higher returns, the government relaxed the policies for holding these as investments. As noted in Chapter 8, China is now the world's second-largest market for gold (after India). And while much of it goes toward the making of jewelry, a large portion is held as an investment. The rules on individuals holding foreign stocks and foreign currency were relaxed beginning in 2006, and Chinese citizens may now purchase up to US$50,000 in foreign exchange annually.[10]

It is interesting to note that 23.7% of the men and 29.5% of the women report they use none of the listed investment vehicles. This is much higher than the level who indicate they do not have any savings whatsoever. Thus, it is likely some individuals simply have funds stashed away under the bed, in a cabinet or in a locked box somewhere. Or, they may have placed their investments outside the organized financial services marketplace, such as an investment in their own business, in real estate in China, Canada, the US or in other types of investment.

Overall, Chinese respondents have a greater interest in variable return investments than do their counterparts in the US, as shown in Figure 10-12.

China's digital generation clearly has a preference for higher risk investments such as mutual funds, stocks or options and bonds compared with the more conservative investments (savings accounts and life insurance) that are popular in the US. Part of the reason for

---

10. Kathy Chu and Julie Schmit, "US Home Market Pulls In More Chinese Buyers," USAToday.com, April 3, 2012, http://usatoday30 .usatoday.com/money/economy/housing/story/2012-04-03/us-homes -lure-chinese-buyers/53977638/1

this is that US financial institutions generally offer a wider range of savings products, including certificates of deposit and the like, that offer a higher guaranteed rate of return than is typically available in China. The only other investment US respondents mentioned more often than the Chinese participants is an individual retirement account (IRA). As discussed in the opening sections of the chapter, retirement planning in China generally lags behind that of the West. The type of long-term investment approaches usually used in retirement planning—that is, "buy and hold" strategies, dollar cost averaging and an emphasis on dividend-paying, blue-chips stocks—have, for the most part, yet to generate much interest among Chinese consumers.

FIGURE 10-12: INVESTMENT VEHICLES CURRENTLY HELD BY BOTH CHINESE AND AMERICAN CONSUMERS

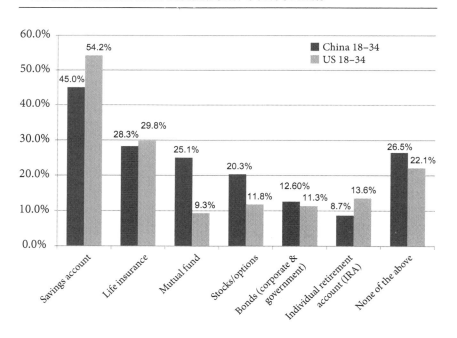

Source: ProsperChina.com

(Note: The MBI survey in the US does not include mention of gold or foreign currency, so there is no comparative information on those investments.)

Chinese investors logically see variable return investments such as stocks, options and gold as a hedge against inflation and a way to achieve better returns than the low rates offered by banks. However, the popularity of these investments also speaks to another side of Chinese culture: the strong belief in luck and the widespread love of gambling. While Chinese people are generally conservative and cautious by nature, for many, these traits are balanced by the willingness to take risks on the spin of a wheel, the throw of the dice or an investment in this week's hot IPO.

Formal securities trading in China dates back to the 1860s during the formation of foreign concessions in Shanghai. Except for the period of the Japanese occupation (1941–45), the Shanghai Stock Exchange was the heart of the financial world in the Far East until the Communists took control in 1949. Trading resumed in 1990 with the establishment of two stock exchanges, one in Shanghai and the other in Shenzhen. The Shanghai Stock Exchange, with a market capitalization of US$2.3 trillion as of December 2011, is now the fifth-largest exchange in the world.[11] The Shenzhen Stock Exchange is smaller, with a market capitalization of approximately US$1 trillion in 2011.[12]

Investing in the Chinese stock market is not for the faint of heart. Historically the markets have been plagued by exceedingly high volatility, weak regulation of trading practices, little concern for shareholder rights and a lack of financial transparency among listed companies. Decrying the situation in 2001, the eminent economist Wu Jinglian described the markets as worse than a casino, because "in a casino at least you cannot see the other people's cards."[13] Meaningful improve-

11. "Shanghai Stock Exchange," *Wikipedia*, last modified on May 4, 2012, http://en.wikipedia.org/wiki/Shanghai_Stock_Exchange

12. "Shenzhen Stock Exchange," *Wikipedia*, last modified on May 4, 2012, http://en.wikipedia.org/wiki/Shenzhen_Stock_Exchange

13. Huang Xiangyang, "It's Time to Clean Up the Stock 'Casino,'" *China Daily*, March 8, 2012, http://www.chinadaily.com.cn/cndy/2012-03/08/content_14784047.htm

ment appears to be in the works, however. In late 2011, the reform-minded Guo Shuqing was appointed chairman of the China Securities Regulatory Commission. In just a few months, he instituted changes to shore up investor confidence, wean business off state-backed financing and introduced stricter requirements for pricing IPOs.[14]

PCQS participants are of mixed attitudes regarding the Chinese stock market. Fully 52% of the men say they probably or definitely would invest in the market, higher than the 41.8% of women who say the same. From this it appears that some segments of the population have taken to the equity market with gusto. On the other hand, 48% of men and 58.2% of women eschew stock market investments, expressing either little or no confidence in the Chinese stock market, or avoiding the market altogether.

When one considers the culture of the Chinese, the interest in equity trading is not surprising. The Chinese have long-held, strong beliefs about "luck," considered one of the "five-fold happinesses" (along with prosperity, longevity, wedded bliss and wealth). One need only recall the importance the Chinese place on acquiring "lucky numbers," "lucky characters" and images of "lucky symbols" to recognize the role this plays in shaping attitudes toward gambling and stock trading.

In an earlier section, we referred to the yin and yang of Chinese consumer behavior. On one hand they desire to surround themselves with the material artifacts of "the good life"—the latest mobile phones, branded leather goods, a late model car, and so on. On the other hand, they know they need to save, and, indeed, they put away sizable portions of their earnings. However, even with the money thus set aside, there is another aspect of yin and yang— balancing conservative, low-risk, low-return investments over the long-term against the lure

---

14. Matthew Philips and Bloomberg News, "China's Top Regulator Woos Investors," *Bloomberg Businessweek*, June 21, 2012, http://www.businessweek.com/articles/2012-06-21/chinas-top-regulator-woos-investors

and excitement of aggressively pursuing high-risk, high-reward investments such as stock, options, gold, for short-term profits.

FIGURE 10-13: Would you invest in the Chinese stock market? Chinese consumers by gender

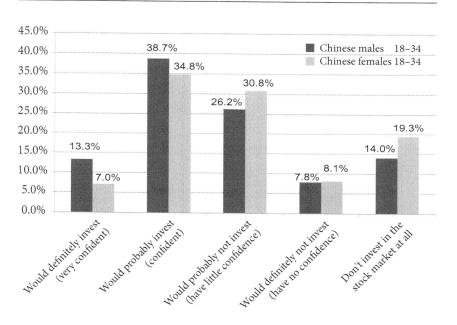

Source: ProsperChina.com

Credit Card Usage

The years of early adulthood are often high-spending years in both mature and emerging economies. Middle-class young people are outfitting their career wardrobes, setting up house and acquiring the accessories of adult lifestyle. However, these are also years where income is often outstripped by an individual's needs and wants. The popular solution in the West? Consumer credit—in the form of mortgages, auto loans, student loans and, of course, a wallet stuffed with multiple credit cards.

While young adult Chinese consumers are beginning to adopt credit and credit cards, how, when and where they use them is significantly different than their counterparts across the Pacific.

Up until the early 2000s, credit cards were relatively rare in China. Few Chinese people had a credit card, and few merchants would accept them. However, in the run-up to the 2008 Olympics, it was recognized that tourists from around the world would be arriving in Beijing with the expectation that they could charge hotels, dinners and souvenir purchases on their favorite global cards. Thus began an intensive campaign over a period of several years to encourage merchant acceptance and to achieve more widespread credit card ownership among domestic consumers.

Today, it has become common for urban Chinese consumers to have one or more credit cards. In fact, among PCQS participants, the percentage that have a credit card (60.4%) is only a little under that of their US counterparts (69.8%), as seen in Figure 10-14. As might be expected, card ownership is somewhat higher for men than for women, and higher in Tier 1 cities than in other regions.

FIGURE 10-14: HAVE A CREDIT CARD
◆ CHINESE AND AMERICAN CONSUMERS

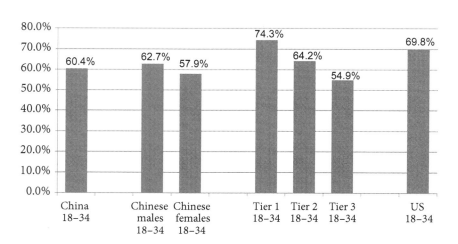

Source: ProsperChina.com

While credit card penetration may be almost as high as in the US, the Chinese use their cards in a very different manner than Americans. Most Chinese consumers are wary of any form of debt, and those that do have a credit card use it largely as a surrogate for cash, paying off the entire balance at the end of each month. Americans, on the other hand, seem to be quite comfortable carrying debt, and frequently revolve their credit from one month to the next. Figure 10-15 depicts the credit card payment practices reported by Chinese and American study participants.

FIGURE 10-15: REGARDING CREDIT CARD DEBT DO YOU...?
CHINESE AND AMERICAN CONSUMERS

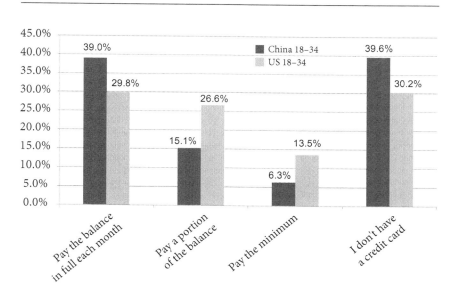

Source: ProsperChina.com

As Visa was a sponsor for the Beijing Olympics, it took an aggressive lead in promoting credit cards in the years leading up to 2008. Thus, it is no surprise that PCQS participants mention Visa as the credit card used most often for personal purchases. As seen in Figure 10-16, MasterCard is well behind Visa, but it recently has narrowed the gap through a local adaption of its successful "Priceless" campaign. American Express and Discover have yet to achieve the penetration they enjoy in the US, while store credit cards are limited to only a few large chain retailers.

FIGURE 10-16: CARDS USED MOST OFTEN FOR PERSONAL EXPENDITURES ◆ CHINESE CONSUMERS BY TIER

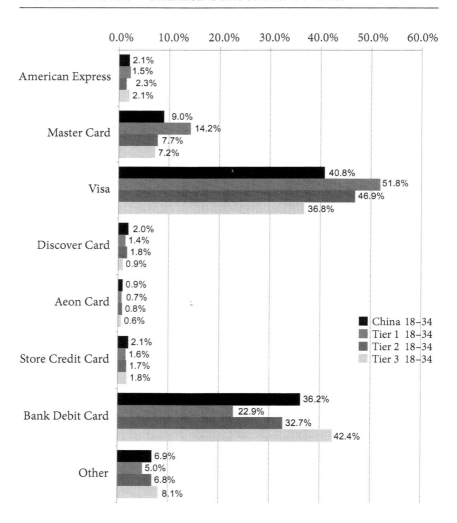

Source: ProsperChina.com

As the EFTPOS (electronic funds transfer at point of sale) technology to support credit cards was introduced to check-out points across Chinese cities, so were bank debit cards enabled as an alternative form of payment. Over one-third of all PCQS respondents report having a bank debit card, a figure that increases to 42.4% in Tier 3 cities. The popularity of the debit cards is that they provide the safety and convenience of carrying a plastic card, but they are in essence a direct cash payment. In a cash-based economy, that is an attractive proposition.

Purchasing Goods and Services: Cash versus Cards

Chinese consumers are evolving in the way they use paper currency, debit cards and credit cards. Having moved from an almost exclusively cash economy just a decade or so ago, they will now vary their payment methods depending on the options different merchants allow as well as their personal preferences.

Figure 10-17 shows the method of payment PCQS respondents say they use the most often in each of 7 different categories of goods and services. Clearly, there is a strong tendency for Chinese consumers to pay either with cash or a debit card, with few purchases going on either a credit card or store card.

The majority of purchases in all categories are made either with cash or a debit card. Of course, card usage will depend on merchant acceptance of plastic, so it is not surprising that card payment is low in categories where there may be many small merchants who choose not to offer card payment options. This would be true with local restaurants and even neighborhood grocery and general merchandise stores.

Cash payments are the consumer preference for dining out, groceries, gasoline and utility payments. Two-thirds or more of all PCQS respondents report they use cash to pay for these items. In some categories, for example, clothing, health and beauty aids and electronics and furniture, major credit cards are increasingly important forms of payment

FIGURE 10-17: Payment method most often used by category ⬦ Chinese consumers

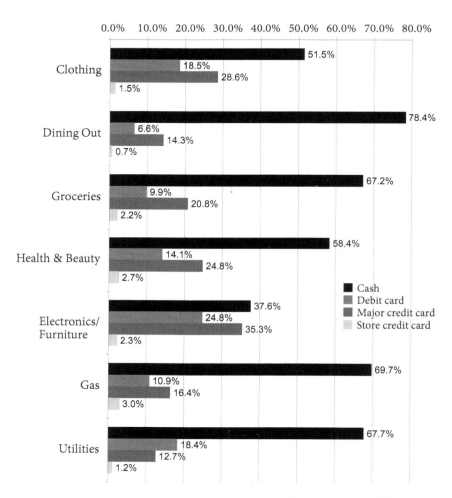

Source: ProsperChina.com

As might be expected, consumers in Tier 1 cities are heavier users of credit cards than are those in Tiers 2 or 3. In fact, in the apparel category, credit card usage exceeds cash payment (44.9% Tier 1 respondents report using a credit card versus 34.8% preferring cash).

Additionally, among Tier 1 residents, credits cards are also the preferred method of payment for purchasing health and beauty products as well as electronics and furniture. This preference is likely the result of the greater penetration of credit cards among Tier 1 consumers than in Tiers 2 and 3. However, it also reflects, at least in part, more widespread merchant acceptance in Tier 1 cities. As the practice of installing EFTPOS systems spreads to small and mid-size merchants in Tiers 2 and 3, it is likely that card usage will become more common across the country.

Media Influence in Shopping for Financial Services and Insurance

As we have done in the previous chapters, we close this discussion with a review of which media forms Chinese and American respondents most often say influence their decision to purchase financial services or insurance (Figure 10-18).

The three leading forms of media that Chinese respondents most often say influence them are broadcast TV (22.0%), word of mouth (21.2%) and "read an article"(16.5%). These are also the three most frequently mentioned influences among the Americans, although the order is somewhat different. The American respondents rely much more heavily on word of mouth (22.6%), while broadcast TV is only mentioned by 12.4% and those citing "read an article" is 11.3%.

A key point about Figure 10-18 is the wide variety of media forms that have some reported influence on decision making. For example, a dozen listed media forms are cited by 10% or more of all PCQS respondents. Chinese consumers are clearly hungry for knowledge in this category, and appear to use almost all forms of media to a greater extent than their US peers.

On the other hand, American consumers are more likely than their Chinese counterparts to report being influenced by direct mail, radio

FIGURE 10-18: Media influence in financial services/
insurance ◆ Chinese and American consumers

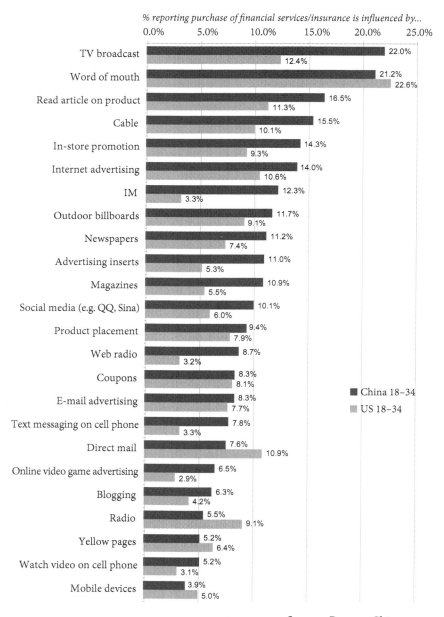

% reporting purchase of financial services/insurance is influenced by...

Source: ProsperChina.com

and the yellow pages. These media forms are mainstays of financial services marketing in America, especially at the local broker and agent level, but have little reported impact among PCQS respondents.

This fragmentation of media sources is clearly one of the major issues facing marketing organizations in China. While the population is huge, there are few dominant media forms, other than television, which gather audiences in large numbers.

Five Key Takeaways

1. The Chinese economy will continue to grow, albeit at a more moderate pace than in recent years. Unlocking the vast hoard of consumer savings is one of the goals of the Chinese government as the country migrates from an export-based economy to encouraging greater domestic consumption.

2. Members of China's digital generation express guarded confidence in the government's ability to sustain a strong economy in the near future, but are concerned about the possibilities of lay-offs, and are uncertain on how to balance their desire to "live for today" versus the strong cultural beliefs in saving for the future.

3. Chinese consumers must balance the yin and yang of risk and reward in managing their money. They are avid savers, but have seen the value of their savings diminish through inflation and plunging prices in the housing and equities markets. Many seek higher returns through variable return investments such as stocks, options, gold and foreign exchange. The extreme volatility of these vehicles, however, is often more akin to gambling than to long-range financial planning.

4. China lacks an adequately funded pension system to provide for citizens' retirement, and private pension plans are still quite limited. Unless significant reforms are made to the capital markets to bring

greater clarity, transparency and stability, it will be difficult for the digital generation to plan adequately for their retirement years. Thus, most survey respondents express grave doubts that they are saving a sufficient amount, even though they are setting aside a much larger share of their income than their American counterparts.

5. Credit cards are now common across urban China, but Chinese consumers are wary of debt and generally pay off the entire balance at the end of the month. That said, the convenience of not having to carry cash will likely lead to increasing use of credit and debit cards as surrogates for bills, especially as electronic point-of-sale payment systems are more widely installed by merchants in Tiers 2 and 3.

Moving On

In this and the previous chapters, we have examined the attitudes and behavior of China's first post-revolution generation on many fronts—their leisure activities, their interests in all things digital, their connection to their Confucian heritage and their offline and online shopping for daily needs, discretionary goods and financial services. Where possible, we have attempted to put information on Chinese study participants in perspective by comparing it with what we know about Americans of the same age.

In the next and final chapter, we will turn our attention to summarizing the key themes that have emerged, and will make some observations on the implications for marketers hoping to serve China's digital generation.

Chapter 11

The Way Forward: Opportunities and Challenges in Marketing to China's Digital Generation

For marketers of consumer products and services, China is a land of tremendous opportunity. But, make no mistake, it is one fraught with many challenges and potential pitfalls. In this final chapter, we draw some overall observations from the ProsperChina™ Quarterly Study (PCQS) data to give our view of the marketing opportunities presented by China in general, and its digital generation in particular.

The power of contemporary marketing is derived from its strong emphasis on understanding customer wants and needs. Leading marketers focus on gathering customer insight and then developing the appropriate products, services and marketing communication activities to address customer interests in a relevant, compelling fashion. In developed markets this has led to sophisticated product development approaches and highly refined segmentation schemes based on buying behaviors, psychographics, lifestyle considerations and so on. All too often, however, we see Western managers stumble when they apply their approaches to a developing market such as China. Frequently the assumption has been that human wants and needs are universal, and that the same customer insight and brand value propositions that are successful in one country can be applied across borders.

This tendency is particularly problematic when applied to China. The country's 1.3 billion citizens present a vast, complex and rapidly changing audience of current and potential consumers. As has often been said before, there is no one China, there are multiple Chinas. This is clearly reflected by the very simple comparisons we have shown between Tier 1, 2 and 3 cities.

While there is increasing diversity, it is true that Chinese consumers are bound together by a common culture, a common history and a common language (albeit with many local tongues and dialects). There are clearly significant regional differences, however, which must be taken into account in the development of marketing plans. The key variables often tend to deal with issues such as local tastes, climate, ethnic mix, level of technological and economic development, infrastructure, education and feelings about foreign brands. The challenges of marketing in this complex environment have been compounded by the lack of reliable longitudinal market research that could assist managers in understanding the evolving interests, shopping behaviors and media usage of Chinese consumers. This is the gap that ProsperChina is filling with its ongoing quarterly studies on which we have drawn heavily.

The goal of this text has been to help marketers understand the attitudes, behaviors, aspirations and even fears of one very specific group: China's digital generation. It does not purport to be a representative picture of all Chinese consumers. Drawing on the PCQS, this book has instead focused on the educated, urban and digitally connected 18–34-year-olds who are at the forefront of China's nascent consumption economy. Since this age group is at the core of many marketing plans in the US, we have used a group of similar US study participants to help put the data on Chinese consumers into a familiar and meaningful perspective.

As we have seen throughout this book, young adult Chinese appear similar to their American counterparts in many regards, at least on the surface. Yet, below the surface there are crucial differences in their attitudes, aspirations, beliefs, fears and purchase motivations that need to be considered in developing brand and marketing communication plans.

In the course of developing this text, five broad marketing opportunities have emerged that we believe are inherent in China's digital generation. The opportunities identified are not easily separated, as many of the strategic and implementation issues are intertwined. Thus, these need to be considered holistically, and the steps needed to achieve meaningful success will require careful planning and decision-making. Therefore, under each topic area, you will find what we believe are the key challenges or obstacles marketers will face on the road to success.

Opportunity 1: Members of China's digital generation are approaching their peak earning years. As incomes rise, they will enjoy greater capacity for discretionary spending and trading up.

As current economic data suggest, the soft global economy is having an impact on China's once double-digit growth rate. Its dependence on low-cost manufacturing has left the country vulnerable to these increasingly challenging global demand cycles. Thus, government officials, as well as business executives, have come to recognize the need to broaden the economy, build more value-added manufacturing, spur real innovation and strengthen the consumer sector. China cannot survive and grow on exports alone. Domestic consumption must be a major focus in the future. Regarding the latter point, McKinsey predicts that by 2020 internal Chinese consumption will account for 43% of total GDP.[1] This goal, however, is dependent on at least two variables: continuing increases in per capita disposable income; and greater willingness by Chinese consumers to spend, rather than save, their increased earnings.

Beyond the immediate, short-term ups and downs of the global economy, most economists agree that over the long term China will continue to grow at an inflation-adjusted rate of around 8–9% a year. However, the rate of growth is expected to vary considerably by region, as more emphasis is placed on development inland and away from the major coastal Tier 1 cities.

The macro trends bode particularly well for those in the 18–34 age group, as they are in the early stages of their careers and can look forward to professional advancement and rising salaries. While McKinsey predicts per capita disposable income of all urban consumers will double by 2020, the educated, connected and mobile members of the digital generation stand a good chance of seeing even more dramatic increases in their personal income.

The consumer goods and services discussed in this book represent a significant portion of study participants' current income. Figure 11-1 recaps by demographic group the average monthly spending by PCQS respondents in seven key categories. As can be seen, groceries represent the largest category of spending among study participants, followed by apparel and fast food.

On average, PCQS participants spend US$249.02 per month on the seven measured categories. Men and women spend at about the same level each month, US$246.63 and US$251.65 respectively. However, there is considerable difference between tier- cities, reflecting

---

1. Yuval Atsmon, Max Magni, Lihua Li and Wenkan Liao, *Meet the 2020 Chinese Consumer*, McKinsey Insights China, (March 2012), http://www.mckinseychina.com/wp-content/uploads/2012/03/mckinsey-meet-the-2020-consumer.pdf

the different purchasing power in each region. In Tier 1, spending across these categories totals US$302.11, while it drops to US$247.79 in Tier 2 and US$227.16 in Tier 3. Overall, Tier 1 residents spend 21.9% more a month on these items than do residents in Tier 2, and 33.0% more than those in Tier 3.

FIGURE 11-1: RECAP OF MONTHLY SPENDING BY CATEGORY CHINESE CONSUMERS BY GENDER AND TIER

	China 18–34	Chinese males 18–34	Chinese females 18–34	Tier 1 18–34	Tier 2 18–34	Tier 3 18–34
Groceries	$74.38	$73.78	$75.03	$86.96	$76.01	$68.21
Apparel	$56.23	$54.22	$58.38	$68.40	$55.32	$51.73
Fast food	$37.08	$37.88	$36.27	$44.63	$36.52	$36.02
Electronics	$22.81	$23.25	$22.33	$29.07	$22.96	$20.30
Telecommunications	$20.96	$23.48	$18.26	$25.14	$20.11	$18.08
Beauty products	$20.77	$17.62	$24.15	$27.53	$20.67	$17.62
Health products	$16.80	$16.40	$17.23	$20.38	$16.20	$15.20
Total measured categories	$249.02	$246.63	$251.65	$302.11	$247.79	$227.16
Average monthly income	$786.50	$784.33	$788.75	$1,164.75	$824.25	$602.25
Spending in measured categories as % of income	31.7%	31.4%	31.9%	25.9%	30.1%	37.7%

Source: ProsperChina.com

While the absolute level of spending is insightful, it is also important to consider spending in relation to income. It is a basic economic principle that at low levels of income, i.e., generally the subsistence level, consumers must spend a relatively high proportion of their earnings on food, housing and other basic necessities. We see the impact of this principle in Figure 11-2, which looks at spending in each of the seven categories as a percentage of monthly income.

Overall, PCQS respondents report spending 31.7% of their income on the seven measured categories. While residents of Tier 1 spend more in absolute terms than those in other tiers, expenditures in the seven categories represent a much lower percentage of their total income.

FIGURE 11-2: SPENDING IN MEASURED CATEGORIES AS PERCENTAGE OF MONTHLY INCOME ◆ CHINESE CONSUMERS BY GENDER AND TIER

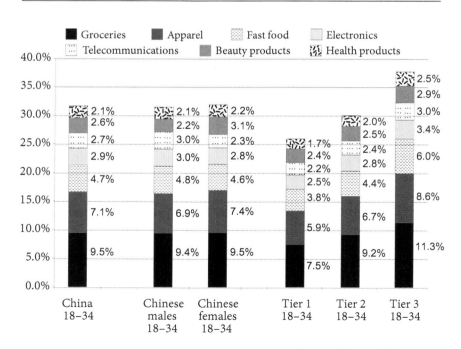

Source: ProsperChina.com

For example, groceries take up, on average, 9.5% of monthly income for all PCQS respondents. For those in Tier 1, however, the US$86.96 spent on groceries represents only 7.5% of income, while the US$68.21 that those in Tier 3 spend on groceries accounts for 11.3%

The most obvious implication for marketers is to appreciate the spending restrictions that most Chinese households still face, even those in Tier 1. There is little wonder that consumers will continue to search for low prices, bargains, promotions and deals in order to stretch their limited resources.

Going forward, as the digital generation advances professionally and economically, it will have greater latitude in spending for daily needs and considered purchases. They will be able to trade up in some categories, and to buy goods or services they cannot currently afford, As a result, household spending will be realigned, with a higher proportion spent on discretionary purchases. Even spending on groceries items will likely increase, although it will probably reflect a declining percentage of overall income.

In order to take advantage of the opportunities inherent in rising incomes among the digital generation, marketers must recognize and address a number of factors that represent potential difficulties.

Key Challenges

- To attract Chinese consumers' attention, a brand must have size, scale, authenticity and authority. In China, these qualities are associated with soundness and stability, which in turn, lead to trust. This means that a brand must be well known, visible and readily available. (More on this later.)

- Pricing will become increasingly complex. As we have seen, Chinese consumers are highly sensitive to price and value. However, as their income rises they will have the ability to trade up for those brands that offer enhanced value for a modest increase in price. Thus, it is likely we will see more marketers offering low-, mid- and high-priced options, and they will encourage consumers to migrate through a portfolio of offerings with different features, qualities and attributes.

- Much of the growth in the past dozen years has come from newly affluent consumers making first-time category purchases. First-time buyers are still an important segment in categories such as automobiles or other high-ticket items. However, in many product categories Chinese consumers are now knowledgeable users, and their expectations have risen accordingly. It is important to consider that China will not always be an "acquisition" market. At some point, marketers must begin to focus on "retention," which comes from ongoing purchases and brand loyalty.

- In categories where there are few new entrants, marketers must look for additional sources of organic growth. They can attempt to capture consumers from competitors or they can seek ways to increase brand consumption, perhaps by suggesting additional applications, finding justification to use the brand in greater volume or moving a brand from special occasions to more regular usage.

- Consumer products and services have proliferated in China at an amazing rate, and competition is fierce among multinational and domestic providers. While shoddy, low-cost domestic brands are everywhere, it is a grave mistake to dismiss all domestic competitors as purveyors of inferior goods. The truth is that Chinese consumer goods manufactures have become very adept at not only matching the quality of multinational products, but also introducing clever incremental innovations that make their products particularly relevant to local customers. Where Chinese companies generally continue to lag behind multinationals is in the broad areas of marketing and branding. That comes from their limited experience in market research, customer segmentation and developing a strong brand value proposition. However, even here they are making strides, and increasingly turning to experienced external marketing agencies and consulting groups for assistance.

- Chinese consumers may be willing to trade up in price, but a brand still must deliver value. At the lowest level, it must represent functional value—that is, be of good quality, be reliable, durable and free from defects or tainted ingredients. Beyond this, a brand must help the consumer achieve a desirable projective or protective outcome. It must help them prepare for advancement, demonstrate their achievement or avoid risk. Practical considerations outweigh brand aesthetics—the beauty and craftsmanship of an Hermès bag is not nearly as important as making sure the logo is placed where a colleague or prospective boss will see it.

Opportunity 2: Affluence is spreading beyond Tier 1, opening up new territories for brand cultivation.

The majority of multinationals operating in China have established their presence in relatively internationalized cities such as Beijing, Shanghai, Guangzhou and perhaps even Shenzhen, or Tianjin. However, as big, vibrant and developed as these cities are, they represent only the visible tip of the Chinese market. Increasingly, the game board is tilting away from these mega-cities and towards Tier 2 and 3 cities such as Chengdu, Xi'an, Nanjing, Hefei, Xiamen, Chongqing, Jinan, Urumqi and dozens of others.

In fact, McKinsey estimates that by 2025 China will have 221 cities with a population of one million or more, compared with only 35 cities of this size in Europe today. Furthermore, that same estimate suggests China will add 350 million people to its urban population over the next twenty years—an incoming audience of prospective consumers that is greater than the current population of the United States.

The economic and consumption implications of these predictions are compelling reasons for marketers to consider geographic expansion.

In moving beyond Tier 1, marketers will face enormous variations in income, standards of living, tastes, housing, personal care practices, media access, and exposure to Western ways. Additionally, since traditional, small format retailing is far more prevalent in these emerging markets than in Tier 1 cities, and distribution networks are highly fragmented, the sell-in process becomes infinitely more complicated. The importance of this cannot be understated. To this point, John Quelch, former Harvard professor and now dean of the China Europe International Business School (CEIBS), has observed that distribution issues are the element that most often constrains or trips up multinationals in their marketing efforts in China.[2]

Per capita income, while increasing, will remain lower than in Tier 1 cities for the foreseeable future. Marketers, therefore, need proper product, distribution and marketing strategies that take into account the need to keep prices low and within the reach of target customers. This may entail modifying products to reduce or eliminate non-critical features, creating single-serve or single-use package sizes, eliminating extraneous packaging and streamlining supply chains, manufacturing and logistical processes.

Key Challenges

- Marketers need to develop the proper expansion strategies, using the most suitable business model, and targeting expansion markets in the most practical sequence. The choice of which regions to focus on also will influence marketing plans going forward, and will depend on a number of factors, including the extent to which the category is already familiar to consumers, the complexity of

---

2. John Quelch and María Ibánñez Gabilondo, "Western Multinationals Expand into China," *Market Leader*, (Q4, 2010), pp 42–45

local supply chains, local income levels, presence of competitors and the general level of acceptance of foreign brands.

- Expanding to 25, 50 or 300 cities is a difficult, multi-faceted process, and requires establishing productive, transparent relationships with local partners and government authorities. It is important to select local partners carefully, and to build a sound organizational infrastructure to oversee and manage local operations and relationships.

- The high proportion of small independent grocery and mom-and-pop stores requires developing multi-layered sales, logistics and customer service strategies, as well as reworking local promotions, displays and packaging for both large- and small-format retail environments.

- Consumers in Tiers 2 and 3 are less likely to be familiar with the full range of consumer products that has become the norm in Tier 1 cities. Thus, marketing strategies may need to recognize that there will be a high proportion of prospects buying in the category for the first time. Communication plans likely need to address issues such as customer education, product demonstrations, technical assistance and post-sales service and guidance.

- Offerings that are successful in Tier 1 cities may need to be adapted or adjusted to the unique characteristics, habits and economic realities of lower-tier cities. Just how this is to be accomplished depends to a large extent on the nature of the category and the region to be penetrated. For example, food preferences are highly regionalized, with some regions preferring highly spiced foods while others lean toward subtle and more nuanced flavors. Food manufacturers are well advised to study local tastes and adapt offerings to be relevant to expansion markets.

- Stripping costs, reducing product features and otherwise adjusting the offering to put products within the reach of less affluent customers introduces the risk of cannibalization and devaluing the brand in the eyes of current customers. For this reason, some companies have created sub-brands specifically for Tier 2 and 3 markets, in order to clearly distinguish them from the full-priced, full-featured parent brand.

- Consumers in Tiers 2 and 3, especially away from the coastal areas, are generally more traditional and less open to Western ways than their counterparts in Shanghai or Beijing. Additionally, they frequently have a high level of distrust for products that are not indigenous. (Recall in our discussions of country-of-origin preferences that consumers in Tiers 2 and 3 lean strongly toward Chinese brands in every category discussed.) Several multinational brands have softened this resistance by giving their brands a Chinese name and identity, by adapting to local tastes and by communicating the brand's functional benefits in ways that are highly relevant to local concerns.

- Extreme care must be given to converting marketing materials or campaigns used in other countries. Chinese consumers live in a world rich in symbols, imagery and traditions, with much importance attached to certain colors, numbers, fruits, flowers, animals and shapes. More than one Western campaign has failed for lack of attention to these subtle but critical brand elements.

Opportunity 3: Chinese consumers are highly brand conscious, and associate established Western brands with quality, reliability, safety and sophistication.

The Chinese fascination with successful brand names, and their concern for safety and consistency, work to the advantage of multinational brands that can demonstrate their strength, leadership and authority in a category. On the other hand, it appears Chinese consumers are wary of brands they have never heard of before, especially in a category in which they are not an experienced user. Thus, for any brand, domestic or imported, it is essential to achieve a substantial presence within a given region, usually by using a combination of awareness-building mass media (TV, outdoor, print advertising) and using events and other promotional activities to generate active word of mouth. In a society that requires peer approval on almost everything that an individual wears, eats, drives or carries, niche brands stand little chance of gaining a sufficient following.

Some of the attraction of Western brands can be traced back to the numerous food contamination and product safety scandals in China in recent years. Milk laced with poisonous melamine, urine in milk powder, lead-tainted children's shoes, fake contraceptives, poisoned preserved fruit, glow in the dark pork… the list goes on and on. Added to that are the never-ending stories of outright counterfeits passed off as the real thing to unsuspecting consumers—fake Smart cars, fake Bordeaux wine, fake Maotai liquor, fake iPhones, even a fake Apple store so convincing that its own employees thought they were working for the real Apple.[3] There is little wonder that cautious Chinese consumers search for authenticity and reliability wherever they can find it.

That does not mean, however, that Chinese consumers eschew Chinese brands, as is often assumed by Western marketers, or buy them only because they are cheap. Throughout this book we have provided several examples of categories where PCQS respondents show a strong preference for Chinese brands over those from the US, Europe, Japan or Korea. Those results are recapped by category in Figure 11-3.

---

3. Abe Sauer, "Chinese Are Fear-Buying, Not in Love with, Western Brands," Brandchannel.com, June 8, 2012, http://www.brand channel.com/home/post/2012/06/08/Chinese-Consumers-Fear-Buying-060812.aspx

FIGURE 11-3: COUNTRY-OF-ORIGIN PREFERENCE IN FIVE
CATEGORIES ◆ CHINESE CONSUMERS

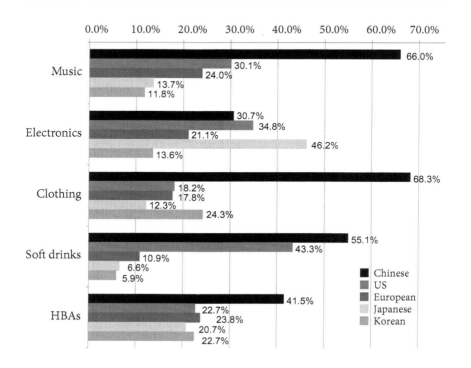

Source: ProsperChina.com

Over the years, when these country-of-origin questions have been asked, the results have remained generally quite stable. There is some evidence that preference for Japanese brands has eroded in the electronics category in recent years, in favor of brands from the US and Korea. And, there is a small increase in interest in American and European clothing brands, but these have made only a small nick in the overwhelming preference for Chinese brands.

As Chinese manufactures improve their quality standards, as many have already done, and as they become more adept at brand building, multinational marketers can no longer assume they have an automatic, built-in advantage over domestic brands. Imported brands will need to meet the Chinese consumer on his or her own terms, and must bring more to the table than just their foreign origin. Young Chinese consumers are interested in the world beyond their borders, and want to be seen as forward thinking and modern. Many have embraced Western concepts and practices, including even a degree of individual freedom of self-expression. However, the trend to modernization and internationalization are not the same as Westernization. They remain deeply rooted in Chinese traditions, communal norms and pride in culture and country. While some brands can drive success based on their inherent "Western-ness"—for example, Apple, Coke, Disney and Ralph Lauren—others have found the path to success requires relating brand benefits to uniquely Chinese concerns, tastes and habits.

For this reason, the country-of-origin question is clouded by the fact that many of the strongest imported brands have been thoroughly adapted to the Chinese market, to the extent that that they are often mistaken for domestic brands. Many imported brands are now manufactured in China, and therefore some consumers view them as domestic brands. Other brands have been very effective in using Chinese celebrities to promote their products, or have adopted Chinese names and imagery in order to appeal to local audiences. A study conducted by the Boston Consulting Group (BCG) found, consistent with the PCQS data, that in most categories Chinese consumers report preferring Chinese brands to imports. However, when BCG dug deeper it found that 90% of the respondents perceived Tide, a long-standing brand of P&G, to be a Chinese brand, while 86% thought the same of Pantene and Head & Shoulders, also part of the P&G stable.

In spite of the affinity that Chinese consumers have with brands, building and sustaining brand equity in China is loaded with several formidable issues.

Key Challenges

- Brand loyalty in most categories is low. Chinese shoppers are curious and willing to try new products and services, especially those offered by brands they recognize. Unlike their counterparts in the US, they did not grow up in brand-conscious households, where they were taught "our family always uses Crest toothpaste," "Mom only bakes with Hershey's chocolate," or "Dad only drives a Chevrolet." Instead of having a favorite brand, Chinese consumers are more likely to rotate their purchase across a rather large consideration set of familiar brand names. Marketers who rely on predictive models based on lifetime customer value calculations must adapt their underlying algorithms to this high-churn environment, and align their spending (and expectations) accordingly.

- Given this "promiscuous" brand behavior, combined with the rapid proliferation of new products, marketers must constantly refresh their brands in ways that are compelling and relevant. This means commitment to ongoing research, product development, finding new applications for the brand and using the full range of communication tools to engage consumers and encourage active, positive word of mouth.

- Traditionally, most brand building in China has focused on functional benefits (gets hair cleaner, makes skin soft, more nutritious, and so on). This type of positioning approach is appealing to pragmatic, value-conscious Chinese consumers, but is vulnerable to competitive one-upmanship. Marketers need to establish a clear, differentiating brand value proposition that encompasses functional benefits linked to higher-level emotional appeals.

- Chinese consumers focus intently on price and value. In the end, practical considerations will win out over more intangible issues such as loyalty or personal indulgence. With the exception of luxury goods with high-status appeal, there is a practical limit to the premium that imported brands can charge in the marketplace. Chinese consumers, especially upwardly mobile consumers such as the digital generation, have the capacity to pay a modest premium for goods that offer a good mix of functional, projective and protective benefits. However, pricing decisions must realistically take into consideration consumers' ability to pay, involvement with the brand or category and the availability of lower-priced, acceptable alternatives.

- Direct and indirect challenges to intellectual property are an ever-present risk. Marketers must police against outright counterfeiting, and take all necessary precautions to protect their trademarks, patents and other IP.

- There are fewer defensive measures against clever "copycat" competitors who duplicate many or most of a brand's look and functional attributes, leaving just enough subtle difference to be legally acceptable. These can blur a brand's identity in the marketplace, undermine its differentiation and enable the copycat to ride on the coattails of the investments made by the legitimate brand owner in marketing programs to build awareness and cachet.

Opportunity 4: E-commerce is expanding rapidly, and China's digital generation is leading the charge.

China will undoubtedly become the world's largest e-commerce market within a few years. The country's total Internet population is currently around 457 million users, but only about a third currently buy goods online. By comparison, in the US, over 70% of the country's 238 million Internet users engage in e-commerce—a population of 170 million online shoppers. BCG predicts that by 2015 China's Internet population will more than double to just over 700 million users, and 47% (329 million) will be shopping online for a range of consumer goods and services.[4]

According to BCG, there are a number of factors driving the growth of e-commerce in China. First, the Internet is affordable and widely available, at least in urban areas. The central government has made it a priority in the Twelfth Five-Year Plan to improve the broadband infrastructure, and has encouraged providers to lower prices to consumers. As these improvements take effect, consumers will have affordable, high-speed service available to them at home, at work and on their mobile phones, and they will be less reliant on Internet cafes for access.

Secondly, modern retailing is highly fragmented and has limited reach in China. Even Walmart currently only has stores in fewer than 120 cities, and China's top 20 retailers account for only 13% of total urban sales. Skyrocketing real estate prices make it difficult for retailers to step up the pace of their expansion plans to smaller municipalities. Furthermore, for consumer products companies, the complicated, multi-tiered distribution systems required to reach small local retailers eats into operating margins. On the other hand, shipping costs are about one-sixth of US levels, so it can often be more economical to sell directly to consumers through online shopping.

For consumers, online shopping offers a broad range of up-to-date products, with a wider choice than would typically be available outside of Tier 1 malls. They are attracted, in part, by the many promotional offers and discounted goods that are available online. However, as we saw in Chapter 7, price and good deals are not the only attractions.

---

4. Jeff Walters, Youchi Kuo, Waldemar Jap and Hubert Hsu, "Selling to China's E-Shoppers," BCG Perspectives, November 10, 2011, https://www.bcgperspectives.com/content/articles/consumer_insight_marketing_sales_and_channels_selling_to_chinas_e-shoppers/

Chinese consumers are increasingly sophisticated in their online shopping, and expect good customer service, flexible return policies, ease of use and free shipping.

While all of these factors combine to paint a glowing future for e-commerce, it is important to keep in mind that at present, it still represents only a small portion of overall retail sales. Again according to BCG, e-commerce currently represents approximately 3.3% of total retail sales, a figure it predicts will rise to 7.4% by 2015. That would equate to a total volume of about US$315 billion, surpassing all other countries in online retail sales.

China's savvy, highly connected digital generation will be leading the charge in the expansion of e-commerce. In Chapter 6, we learned that they heavily use the Internet to gather pre-purchase information, particularly in categories such as apparel, shoes, electronics, appliances and HBAs. And, we learned that over 90% say they either regularly or occasionally shop online.

Tapping into China's growing e-commerce market is a practical way multinational marketers can expand their reach to Tier 2 and 3 consumers. This does not mean they can forgo having a physical presence in these regions altogether. However, it does mean that online selling is an important part of an overall, multi-channel strategy to penetrate these growing areas.

Key Challenges

- Chinese consumers, especially women of the digital generation, love to shop, and see it as a form of entertainment and an opportunity for socializing. Additionally, an outing to the mall with friends or family is a chance to solicit feedback and advice on goods under consideration. While e-commerce offers broad choice and conveniences for time-pressed shoppers, it is not likely to replace the social rituals of shopping and the giving and getting of advice that is so much a part of Chinese culture. Chinese consumers often will use store visits to touch, feel and try on merchandise, but then turn to the Internet for comparison shopping and making an actual transaction. Marketers, therefore, need to put their best foot forward in offline and online environments, and integrate their physical and virtual operations.

- There is still a significant level of distrust surrounding e-commerce. There have been many highly publicized cases of shoppers who complained of shoddy or inferior merchandise, products that were clearly counterfeits or never even receiving the ordered goods. While the overall e-commerce ecosystem of vendors, payments systems and delivery services has improved in recent years, many consumers are still wary. As a result, they tend to stay with well-known e-commerce providers such as Taobao.com, place high value on return privileges and customer complaint handling, and actively blog about companies that have not lived up to their expectations.

- As discussed in Chapter 6, three e-commerce operations from Alibaba dominate consumer online sales in China. The first, Taobao. com, is primarily for consumer-to-consumer transactions, while sister site Tmall.com operates an online storefront for retailers and brand owners. The latter has been active in widening the range of foreign goods on its site, and recently signed brands such as Levi Strauss, Gap and Adidas to open online stores.[5] Additionally, the CEO of Alibaba, Jack Ma, controls the country's leading escrow payment service, Alipay. Together, these three consumer-oriented operations have brought scale, good customer service and greater reliability to e-commerce in China. However, it has also given Alibaba tremendous power over brand owners and it puts the

---

5. Mark Lee, "Alibaba's Tmall Woos US Retailers as Chinese Buy Brands," Blomberg.com, July 20, 2012, http://www.bloomberg.com/news/2012-07-21/alibaba-s-tmall-woos-u-s-retailers-as-chinese-buy-brands.html

company in the position of being able to heavily influence future developments of e-commerce.

- Marketers need to keep up with rapidly evolving technologies, and be ready to adapt their online presence to new formats and environments. For example, PCQS consumers are much more likely to use their cell phone for accessing the Internet than their American counterparts. The next pioneering development may be digital shopping "walls." Online grocer Yihaodian has tested these in Shanghai's underground stations and on billboards. These go well beyond the use of QR codes, and are attractive displays depicting merchandise that can be scanned and ordered via a smartphone, with goods delivered within twenty-four hours.[6] Going forward, a successful e-commerce strategy must encompass multiple environments ranging from PC to laptops, tablets, interactive displays and various phone environments, and must be able to adapt rapidly to changing technology.

Opportunity 5: Chinese consumers are conscious of making a "correct" purchase decision. They actively seek information about brands from the media, and turn to friends and family for advice, guidance and approval.

Members of China's digital generation are particular, thoughtful shoppers. Any important purchase usually will be preceded by extensive research into the category, a careful examination of the various competitors, weighing the merits of different product features and, of course, a search for the best available price. The purchase process can

---

6. "Mcommerce Surges in China," Warc.com, Aug 30, 2011, http://warc.com/LatestNews/News/Mcommerce_surges_in_China.news?ID=28739&isUS=True

sometimes drag for weeks and months, often including multiple dealer or retail visits, until the shopper feels he or she has come to the best decision.

During this period, consumers will actively seek information about the brands in the category, and even the companies behind them. In this text, we have examined the media forms that PCQS participants most often say influence their purchase decisions in various categories. Three overall findings stand out as remarkable. First, broadcast TV and word of mouth are by far the most frequently mentioned influencers in virtually all categories. Second, consumers draw on a wide range of media forms to inform their buying decisions. Third, personal experience, opinions and recommendations, whether delivered face-to-face or through digital media, have tremendous weight in China.

It can be argued that word of mouth and marketing communication are not distinct alternatives. In fact, in the truest sense, the latter feeds and shapes the former to a large extent. Thus, a brand that has an effective and memorable TV campaign, which it then parlays to public events, product demonstrations and clever promotions, will be talked about by consumers. In the parlance of Madison Avenue, this is about creating "buzz."

In China, however, word of mouth, both in person and via social media, plays a particularly potent role. For example, in a study conducted by McKinsey, 66% of Chinese consumers said they would consider recommendations from friends and family when choosing a moisturizer, compared with just 38% in the US and the UK.[7]

According to the online video magazine, Thoughtful China, there are two reasons why word of mouth is so important in China. "First, China is a low-trust society, and people here are generally skeptical and

---

7. Max Magni and Yuval Atsmon, "The Power of Word-of-Mouth in China," Harvard Business Review Blog Network, March 30, 2010,   http://blogs.hbr.org/cs/2010/04/the_power_of_word-of -mouth_in.html

take nothing for granted. China's media, meanwhile, is neither neutral nor independent and doesn't play a watchdog role. So, word of mouth is inevitable. Where else can shoppers turn but to each other? That explains the massive volume of brand reviews and product experiences that fill China's bulletin boards."[8]

For this reason, brand building in China must take into consideration not just target customers, but also the circle of influence that envelops them. Media plans must be both broad and narrow. Broad, to establish general brand presence and influence public opinion, and narrow to enhance salience, preference and engagement with actual users.

Two popular shortcuts to achieving brand familiarity and acceptance is the widespread use in China of celebrity spokespeople and product placement. In essence, these serve as surrogates for a personal recommendation from an admired celebrity, and help give a brand immediate credibility and status.

Key challenges:

- Media costs are skyrocketing across China. Although consumption of traditional media such as TV and print is declining, there is an ever-increasing demand for advertising time and space as more and more companies enter the market. The situation was exacerbated recently when the central government put limitations of the amount of advertising time available during popular drama programs.

- Online communication environments are a natural fit for marketing to China's digital generations. However, to facilitate peer approval, offline communication will be still be necessary to achieve awareness and familiarity among their friends and family.

---

8. "Community Engagement," video, 15:25, posted on ThoughtfulChina.com, Feb 28, 2012, http://www.thoughtfulchina.com/en/community -engagement-in-china-en.html

- The Chinese social media scene is highly fragmented across many providers and platforms, making it complicated for brands to use such sites as a listening post or framework for engaging with consumers. Nevertheless, it is important to have a holistic online and social media strategy to know, on one hand, what consumers are saying about the brand and, on the other, to have a means to engage with them on their own terms. This requires tracking, monitoring and maintaining a presence on a constantly changing range of digital communication options from the brand's own website to discussion groups, bulletin boards, microblogs, social networks and video sharing sites.

- Brands need to go beyond simple name awareness and recognition. They need share their story, heritage and values. Chinese consumers prefer to do business with established companies that are leaders. Digital media platforms provide an appropriate forum for disseminating more information about the company, its brands and its history than would be feasible in traditional mass-media advertising.

- The long lead time that some Chinese consumers require to come to a purchase decision can distort reading the results of a given marketing campaign. This is particularly true for considered purchases such as an automobile, appliance or other high-ticket item. Multinationals need to be cautious in adapting their marketing mix models and other metrics to the timeframes of the Chinese market.

Opportunity 6: Members of the digital generation are influencing markets around the world, not just in China.

While this book has concentrated on the issues of marketing to the digital generation within China's borders, it should be apparent that this connected and mobile audience is making its presence felt well beyond the mainland.

Consider the matter of outbound tourism. In Chapter 3, we discussed the fact that Chinese study participants express higher interest in travel than do their American counterparts (56.2% for PCQS respondents versus 45.6% in the US).

With rising incomes, the relaxation of travel restrictions by the central government and the appreciation in the renminbi, Chinese consumers are heading for overseas travel in record numbers. According to Thoughtful China, 66 million Chinese traveled overseas in 2011, a 15% increase over the prior year. The World Travel Organization estimates that 100 million Chinese will be global travelers by the year 2020.[9]

Among the favorite destinations are those that can combine exposure to contemporary culture, history, a touch of glamor, casinos and especially high-end shopping. Popular tours from China that include a mix of these include destinations such as New York, Las Vegas, Los Angeles and San Francisco. In Europe, favored destinations on the Chinese version of the Grand Tour includes France, Italy, Monaco and Germany, perhaps with brief stops in Switzerland, Belgium or Luxembourg.

A major factor driving tourism to these destinations is the desire to shop for fashion and luxury goods, which are often 30–50% higher in China due to a suite of customs tariffs, value-added taxes and consumption taxes. The impact of Chinese tourism is so great that the World Luxury Association estimates that Chinese consumers alone accounted for 62% of European luxury goods sales in 2011.[10]

---

9. "Travel Trends: Chinese Heading Overseas in Record Numbers," ThoughtfulChina.com, Aug 16, 2011, http://www.thoughtfulchina. com/zh/Travel-Trends-Chinese-Heading-Overseas-in-Record-Numbers.html

10. Harvey Morris, "Chinese Tourists to the Rescue" IHT Rendezvous *New York Times*, Feb 3, 2012, http://rendezvous.blogs.nytimes.com/ 2012/02/03/chinese-tourists-to-the-rescue/

Clearly, during a period of problematic economic conditions in the developed markets, and soft travel among American and Europeans consumers, Chinese tourism may be one of the few bright spots for hotels, entertainment venues and retailers. International hotel chains, airlines and tourism organizations are increasingly promoting their destinations to Chinese audiences. Yet, for the most part, most of these organizations have barely begun to address the myriad of issues necessary to make arriving Chinese tourists feel welcomed, appreciated or well served.

Chinese consumers are directly impacting Western markets in other ways as well. For example, in the US, affluent mainland Chinese businessmen are taking advantages of the real estate crash to snap up houses, apartment building and commercial buildings in New York, Los Angles, San Francisco and other cities. According to *USA Today*, the Chinese are now the second-largest foreign buyers of homes, behind the Canadians, accounting for US$7.4 billion of sales in the 12 months up to March 2011, a 24% increase over the prior period. While some of these purchases are purely for investment purposes, the paper estimates that 60% are in anticipation of living in the US part-time in order to conduct business, and to send their children to US schools.[11]

Which brings us to another increasingly visible group of Chinese in the US and other developed markets: the waves of university and high-school students leaving the mainland to study abroad. According to the Institute of International Education and the State Department's Bureau of Educational and Cultural Affairs, Chinese enrollment in US universities rose 23% to 157,558 undergraduate and graduate students in the 2010–11 academic year. This put Chinese enrollment ahead of India (103,895) and South Korea (73,351).[12]

---

11. Chu and Schmit, "US Home Market Pulls In More Chinese Buyers"
12. Shaun Rein, "China Needs American Education. Here's How to Bring It There," *Forbes,* June 20, 2012, http://www.forbes.com/

Tourists, part-time residents and students represent diffused, difficult to reach populations. However, their sheer numbers and spending power warrant attention from local marketers in areas where they visit, live or study.

Key challenges

- Hotels, retailers and service organization may want to consider adding Mandarin-speaking staff, creating special materials and services to help Chinese navigate their way through unfamiliar physical and cultural territory, and develop special outreach programs to meet local Chinese customers' expectations.

- The pragmatism, caution and frugality that characterize Chinese consumers at home are just as true when they travel. Thus, as one European travel industry report noted, they "sleep cheap, shop expensive."

- Chinese consumers are most attracted to brands that they already know and recognize, putting local brands that do not export to China at a disadvantage. Furthermore, the value propositions that have made the brands popular with domestic customers may not have the same relevance to Chinese customers. Nevertheless, the insights into Chinese consumer attitudes and behavior that have been covered in this text can be applied to recast the value proposition in ways that will be relevant to visiting Chinese consumers.

sites/forbesleadershipforum/2012/06/20/china-needs-american
-education-heres-how-to-bring-it-there/

A Final Comment

The Chinese consumer market is a kaleidoscope of evolving attitudes, behaviors, needs, wants, aspirations and fears. While core values are deeply rooted in cultural history, the outward manifestation of these values and the manner in which they shape consumer behavior are constantly changing. Therefore, it is critical for marketers to have a reliable, consistent flow of information on developing concerns, preferences, habits and purchase intentions.

The data and insights we have provided here into China's digital generation barely scratch the surface of the information that is contained in the ProsperChina database. We have focused on those issues and segments felt to have the greatest practical application to prospective readers marketing to young Chinese adults. However, behind the data presented here there are additional tools to drill down into the information using more refined and granular segmentation approaches.

The Chinese market is dynamic, complex and competitive—and will only continue to be more so in the future. The days of scarcity and pent-up consumer demand are long gone. Success for consumer products marketers will depend on targeting the right customer segments, in the right regions, with the right mix of offline and online media delivering a relevant brand value proposition. For those that approach the market with forethought, who use customer insights to drive their business, and who are willing to take risks and learn from their mistakes, the long-terms benefits are potentially enormous.

As we close, we are reminded of two Chinese proverbs that may offer encouragement to those seeking to market to China's digital generation:

Be not afraid of going slowly, be only afraid of standing still.

Failure is not falling down, but refusing to get up.

Appendix

A Short Guide to
Major Chinese Digital Media

China's digital media scene is made up of an ever-changing list of players. While Baidu dominates search, and QQ dominates IM, other segments are highly fragmented. Dozens of providers offer news and information portals, social networks, bulletin boards (BBS), blogging, micro-blogging, video sharing, gaming sites and e-commerce. Audience figures are difficult to come by and often unreliable, but here is a brief guide to the organizations that most frequently are mentioned by respondents to the PCQS.

163.com	*Web portal owned by NASDAQ-traded NetEase, founded in 1997.*
360buy.com	*Privately held online B-to-C retailer founded in 1998.*
51.com	*Social network established in August 2005. Its strength historically has been in rural areas and lower-tier cities.*
Baidu	*China's dominant search engine provider, established in 2000. Listed on NASDAQ.*
Dangdang	*Online shopping company founded in 1999, offering books and other products. Listed on NYSE in December 2010.*
Google	*Hong-Kong-based operation of multinational search engine company Google.*

Hainei	*Real-name social network launched in 2007 by one of the founders of Xiaonei.*
Joyo	*Online shopping company acquired by Amazon in 2004 and now renamed Amazon China.*
Kaixin001	*Real-name social networking site for white-collar workers, known for social games and post-forwarding features. Its strength is primarily in Tier 1 and 2 cities.*
Mop	*Entertainment- and technology-related BBS established in 1997.*
MySpace	*Chinese operation of international social networking site.*
Paipai	*C-to-C auction site launched in September 2005 by Tencent Holdings.*
Pengyou	*Real-name social network launched by Tencent Holdings in July 2010.*
QQ	*Popular portal integrating news, interactive communities, entertainment products and other services—owned by Tencent Holdings.*
Qzone	*Nickname-based social networking site established by Tencent in 2005. In March 2011 company claimed more than 480 million users.*
Renren	*Real-name social network originally founded as an on-campus network called Xiaonei.com. Company claims a total of 147 million cumulate activated users. Traded on the NYSE since April 2011.*
Sina.com	*News and information portal network encompassing four region-specific sites (mainland China, Taiwan, Hong Kong and overseas Chinese in North America), with interest-based channels covering sports, automotive, finance, entertainment, news, technology and so on. Parent company Sina Corp was founded in 1997 and is traded on the NASDAQ.*
Sina Weibo	*Micro-blogging site offered by Sina Corp, launched in August 2009.*

Sogu   *Search engine owned by Sohu.*

Sohu   *Founded as China's first search engine in 1998, the company now offers an expanded range of information, online video and multi-player gaming services. Listed on NASDAQ since 2000.*

Taobao   *Dominant online shopping company owned by Alibaba Group. Taobao Marketplace is a C-to-C transaction platform using auctions and fixed pricing. Company also provides a dedicated B-to-C e-commerce platform through its Tmall.com site.*

Tencent QQ   *Widely used free IM service, launched in 1999 by Tencent Holdings and claiming more than 711 million active user accounts. Services include text messaging, video and voice chat, multi-player games, as well as file transmission. Revenue is largely derived from users via membership fees and micro-transactions for games and virtual goods.*

Tianya   *Popular Internet forum providing BBS, blogging, micro-blogging and photo album capabilities. Established 1999.*

Tom   *Web portal owned by NASDAQ-traded Tom Online. Parent company also offers the Chinese version of Skype.*

Tudou   *China's second-largest video-sharing site, established in April 2000. A stock-for-stock merger with category leader Youku was announced in March 2012.*

Wangyou   *Youth-oriented social network focusing on user-generated content.*

Xiao Yuan Wan   *Not a media provider per se but a reference to campus intranets used by students to access the Internet as well as school-specific information and services.*

Xunlei   *Download management software used for peer-to-peer file sharing and downloading video on-demand.*

Youku   *Largest Chinese video-hosting site, launched in December 2006. Listed on NYSE since December 2010. In March 2012, announced a merger with number-two provider Tudou to form a new company Youku Tudou.*

About the Authors

Heidi Schultz is an author, consultant, and adjunct lecturer at the Medill School of Journalism, Media, Integrated Marketing Communications. She is also Executive Vice President of Agora Inc, a global marketing, communication and branding consultancy based in Evanston Illinois. She has extensive experience in China, having lectured at numerous universities, executive education seminars, and industry events. Along with her husband, Don Schultz, she is the co-author of *IMC: The Next Generation*, and *Brand Babble*, both of which have been translated into Chinese, as well as other books and articles. She is the former publisher of CHICAGO magazine, and has worked with media organizations in both the US and China on developing strategic business plans. She holds a Bachelor's degree in Journalism from the University of Southern California, and a Master's degree from the Northwestern University Kellogg School of Business.

Martin P. Block is a Professor in the Integrated Marketing Communications Division of the Medill School at Northwestern University. He is currently sector head for Entertainment and Gaming. He teaches graduate level marketing research, sales promotion, advertising, and direct marketing courses. Previously, Martin was a Professor and Chairperson of the Department of Advertising at Michigan State University. Martin is co-author of Analyzing Sales Promotion (Dartnell, 1994), Business-to-Business Market Research, (Thomson, 2007). His recent chapter "Post Promotion Evaluation" appears in The Power of Marketing at-Retail (POPAI, 2013). He was also co-author of Cable Advertising: New Ways to New Business (Prentice-Hall,

1987). He has published in academic research journals and trade publications. He has been the principal investigator on several Federally funded research projects and has served as a consultant to the Federal Trade Commission (FTC).

Don E. Schultz is Professor (Emeritus-in-Service) of Integrated Marketing Communications at Northwestern University, Evanston, IL. He is also President of Agora, Inc., a global marketing, communication and branding consulting firm also headquartered in Chicago, IL. Schultz lectures, conducts seminars and conferences and consults on five continents. He is the author of twenty-seven books and over 150 trade, academic and professional articles. He is a featured columnist in MARKETING NEWS and was founding editor of THE JOURNAL OF DIRECT MARKETING. Schultz is recognized as a leading authority on new developments in marketing and communication and has helped develop the Integrated Marketing and Integrated Marketing Communication concepts around the world along with pioneering work in marketing accountability, branding, internal marketing and marketing metrics/ROI.

The Prosper Foundation is a Not-for-Profit supporting entrepreneurship and innovation. It facilitates transdisciplinary collaboration using consumer insights as the common language. Founded in 1993 by Gary Drenik and Philip Rist, the Prosper Foundation currently provides information grants to more than 15 leading academic institutions. For more information please visit our website.

http://www.goprosper.com/prosperfoundation.html